Career Exploration and Development in Childhood

Career development is a lifespan process, but to date the early part of the lifespan has received little attention. This book represents a much-needed impetus to change this. Watson and McMahon have assembled a diverse group of scholars to document how childhood experiences serve as precursors of future occupational roles and identities and to review the functions of theory, research, and practice in understanding and facilitating the underlying processes. This book will expand the scope of the field and should be required reading for students of career development and career counselling.

Fred W. Vondracek, Professor Emeritus of Human Development,
Pennsylvania State University

Career Exploration and Development in Childhood presents chapters from leading figures in the field of childhood career exploration and development. As the first substantive edited collection of its kind, this book makes an important contribution to our understanding of children's career development. It provides cutting-edge theory, research, and practice for understanding and fostering career exploration and development during childhood across a wide spectrum of international settings.

Divided into five sections that reflect the authors' perspectives on critical aspects of children's career development, chapters include relevant research as well as the practical application of concepts, issues, and strategies for career interventions with children. The book includes sequential sections on theory, research, contextual influences, assessment, and the facilitation of career exploration and development. Perspectives from both developed and developing world contexts consider traditional approaches to career education as well as career development learning in childhood. The collaborations evident in the chapter authorship reflect the significant internationalisation of the field of child career development.

The book synthesises key issues and presents innovative recommendations that will not only enhance our understanding of children's career development but also set the agenda for the future of the field. It will be of key interest to researchers, academics and postgraduate students in the fields of career development, career guidance, education, childhood, child development, and counselling.

Mark Watson is Distinguished Professor in the Department of Psychology, Nelson Mandela University, South Africa.

Mary McMahon is Senior Lecturer in the School of Education, The University of Queensland, Australia.

Career Exploration and Development in Childhood

Perspectives from theory, practice and research

Edited by Mark Watson and Mary McMahon

LONDON AND NEW YORK

First published 2017
by Routledge
2 Park Square, Milton Park, Abingdon, Oxon OX14 4RN

and by Routledge
711 Third Avenue, New York, NY 10017

First issued in paperback 2018

Routledge is an imprint of the Taylor & Francis Group, an informa business

© 2017 selection and editorial matter, M. Watson and
M. McMahon; individual chapters, the contributors

The right of the editor to be identified as the author of the
editorial material, and of the authors for their individual chapters,
has been asserted in accordance with sections 77 and 78 of the
Copyright, Designs and Patents Act 1988.

All rights reserved. No part of this book may be reprinted
or reproduced or utilised in any form or by any electronic,
mechanical, or other means, now known or hereafter invented,
including photocopying and recording, or in any information
storage or retrieval system, without permission in writing from
the publishers.

Trademark notice: Product or corporate names may be trademarks
or registered trademarks, and are used only for identification and
explanation without intent to infringe.

British Library Cataloguing in Publication Data
A catalogue record for this book is available from the British Library

Library of Congress Cataloging in Publication Data
Names: Watson, Mark, 1956– editor. | McMahon, Mary, 1955– editor.
Title: Career exploration and development in childhood :
  perspectives from theory, practice and research / edited by
  Mark Watson & Mary McMahon.
Description: Abingdon, Oxon ; New York, NY : Routledge, 2017.
Identifiers: LCCN 2016019634 (print) | LCCN 2016033410
  (ebook) | ISBN 9781138926288 (hbk : alk. paper) |
  ISBN 9781315683362 (ebk)
Subjects: LCSH: Career education. | Occupations—Study and
  teaching (Elementary) | Occupations—Study and teaching
  (Secondary) | Professions—Study and teaching (Elementary) |
  Professions—Study and teaching (Secondary)
Classification: LCC LC1037 .C365 2017 (print) | LCC LC1037
  (ebook) | DDC 370.113—dc23
LC record available at https://lccn.loc.gov/2016019634

ISBN 13: 978-1-138-60201-4 (pbk)
ISBN 13: 978-1-138-92628-8 (hbk)

Typeset in Bembo
by Apex CoVantage, LLC

Contents

Preface	viii
Acknowledgements	x
Contributors	xi

1 Telling stories of childhood career development   1

MARK WATSON AND MARY McMAHON

PART I
Theoretical perspectives   9

2 Theories of career development in childhood and early adolescence   11

ASHTON D. TRICE AND HUNTER W. GREER

3 Childhood: Career construction's opening act   24

PAUL J. HARTUNG

4 Systems and relational perspectives in understanding children's career development   34

WENDY PATTON

5 Supporting the career development of children: The concepts of career choice and attainment model   48

KIMBERLY A. S. HOWARD, ELEANOR CASTINE, SEAN FLANAGAN, AND YERANG LEE

6 Children as storytellers: Constructing identity through story   60

MARY McMAHON AND MARK WATSON

vi Contents

PART 2
Research perspectives
71

7 Children's career exploration and development:
Research overview and agenda
73

ÍRIS M. OLIVEIRA, ERIK J. PORFELI, AND MARIA DO CÉU TAVEIRA

PART 3
Contextual perspectives
87

8 The antecedents of children's aspirations
89

EIRINI FLOURI, HEATHER JOSHI, ALICE SULLIVAN, AND
VANESSA MOULTON

9 Child career development in family contexts
101

JIANWEI LIU AND MARY McMAHON

10 Child career development in developing world contexts
114

ANURADHA J. BAKSHI

PART 4
Assessment perspectives
127

11 Career assessment of children
129

TERENCE J. G. TRACEY AND SANDRO M. SODANO

12 A review of assessment in child career development
143

GRAHAM B. STEAD, DONNA E. P. SCHULTHEISS, AND ASHLEY OLIVER

PART 5
Facilitating career exploration and development
157

13 School-based approaches promoting children's
career exploration and development
159

RICHARD T. LAPAN, BECKY L. BOBEK, AND JOHN KOSCIULEK

14 Targeted career exploration and development
programmes
172

ANTHONY BARNES AND BARBARA McGOWAN

Contents   vii

15 Career development learning in childhood: Theory, research, policy, and practice   186

EWALD CRAUSE, MARK WATSON, AND MARY McMAHON

16 Epilogue   199

MARY McMAHON AND MARK WATSON

Index   205

Preface

In a sense, the content of this book prefaces lifespan career development, for it describes the foundational lifespan stage of childhood career development. It is the first book in the discipline of career psychology, a field with a history that has its origins in the start of the last century, to focus solely on children from a broad range of international perspectives. The book is long overdue. Throughout the book, chapter authors have commented on the increasing chorus of voices in recent decades for greater attention to be paid to childhood career development. The call for a more cohesive focus on children's career development has also arisen out of the piecemeal growth of literature in this field, all of which is sited in journal articles, special journal issues, or isolated book chapters.

There have been several persistent criticisms of extant literature on children's career development that the editors of this book were sensitive to. One criticism is the need for a more unified definition of childhood in relation to career development. In this book, authors were requested to define childhood specifically within a chronological age range that had an upper limit of 14 years. This definition helps to differentiate childhood from its present blurring with adolescent career psychology in the literature.

A further criticism of literature on children's career development has been the predominant focus on theoretical perspectives. This book considers several perspectives on children's career development: theoretical, research, contextual, assessment, practice, and policy. This broader range of perspectives provides the reader with a more holistic, integrative understanding of foundational career development in childhood and the relationship of this development stage to later lifespan career development in adolescence and adulthood.

In career psychology in general, and childhood career psychology in particular, concern has been expressed about the culturally skewed nature of the literature, much of which has been written in North America. In this regard, the editors invited chapter contributions from 30 authors representing 7 countries: Australia, China, England, India, Portugal, South Africa, and the United States. Among the invited authors are internationally recognised academics in the field of children's career development. In addition, there are emerging authors who have co-authored several of the chapters – a most promising development for the future of the discipline.

The book is structured in five sections. Section 1 consists of five chapters that describe both established as well as more recent emerging theoretical perspectives on children's career development. Section 2 consists of a chapter that comprehensively reviews research on children's career development and considers a future research agenda. Section 3 consists of three chapters that explore a variety of contexts within which children's career development occurs. Section 4 consists of two chapters that explore assessment perspectives on children's career development. Section 5 contains three chapters that provide perspectives on the facilitation of career exploration in children's career development. The book concludes with an epilogue that reflects on the perspectives emerging from this first book on children's career development.

It is the editors' hope that the voices heard in this book will help lift the study of children's career development from its present Cinderella status in the career literature to a greater appreciation of the critical foundational roots that this developmental stage provides in the study of lifespan career development. Childhood is an exciting time of exploration and imagination, a time which, if proactively engaged with by career theorists, researchers and practitioners, could help circumvent the reactive issues of later stages of lifespan career development that seem to dominate much of the career literature at present.

Acknowledgements

The publication of this first book on children's career development has been a team effort and an international collaboration. In the first instance, we would like to thank the 30 chapter authors. Despite prominent positions and their busy time schedules, all were willing to be involved and to share their expert knowledge in this field. We appreciated the professionalism with which they responded to our editorial process, and it was a privilege to have worked with them on this book.

We also need to thank Routledge for their commitment to this book and to the professional and understanding support their staff provided in the publication process.

In addition, we would like to thank Nicole Grundlingh for the excellent work she undertook in the formatting and editing of the chapters.

We believe that the publication of it fills a significant gap in the career literature, and we hope that this book stimulates further understanding of this critical developmental stage in lifespan career development.

Mark and Mary

Contributors

Anuradha J. Bakshi is an Associate Professor in the Department of Human Development, Nirmala Niketan College of Home Science, University of Mumbai. She is the Vice-President of the Indian Association of Career and Livelihood Planning and the Career Guidance and Cross-Disciplinary Co-editor of the British Journal of Guidance and Counselling. Many of her recent publications have been in the area of career development.

Anthony Barnes is a UK Fellow of the National Institute for Career Education and Counselling (NICEC) and edits the Cegnet website, which supports career learning and development practitioners in schools (www.cegnet.co.uk). He is an independent consultant, trainer, and materials developer with a strong interest in career-related learning in the primary school.

Becky L. Bobek is a principal research scientist who conducts research on career development constructs and processes and investigates topics such as individual differences in interests and values, education/career exploration, decision making, and goals for education and work transitions.

Eleanor Castine is a Ph.D. student in counselling psychology and applied human development at Boston University's School of Education (USA). A graduate of the University of Virginia, Ellie received her M.S. in counselling psychology from Loyola University Maryland. Her research interests include children's career development, especially among marginalised youth.

Ewald Crause is a psychologist working in private practice and senior psychologist at the Cape Winelands Education Department in South Africa. His fields of interest include career program development and using ICT within learning environments.

Sean Flanagan is a Ph.D. student in counselling psychology and applied human development at Boston University's School of Education, USA. His interests include children's vocational development with emphases on cognitive developmental and social justice approaches to investigating the ways that children understand the world of work.

xii Contributors

Eirini Flouri is a Professor of Developmental Psychology at the UCL Institute of Education, University College London. She is interested in the role of contextual risk in children's emotional and behavioural problems and the development of emotional and behavioural resilience in children.

Hunter W. Greer is a counselling graduate student in the Department of Graduate Psychology at James Madison University.

Paul J. Hartung is Professor of Family and Community Medicine at Northeast Ohio Medical University and Adjunct Professor of Counselling at the University of Akron, USA. He is the current editor of *The Career Development Quarterly* and fellow of the American Psychological Association, International Association of Applied Psychology and National Career Development Association.

Kimberly A. S. Howard is an Associate Professor in Counselling Psychology and Applied Human Development as well as an Associate Dean for Faculty Affairs in Boston University's School of Education (USA). Her research focuses on the reasoning processes used by children and youth to understand career choice and career attainment.

Heather Joshi, an economic demographer, was the founder/director of the UK Millennium Cohort Study and the first president of the Society for Lifecourse and Longitudinal Studies. Currently Emeritus Professor at University College London, Institute of Education, she was awarded a CBE for services to longitudinal and women's studies in 2015.

John Kosciulek is a Professor in the Department of Counselling, Educational Psychology and Special Education in the College of Education at Michigan State University. His teaching and research interests include rehabilitation counselling, transition from school to adult life for youth with disabilities, career development, and family adaptation to disability.

Richard T. Lapan is a Professor in the College of Education at the University of Massachusetts Amherst, USA, where he teaches comprehensive school counselling in schools. This includes a focus on college and career readiness, adolescent development, and vocational psychology.

Yerang Lee is a Ph.D. student in counselling psychology and applied human development at Boston University's School of Education, USA. A graduate of the University of Michigan, she received her M.A. in mental health counselling from Boston College. Her current research focuses on vocational psychology and cultural considerations.

Jianwei Liu is a graduate from the School of Education at The University of Queensland. Jianwei's research interests focus on career development, in particular child career development and the influence of parents, and also on qualitative research methods.

Barbara McGowan is a NICEC Fellow with extensive experience with curriculum development in the area of career learning. She has contributed to its development and management nationally and internationally, and for the past 20 years has argued for the need to lay the foundation for this area of learning at the primary level.

Mary McMahon is a Senior Lecturer in the School of Education at The University of Queensland, Australia, where she teaches career development and career counselling. She researches and publishes in child and adolescent career development, narrative career counselling, and qualitative career assessment.

Vanessa Moulton is a doctoral student and Teaching Fellow at the UCL Institute of Education, University College London. Her research interests include aspirations, child behaviour, social disadvantage and gender differences. Her thesis, supervised by Flouri, Joshi and Sullivan, explores the role of aspirations in young children's emotional and behavioural problems.

Ashley Oliver is a counselling psychology doctoral student in the College of Education and Human Services at Cleveland State University. Her current research interests include job placement rates of ex-offenders and how to increase their job opportunities upon release from prison, as well as general areas of unemployment.

Íris M. Oliveira is a doctoral student of applied psychology at the University of Minho (Portugal). Íris is a grant holder from the Portuguese Foundation for Science and Technology. She is interested in childhood career development, career assessment and counselling. She writes for international publications and delivers professional presentations in her areas of interest.

Wendy Patton is Executive Dean, Faculty of Education at Queensland University of Technology, Brisbane, Australia. She has taught and researched in the areas of career development and counselling for more than 20 years. She has co-authored and co-edited a number of books and is currently Series Editor of the Career Development Series with Sense Publishers. She has published widely, including more than 150 refereed journal articles and book chapters. She serves on a number of national and international journal editorial boards.

Erik J. Porfeli received his doctorate in human development and family studies from Pennsylvania State University. He is Associative Dean for Community Engagement and Admissions and an Associate Professor at NEOMED. Erik is interested in the intersection of career and academic development from childhood through emerging adulthood. He leads initiatives translating career development research into health professions' programs, admissions, learning, and web-based tools.

Donna E. P. Schultheiss is Interim Dean at the College of Graduate Studies and Professor and Co-director of Training of Counselling Psychology at Cleveland State University. Her research interests include the interface of work and relationships, childhood career development, international and immigration issues in vocational psychology, and women's work.

Sandro M. Sodano, Ph.D., is an Associate Professor of Counselling, School and Educational Psychology at the State University of New York at Buffalo, USA, where he is the Director of the master's program in mental health counselling. Sandro is Past-President of the Society for Interpersonal Theory and Research (SITAR).

Graham B. Stead is a Professor and Director of Doctoral Studies in the College of Education and Human Services at Cleveland State University. He is a core faculty member of the doctoral counselling psychology program. His interests are in career psychology, statistics, meta-analysis, and social constructionism.

Alice Sullivan is Director of the 1970 British Cohort Study (BCS70) at the UCL Institute of Education. Her research is focused on social and educational inequalities in the life course. She has published in areas including social class and gender differences in educational attainment, single-sex and coeducational schooling, private and grammar schools, cultural capital, reading for pleasure, and access to elite higher education.

Maria do Céu Taveira received her doctorate in educational psychology. She is Assistant Professor and Coordinator of research in Career Development and Counselling at the School of Psychology, University of Minho, Portugal. Maria's research interests focus on career exploration, well-being, vocational identity, and efficacy of career interventions. She contributes to international publications and presentations in her areas of interest.

Terence J. G. Tracey, Ph.D., ABPP, is a Professor in Counselling and Counselling Psychology at Arizona State University, USA. He is currently serving as the editor of the *Journal of Counseling Psychology*. His scholarship has focused on the topics of the structure and development of vocational interests, client-therapist interaction in psychotherapy, interpersonal models of personality and psychotherapy, and minority student academic success.

Ashton D. Trice received his doctorate from West Virginia University in educational psychology and is currently a Professor in the Department of Graduate Psychology at James Madison University. His research interests include the transition to work and postsecondary education for adolescents with attention deficits and autism spectrum disorders.

Mark Watson is a Distinguished and Emeritus Professor at the Nelson Mandela Metropolitan University, South Africa. He teaches, researches and practices in the field of career development, counselling and assessment. He has co-authored and co-edited a number of books and published 86 journal articles. Mark is on the editorial board of several international career journals.

Chapter 1

Telling stories of childhood career development

Mark Watson and Mary McMahon

There is a story to tell when considering childhood career development within the broader context of lifespan career development. It is a story of an orphaned stage of the lifespan that for decades has been considered divorced from the realities of career development, for theory, research, policy and practice have chosen to emphasise career development stages where career choice must be made, resulting in a skewed dominance towards adolescence and adulthood. Nevertheless, in the second half of the last century and through to the first decade of the present century, there has been a growing awareness that the foundations of career development, as with developmental psychology itself, are to be found in childhood. This awareness has been predominantly theoretical to date, with major career developmental theorists such as Gottfredson (2002, 2005) and Super (1980, 1990), for instance, describing early developmental tasks that provide children with the foundation for later career development and decision making. The lack of a consistent body of research, policy and practice, however, has led to a persistent call for a greater emphasis on child career development.

This introductory chapter to the first book on childhood career development needs to recognise, at the outset, that there has been a growing response to the call for a greater emphasis on childhood career development, although this emergent focus is not without its issues. It is no longer possible to start a publication on children's career development with the statement that there has been a dearth of such literature to date. Rather, the concern is less quantitative and more qualitative; in short, how much has the growing focus on this earliest stage of lifespan career development enhanced our understanding of children's career development? It will become clear from the analysis of issues raised by the definitive reviews in the next subsection of this chapter that the answer seems to be 'not enough'. One critical issue to emerge from research reviews is the definition of childhood, which has varied considerably within the literature over the last decade and a half. There remain definitional issues regarding the developmental boundaries between childhood and adolescence. It is for this reason that we define childhood in the present book as spanning from birth to 14 years in order to maintain consistency across chapters. In addition to the issue of age–span definitions within the childhood career literature, there has been a skewed focus on middle to late childhood (8 to 14 years) rather than on earlier foundational substages of childhood. Further complicating our understanding of children's career development is the fact that earlier career theories' definitions of children reflected those historical times within which children developed. Children growing up in the '50s and '60s of the last century lived a slower-paced, less technologically exposed life, and they faced a more stable future work environment than that faced by children growing up in the new millennium.

There have been several attempts since the middle of the last decade to examine the emerging literature on children's career development. Given that this literature has been almost exclusively research driven, these attempts have predominantly taken the form of research reviews, all of which have appeared as journal articles or as special journal issues. Describing the story of children's career development over the last decade requires a consideration of the purpose of such storytelling. The American novelist, Therese Fowler, argues that storytelling goes way beyond its entertainment value and that it also serves the purpose of instructing us and of challenging the status quo. Indeed, reviewing extant research can often provide challenging perspectives of the status quo. However, it is not the intent of this chapter to review research (Chapter 7 provides the reader with the most recent review in this regard). Rather, this chapter considers the recommendations and conclusions of earlier reviews of children's literature in order to better contextualise how this first book on children's career development advances the field in terms of the known status quo.

Reviewing the story so far

Several reviews of the literature on children's career development have been published since the turn of this millennium. The first two substantive reviews appeared in the *Journal of Vocational Behavior* (Hartung, Porfeli, & Vondracek, 2005; Watson & McMahon, 2005). Hartung *et al.'s* review aimed to describe extant knowledge, propose future research directions, and link earlier career development with later lifespan developmental stages. In this review, children were defined as being between the ages of 3 and 14 years. The authors analysed nearly two hundred publications on children's career development, with the literature "scattered across a wide range of disciplines and journals" (p. 411). The review advocated for a more holistic perspective on children's career development, both within childhood itself as well as between childhood and other career development lifespan stages. The latter recommendation was based on Hartung *et al.'s* concern that the literature emphasises "discrete age-graded periods" (p. 411), with a particular focus on adolescent career development. This fragmented focus of research was criticised by Hartung *et al.* as labouring "under the mistaken assumption that key processes in vocational development take place almost exclusively in adolescence or later" (pp. 411–412).

The second review in the *Journal of Vocational Behavior* was by Watson and McMahon (2005). This review attempted a more holistic perspective by considering extant research within a learning framework. This framework addressed a concern raised by Hartung *et al.'s* (2005) review that most research has focused on what children know about the world of work rather than on how they know this. The definitional inclusion criteria for the review resulted in 76 publications over three decades, with children defined as 13 years and younger. Watson and McMahon concluded, similarly to Hartung *et al.*, that there was a lack of a holistic and cohesive perspective on children's career development which they attributed to several factors: methodological diversity, measurement diversity and conceptual and definitional diversity, as well as a consistent focus on identification rather than exploration of variables researched. Of concern is the fact that Watson and McMahon's resultant call for the literature to "understand more holistically the influences on and processes of career development learning in children" (p. 128) repeated a similar decade-old call in the literature (Gysbers, 1996).

The preceding two reviews focused on extant research on children's career development at the midpoint of the last decade. Since then there has been a book on career development in childhood and adolescence (Skorikov & Patton, 2007). There have also been subsequent reviews (e.g., Porfeli, Hartung, & Vondracek, 2008) – some of which have focused on invited collated publications. For instance, there was a special section in 2008 in *The Career Development Quarterly* (McMahon & Watson, 2008a) that attracted seven articles written by prominent researchers of children's career development. Two articles specifically considered the status quo of research in this field as well as the way forward. McMahon and Watson (2008b) expressed concern about the consistent and persistent disconnect between career theory, research and practice and argued that this limited our understanding of the "dynamic nature of children's career development" (p. 4). In addition, these authors felt that the issues raised about children's career development in this special journal section reflected decades-old concerns.

There was a sense that the field had not moved on in any significant way. This led Watson and McMahon (2008) to state in the concluding article to this special section that children's career development literature remained "in its infancy . . . compared with the maturation of the career literature that has focused on later developmental stages" (p. 76), thus suggesting that the career literature continued to evidence a skewed developmental focus. Several issues were raised in this special issue of *The Career Development Quarterly*. There was concern that there was a lack of an organising and interdisciplinary framework for understanding children's career development, thus raising the question of whether new theories need to be developed. This latter issue is addressed in Chapter 3 of this book, where Hartung considers the relevance of career construction theory for childhood career development, and Chapter 5, where Howard *et al.* describe their theory of children's vocational reasoning. Similar to the 2005 reviews, there was a concern about the methodologies evident in children's career development research, but less so about the diversity of such methodologies and more about the lack of diversity in methodology. In particular, the persistent dominance of cross-sectional research and the absence of substantive longitudinal research were seen as providing a limited and restrictive understanding of children's career development.

As with the earlier reviews, Watson and McMahon concluded that there was a need for a more holistic perspective and that more recent efforts had largely maintained the status quo in reinforcing "the disparate nature of career theory, research, and practice in this field" (pp. 81–82). Of interest to the reader of this book is the concern raised by Watson and McMahon of the skewed and limited samples on which much of the career literature on children's career development is presently founded. In particular, these authors called for a greater focus on children from lower socioeconomic backgrounds, different ethnic populations, and children with special needs. Several chapters in this book address these suggestions as well as Watson and McMahon's call for more international research in order to provide us with "a richer understanding of children's career development" (p. 82).

The most recent review of literature on children's career development is the special issue of the *International Journal for Educational and Vocational Guidance* (Watson, Nota, & McMahon, 2015b). Again, this issue represented seven invited collated publications, two of which explored present and future trends in the field. Watson, Nota, and McMahon (2015a) describe this special issue as focusing on advances in theory, practice, and assessment; the implications of such advancements for policy; and a focus on research on children's career development in diverse settings. These authors considered the percentage of journal articles that have focused on children's career development, as opposed to other life stages of career development, and established that the percentage has remained at the same low level of 3 per cent for the last two decades. This suggests that, while the body of research on children's career development may have grown since earlier decades, it still remains the Cinderella of career developmental stories. The second article of this special issue reviewed the latest contributions to the field of children's career development. This review resulted in Watson, Nota, and McMahon (2015c) proposing five possible directions for future research in the field. The first suggestion was that there was a need to focus on younger children, thus echoing earlier review comments about the skewed nature of children's career development research on middle to late childhood. The special issue reflected several international studies, leading to Watson *et al.'s* (2015c) second suggestion that international collaborative research should become a focus of future research. The third suggestion was a call for future research to focus on theoretical constructs, particularly in order to create a much-needed greater synergy between theory and research in the field. Several chapters in this book specifically address this latter suggestion.

Watson *et al.'s* (2015c) fourth suggestion was that there was a need for action research in order to better inform evidence-based practice. While this call for the consideration of other research methodologies seems to run counter to earlier critiques of too much methodological diversity in the field, it does reflect other criticisms from earlier reviews that criticised the field for having too narrow and restricted methodological perspectives. The fifth suggestion endorses earlier review critiques that established that there remains a limited focus on socioeconomically disadvantaged and disabled populations of children. There are several chapters in this book that specifically address this criticism. Finally, there was the identified need for research on children's career development to be related more closely with policy development in the field through strengthening interdisciplinary research.

Future stories

The chapters in this book respond well to the recommendations and conclusions arising out of reviews of the story of children's career development to date. The book itself is structured in five sections that reflect the chapter authors' perspectives on critical aspects of children's career development. There are sequential sections on theory, research, contextual influences, assessment, and facilitation of career exploration and development. The first section on 'Theoretical Perspectives' is subdivided into established and emergent theories. In Chapter 2, Trice and Greer consider several acknowledged foundational career development theories that emerged from the middle of the last century onwards. These include Ginzberg and associates' theory of occupational choice, Donald Super's career development model, Anne Roe's psychology of occupations, John Holland's theory of vocational personalities and work environments, and Linda Gottfredson's theory of circumscription and compromise. There is also mention of the perspectives of Robert Havighurst and Erik Erikson. Trice and Greer then briefly consider contemporary approaches in terms of four qualities that define current theoretical descriptions of children's career development. This latter description helps to set the scene for the three subsequent chapters that describe emerging theoretical perspectives in the career development of children.

In Chapter 3, Hartung considers the foundations and fundamental principles of career construction theory and the relevance of childhood as the first life stage in the construction of one's career over the lifespan. Patton describes in Chapter 4 the emergence of relational and systemic perspectives of career development by considering a number of theories and metatheoretical frameworks. More specifically, Patton considers these perspectives in relation to children's career development. Howard, Castine, Flanagan, and Lee describe the Conceptions of Career Choice and Attainment (CCCA) model in Chapter 5, a theoretical model of children's career development that was first published at the start of the present decade. Importantly, this model focuses not on what children know and are interested in but rather on how they conceptualise critical career developmental processes. As such, this model attempts to address known criticisms from earlier reviews that have called for this shift in perspective. The authors further advance the literature on this model by summarising its empirical support as well as its implications for intervention with children. In Chapter 6, McMahon and Watson consider children as storytellers and how, through this role, children begin to construct the foundations for their later career development in adolescence and adulthood. The authors consider the implications of a narrative perspective for child career development theory, research, and practice.

The second section of the book, 'Research Perspectives', consists of a single but extensive chapter (Chapter 7) that explores the present and future directions of research in children's career development. Importantly, the chapter reviews the literature subsequent to the seminal reviews described in this chapter. The research reviewed spans the years 2008 to 2015 and is guided by a metatheoretical framework within which the diverse research findings on children's career development can converge around a common theme. The third section of the book, 'Contextual Perspectives', consists of three chapters. In Chapter 8, Flouri, Joshi, Sullivan, and Moulton consider how children's aspirations develop over time as well as the contextual factors that may impact on this development. The authors consider the role of parents in the development of children's aspirations as well as the broader context (for example, the school and neighbourhood) within which such development occurs. In Chapter 9, Liu and McMahon consider further contextual factors in children's career development, with a specific focus on the family context. These authors describe how theory has considered the nature of family influence on children's career development and what research has established about such family influence. The chapter concludes with the authors considering the possible implications of the family context for career theory, research, and practice. Bakshi addresses a significant gap in the literature in Chapter 10 regarding child career development in developing world contexts. This chapter underscores the different contexts for child career development found in developing as opposed to developed world contexts and, in so doing, challenges the application of western career theory and research in developing world contexts. Bakshi describes contexts that are seldom read in the literature on children's career development, including those of child labour, religious identity, discrimination, and violence.

The fourth section of the book, 'Assessment Perspectives', consists of two chapters that explore the developing field of assessment of children's career development. In Chapter 11, Tracey and Sodano identify unique characteristics that need to be considered in the valid assessment of children's career development in order to better inform theories of children's career development. This chapter specifically focuses on the assessment of interests, self-efficacy, general aspects of career development, and personality traits as salient to the career development of children. Stead, Schultheiss, and Oliver (Chapter 12) review eight quantitative and seven qualitative instruments and procedures that are presently in use for assessing both children's career development as well as career intervention programs designed for use with children. The authors identify several diverse factors across quantitative and qualitative assessment procedures that need to be addressed if progress in children's career development is to be effectively evaluated. In the fifth and final section of the book, 'Facilitating Career Exploration and Development', three chapters focus on career interventions designed for use with children. In Chapter 13, Lapan, Bobek, and Kosciulek describe school-based career exploration and development approaches for children. The authors describe the possible positive impact of these interventions in relation to two major career development transitions that occur at ages 6 to 11 and again at ages 12 to 14 years. Critical career constructs as well as developmental tasks are described for each of these developmental transitions. Barnes and McGowan (Chapter 14) argue for the benefit of career exploration and development programmes for children with learning difficulties and disabilities, as well as children who come from socio-economically deprived backgrounds. The authors examine the lack of substantive initiatives to date and suggest key features for effective practice with disadvantaged children and children with specific needs. In the third and final chapter of this section (Chapter 15), Crause, Watson, and McMahon consider career development learning in childhood in relation to career development learning programs. Specifically, the authors consider suggestions from theory, research, policy, and practice in children's career development and propose eight holistic guidelines for the successful development and implementation of career development learning programs for children.

In the final chapter of the book (Chapter 16), Watson and McMahon reflect on the preceding chapters and consider how the field of children's career development should move forward.

Conclusion

There has been no substantive collation of recognised major contributors, to our understanding, of children's career development to date. This book represents the first attempt to do so, and it provides the chapter authors with greater freedom to express and describe their work than is traditionally afforded within the rigorous limitations of journal articles. While scholars in the field of children's career development, indeed of career psychology in general, would recognise these prominent chapter authors, the book collates their contributions into a book for the first time. In so doing, it allows us to consider the way forward for the field of children's career development. Salman Rushdie (1991) urges us to reconsider stories that have dominated our lives (or, in this case, dominated the field of children's career development) to have the power "to retell it, rethink it, deconstruct it . . . and change it as times change" in order that we can "think new thoughts" (p. 480). It is our hope that this book will do just that.

References

Gottfredson, L. S. (2002). Gottfredson's theory of circumscription, compromise, and self-creation. In D. Brown & Associates (Eds.), *Career choice and development* (4th ed., pp. 85–149). San Francisco, CA: Jossey-Bass.

Gottfredson, L. S. (2005). Applying Gottfredson's theory of circumscription and compromise in career guidance and counseling. In S. D. Brown & R. W. Lent (Eds.), *Career development and counseling: Putting theory and research to work* (pp. 71–100). New York: John Wiley & Sons.

Gysbers, N. C. (1996). Meeting the career needs of children and adolescents. *Journal of Vocational Education Research, 21*, 87–98.

Hartung, P. J., Porfeli, E. J., & Vondracek, F. W. (2005). Child vocational development: A review and consideration. *Journal of Vocational Behavior, 66*, 385–419.

McMahon, M., & Watson, M. (2008a). Career development in childhood [Special section]. *The Career Development Quarterly, 57*(1), 4–83.

McMahon, M., & Watson, M. (2008b). Children's career development: Status quo and future directions. *The Career Development Quarterly, 57*, 4–6.

Porfeli, E. J., Hartung, P. J., & Vondracek, F. W. (2008). Children's vocational development: A research rationale. *The Career Development Quarterly, 57*, 25–37.

Rushdie, S. (1991, Dec. 12). One thousand days in a balloon. *New York Times.* New York.

Skorikov, V. B., & Patton, W. (2007). *Career development in childhood and adolescence.* Rotterdam, The Netherlands: Sense Publishers.

Super, D. E. (1980). A life-span, life-space approach to career development. *Journal of Vocational Behavior, 16*, 282–298.

Super, D. E. (1990). A life-span, life-space approach to career development. In D. Brown & L. Brooks (Eds.), *Career choice and development: Applying contemporary theory to practice* (2nd ed., pp. 197–262). San Francisco, CA: Jossey-Bass.

Watson, M., & McMahon, M. (2005). Children's career development: A research review from a learning perspective. *Journal of Vocational Behavior, 67*, 119–132.

Watson, M., & McMahon, M. (2008). Children's career development: Metaphorical images of theory, research, and practice. *The Career Development Quarterly, 57*, 75–83.

Watson, M., Nota, L., & McMahon, M. (2015a). Child career development: Present and future trends. *International Journal for Educational and Vocational Guidance, 15*, 95–97.

Watson, M., Nota, L., & McMahon, M. (2015b). Childhood career development [Special issue]. *International Journal for Educational and Vocational Guidance, 15*, 95–184.

Watson, M., Nota, L., & McMahon, M. (2015c). Evolving stories of child career development. *International Journal for Educational and Vocational Guidance, 15*, 175–184.

Part 1

Theoretical perspectives

Chapter 2

Theories of career development in childhood and early adolescence

Ashton D. Trice and Hunter W. Greer

Asking children what they want to be when they grow up is a fairly common conversation between adults and children in the United States. Most children have an answer, and most of their answers are actual jobs. Often the answers are along gender lines: boys want to play the professional sport that is in season or be doctors or 'cops'. Girls want to be teachers and ballerinas and lawyers and veterinarians. Follow-up questions often reveal the bases for these aspirations to be flimsy: some children think you become a physician by putting in an application; others think they are qualified to be a lawyer because they have been told they like to argue. More than a third want to be what their parents are (Trice, 1991). Children rarely know much about the educational requirements or the pay or more than one thing they would do on that job on a regular basis (Trice, Hughes, Odom, Woods, & McClellan, 1995).

This lack of depth led many of the mid-twentieth-century career development theorists to minimise the importance of childhood and early adolescence. Career development was viewed as entirely a rational process of matching the demands of a career and aspects of the self. It was assumed that children knew very little about the world of work and almost nothing about themselves, and that they were not very rational. Many regarded implementing a career, not as a lengthy process of exploration and examination, but a decision to be made once the facts were in, and those facts might be simply the adolescent's profile of interests and a list of available jobs and training opportunities.

The lack of attention to the early years is not surprising given the history of vocational psychology. The first manifestation of the field, the matching of interests and careers, had just begun (e.g., Strong, 1927) when the Great Depression refocused the attention of those interested in the psychology of work on issues of unemployment and retraining. Many were refocused again by the demands of World War II and then again with the career needs of those exiting the military after 1945. Each of these historical events urgently focused the field on the mature worker facing seismic social change rather than younger persons finding their way. In this chapter, we will trace the theoretical threads that over the past sixty-or-so years have led to the need for a book like the present one. The first significant theoretical work to posit a (limited) role for the early years comes out of this trajectory in the work of Eli Ginzberg.

Occupational choice (1951)

Frustrated over the lack of coherent theory in vocational psychology on which to base aspects of this research, Ginzberg and associates conducted an interview study designed to provide age norms for career development. The resulting work was *Occupational Choice: An Approach to a General Theory* (Ginzberg, Ginsberg, Axelrad, & Herma, 1951). The theory was developmental and divided the career choice process into three stages. The first, which spanned the ages of 6 through 11, was termed *fantasy choice*; the second, which extended from 12 through 17, was called *tentative choice*; the last, which was designated *realistic choice*, started at age 18 and continued into early adulthood. During the fantasy choice period, children are said to 'choose' careers on the basis of *functional pleasure*, which means that simply by doing a particular job they and their family will derive benefit. Ginzberg *et al.* (1951) give an example of a child who says, "I would like to be a physician so that if anyone in my family gets sick I will be able to help" (p. 61). Early in this stage, children often want grandiose and spectacular jobs, but this gives way to more ordinary jobs over time. Children do not consider that some occupations may not be attainable.

The term 'fantasy' does not imply that children want jobs that do not or cannot exist (such as to be angels or minions), but that their understanding is based mostly on their own imaginations and interpretations of jobs:

> The fantasy element grows out of the inability of children to introduce the relation between means and ends into their thinking about the future – that is, to engage in rational considerations, without which they cannot establish or realize appropriate goals in the future. Children in the age group make any and every type of choice and are unaware of the barriers which stand in their way.
>
> (Ginzberg *et al.*, 1951, p. 63)

Since everything is possible, children's aspirations are fluid.

We also need to include what Ginzberg *et al.* (1951) said about the years immediately following the fantasy period. They divided the tentative period into four substages, the first two of which were the *interest stage* and the *capacity stage*. The interest stage is where adolescents select occupations based on their likes and interests, but in the capacity stage, increasingly realistic adolescents begin to think about their capacities and how they will limit their ability to achieve an occupation. During this time, too, the adolescent becomes more aware of different training and preparation and different work demands for different jobs.

The criticisms of Ginzberg (1952) were immediate and several. Many authors criticised the methodology (see Meadow (1955) for a summary). The sample was small (eight boys at two-year intervals from 11 through 24) and biased (high-achieving, white, urban, Christian males from intact families). All the young adults were in college or graduate school; the adolescents came from selective secondary schools. Also at the time, Ginzberg *et al.* (1951) were criticised for a lack of psychoanalytic interpretation of the boys' responses, but no one worried that the entire description of the fantasy choice stage was based on retrospective accounts. It is worth noting that by 1971 in *Career Guidance: Who Needs It, Who Provides It, Who Can Improve It*, Ginzberg was willing to entertain the notion of career guidance in the elementary schools. *Occupational Choice* (Ginzberg *et al.*, 1951) influenced career theory for decades; it made vocational psychologists regard career choice as a long-term developmental process, the origins of which lie in the elementary school years.

Donald Super

Donald E. Super's (1910–1994) work both precedes and antecedes that of Ginzberg. The son of the personnel specialist for the YMCA, Super took some time to find his own career direction. From that experience, he came to understand that the process he was studying was not a moment (occupational choice) but a process (career development) and that it was not a process of selecting one's ideal occupation but of compromising among career, family, location, income, etc.: "It is more important to have a good path and several alternative goals than to have a good goal" was an adage he often used (Savickas, 1995, p. 795). Super's (1953) early work had influenced Ginzberg to adopt a developmental approach to his theory. Super's developmental model, typical of the time, was a single pathway along which all must travel, although some travelled at different rates.

Super played a consultant role on *Occupational Choice* (Ginzberg *et al.*, 1951), and it was its publication, particularly his claim that vocational guidance suffered from having *no* theoretical basis, that provoked Super (1953) to write his most widely quoted article, 'A Theory of Vocational Development.' After specifically addressing Ginzberg's book and the 'shocked' and 'annoyed' reaction of the members of the National Vocational Guidance Association to Ginzberg's address to that organisation, Super (1953) laid out ten propositions for a theory. Three of those propositions are *apropos* to this discussion:

5   This process (of choice and adjustment) may be summed up in a series of life stages characterized as those of growth, exploration, establishment, maintenance, and decline, and these stages may be subdivided into (a) the fantasy, tentative, and realistic phases of the exploratory stage, and (b) the trial and stable phases of the establishment stage.

7   Development through the life stages can be guided, partly by facilitating the process of maturation or abilities and interests and partly by aiding in reality testing and in the development of a self-concept.

9   The process of compromise between individual and social factors, between self- concept and reality, is one of role playing, whether the role is played in fantasy, in the counseling interview, or in real life activities such as school classes, clubs, part-time work, and entry jobs.

(pp. 189–190)

In proposition 5, Super (1953) comes close to adopting the developmental sequence proposed by Ginzberg (1952), but he extends the domain of career theory to include maintenance and decline. As one of the founders of lifespan orientation within developmental psychology, Super insisted not only in extending the process of career development back to include the childhood antecedents of career establishment but also expanding it forward to include the periods of adulthood and old age. While Super acknowledged that some career development occurs in childhood, he did not pay particular attention to what it was. In his classic longitudinal study, published over a period of 20 years, known as the Career Pattern Study, he began following his study group only at age 14 (Super & Overstreet, 1960).

In proposition 7, Super (1953) hints at one of his main contributions to career counselling, the concept of *career maturity*. While children and adolescents are all on the same path, some move more slowly. This may put some individuals in a catch between their stage of career development and their state of life. A college junior is expected to have declared a major, but there are some who are still trying on any and every type of choice. This type of student can be assisted, Super asserts, by professional vocational intervention.

With proposition 9, Super (1953) puts an emphasis on the issue of compromise. Although there was some passing attention paid to this idea by Ginzberg *et al.* (1951), Super is the theorist and practitioner who first made this idea central to the process of career counselling. Unlike the interest inventories on which Super had worked for a decade by this time, which sometimes promised to find *the* occupation that matched one's interests, Super came to believe that career development involved compromising the ideal job for other aspects of life (e.g., should one take a job if the location is far from family and one's other interests? Should one be so set on a specific position that if someone else is deemed more qualified, one's whole self-concept is shattered?). Where this self-concept comes from would be the focus of our next theorist.

Anne Roe's theories

Anne Roe's (1904–1991) dissertation studied the kinds of errors musicians made when sight-reading. During the next 15 years, she took a number of short-term positions examining issues as diverse as the IQ profiles of Native Americans, breastfeeding, alcohol education, and personalities of successful artists. In 1938, she married the well-known palaeontologist George Simpson, and she combined many of her previous areas of research into her own study of the differences among eminent men of science. In this work, she found differences among biologists, physicists, and social scientists that related to their types of intelligence (verbal, spatial, or symbolic) and to their upbringing. This work culminated in the publication of *The Making of a Scientist* in 1953 and *The Psychology of Occupations* in 1956.

The most researched aspect of this work was the proposal that the quality of early family experiences leads to the formation of basic personality types, which in turn lead to occupational choices. She identified three categories of parent interactions with children, each with two subcategories: (a) Emotional Concentration (overprotection and over-demanding), (b) Avoidance (rejection and neglect), and (c) Acceptance (casual acceptance and loving acceptance). Each of these categories/subcategories was hypothesised to lead to a cluster of occupations. Dissatisfied with existing classifications, Roe produced a new one based on two levels: the first level included eight foci of activity (e.g., service, business contact, technology) and the second six levels at which the activity is pursued (from unskilled to professional/managerial).

Because certain parenting patterns lead to unsatisfied needs, those raised that way, when adults, were proposed to turn to occupations to satisfy them:

> Homes in which children are the center of attention provide pretty full satisfaction of physiological and safety needs, and attention to needs for love and esteem, but gratification is usually not entirely routine. The overprotecting home places great emphasis upon gratification and generally upon immediacy of gratification, which keeps lower level need satisfaction in the foreground. Belongingness, love, and esteem are often made conditional upon dependency and conformity, and genuine self actualization may be discouraged.
>
> (Roe, 1957, p. 215)

Children from casually accepting, neglecting, and rejecting homes would not develop a major orientation toward persons, and this would then lead to interest in technology, outdoor, and science careers; those from overprotective and over-demanding homes would develop an orientation to the self and to self-expressive careers in arts, entertainment, and general culture, while those from loving, accepting homes would develop an orientation to others which would play out in service careers. Business careers were associated with loving acceptance, overprotection, and over-demanding parenting.

While the parenting-personality-profession proposition is the most remembered aspect of her theory (it was what she chose to write about in presenting her theory in a 1957 *Journal of Counseling Psychology* article), there were other aspects of her theory, including the general state of the economy, education, special acquired skills, physical capacity, friends, marital situation, cognitive capacity, interests, and values (Lunneborg, 1997). The specifics of the parenting-personality-profession hypothesis failed to withstand empirical testing. At first, Roe (1964) objected to the way studies were operationalised, but by 1964 she had abandoned the proposition. In later writing on careers, she emphasised the multifaceted nature of work patterns: each profession had norms in terms of special skills, education, the role of friends and family, interest, etc. She urged those seeking careers to find careers where they best fit in because it would lead to job and life satisfaction, while at the same time noting that occupations profited from the innovations of those who did *not* fit in. Perhaps her most lasting

John Holland

The theory of John Holland (1959, 1997) seems to bring together a great many of the ideas from the previous theories. It is a person-environment matching system. It is based on personality. It is assumed that people are in search of job environments where they can use their skills and abilities and express their values and attitudes. People who choose to work in an environment compatible with their personality are more likely to be successful and satisfied. 'Matches' are made between the person and large clusters of occupations so that there is a good deal of room for compromise.

Holland (1960) developed a measure, the Vocational Preference Inventory, that produced scores on 12 traits, such as physical activity, conformity, emotionality, and intellectuality and validated these traits against traditional personality inventories. He then found that these traits had power to predict into which of six work clusters adolescents would fit. Originally, the six work environments were called the motoric, the intellectual, the esthetic, the supportive, the persuasive, and the conforming. In later versions of his theory, Holland collapsed his traits to form six personality types. He used the same labels to define the personality types as the work environments, although the labels were less jargonesque. The six types/work environments are noted in Table 2.1.

After the publication of a brief overview of the theory in the *Journal of Counseling Psychology* (Holland, 1959), E. S. Bordin provides the following comment:

> It is debatable how much, beyond greater vividness, is added by the typology of personal orientations. Since it will certainly founder on the discontinuity requirement, as do most typologies, it ends up descriptions of dimension along which persons are distributed and as such becomes a functional duplication of the occupational categories. In this sense we have a series of joint scales on which persons and occupations can be distributed.
>
> (Bordin, 1959, pp. 44–45)

Table 2.1 Holland's six types, occupations, and traits

Type	Occupations	Traits
Realistic	outdoors/making things	practical, concrete
Investigative	scientific, problem solving	inquisitive, analytical
Artistic	arts	innovative, unconventional
Social	helping professions	helpful, outgoing
Enterprising	sales/management	self-confident, persuasive
Conventional	business data	orderly, conscientious

While Bordin's comments are not particularly friendly, they are apt. No doubt the theory's *vividness* helped contribute to its longevity. It makes sense to children as well as adults that if you enjoy doing things with your hands and you have some talent, being a carpenter or a machinist might be a serious career option. Holland's theory and some of his instruments may not be elegant, but in diverse, growing economies, they have proven useful for generations of adolescents and returning workers. Like his predecessors, he acknowledges the importance of early experience in forming interests (Holland, 1997) but there is little specific description in this regard. The examples he uses, however, are positive rather than psychopathological: working with a mother to repaint the living room may teach a child that he or she does not have the patience for detailed work. Going hiking with a father who can explain why hiking is fun may lead to an interest in conservation.

Two brief diversions: Havighurst and Erikson

Two writers contemporary with the early development of Holland's (1959) theory, Robert Havighurst and Erik Erikson, made contributions to career development that did not have much impact at the time but which would gradually influence career theory, particularly for children and adolescents. Along with Super, Robert Havighurst and Erik Erikson were founders of the lifespan approach to developmental psychology. Before the 1950s, the study of human development was mostly limited to the ages of 2 through 16. Infancy, and especially prenatal development, were left to medical specialists (mostly), and it was largely assumed that nothing interesting psychologically happened after adolescence. Marriage and the family were studied by sociologists and work had been the purview of organisational behaviour specialists. The end was again thought to belong to the medicos. Each of these theorists eventually came to a conception-to-death vision of development. With regard to career theory, this meant that it did not begin in mid-adolescence or end there. Both Havighurst and Erikson made one shining, brief contribution to vocational theory in the 1950s.

Robert Havighurst (1900–1991) was trained as a chemist, but turned his attention to education in 1928. He is probably best known for his research showing the limited value of rote learning and the concept of *developmental tasks*. Developmental tasks are *developmental* in that they arise at different ages, or, more accurately, they have different aspects at different ages. They are *tasks* because biological growth, social situations, or societal expectations sets the person to accomplishing them. Among the developmental tasks that Havighurst wrote about was choosing a career. Although he addressed the issue throughout his work, his definitive statement came in 1964. Here he divided the ages we are considering into two periods for the task of choosing a career: (1) Identification with a Worker (ages 5 to 10) and (2) Acquiring the Basic Habits of Industry (ages 10 to 15). The worker with whom the child identifies is often the parent, but it can be a teacher, a neighbour, or even a fictional character. Through identification, the child imitates (or imagines) what it is like to be that person in his or her work role and out of it. Havighurst felt this was the way children learned about the world of work. During the period of Acquiring the Basic Habits of Industry, through various home and school activities, the child learns (or does not learn) to organise time and effort to accomplish goals and to put work ahead of play in appropriate situations. It is not merely that children work on these tasks, but they come to know themselves by the way they succeed or fail at them. A child acquires valuable information about him- or herself: *I am well organised; I am a hard worker; I prefer goofing off to sustained effort; etc.*

It is worth noting that these tasks are not directly 'career exploration.' They are, rather, steps toward career exploration in the future. They should suggest to those who objected to career education in the elementary school years (because career development was impossible since children had little knowledge of the world of work and no knowledge of themselves) that this was the appropriate developmental process through which children acquired that base knowledge.

Erik Erikson (1902–1994) is best known for his eight developmental conflicts and the concept of the identity crisis. While never known as a 'career theorist', his theoretical writings often dealt with careers, and his writing influenced later theorists. In fact, in his most important theoretical writing, the chapter on the eight developmental conflicts from *Childhood and Society* (Erikson, 1950), all but one of his examples about identity are career examples.

The eight developmental conflicts appear to rise from nowhere in the middle of a book on how society bends the route of biology in childhood (Erikson, 1950). There are no references to previous research or theory, although it is usually pointed out that the first three stages map nicely onto Freud's three developmental crises. It is Conflicts 4 and 5 that describe the age range we are interested in: 4. Industry versus Inferiority (ages 5 to 11) and 5. Identity versus Role Confusion (ages 11 to 18).

During Conflict 4, through social interactions with peers, children develop a sense of pride in their abilities and accomplishments. When encouraged by parents and teachers, they develop feelings of competence and beliefs in their skills. These are children who will go on to have high aspirations and career self-efficacy. They develop what Erikson (1950) describes as *Purpose*. Those who are shunned by peers and who receive little or no encouragement from teachers and parents will come to doubt their abilities to become successful and will set low career and educational expectations or have none at all. They may become isolated or cope with their inferiority by become conformists.

Conflict 5 has often been regarded as the most critical aspect of the theory, or at least Erikson's (1950) most original contribution. The adolescent who receives proper guidance and engages in personal exploration will come out of this stage with a strong sense of self (identity) and feelings of independence and control. Much of this is because adolescents are concerned about how others perceive them – how they make their presentation to the world. Career aspirations are particularly important because they put the adolescent into a place in this social world. The adolescent who achieves identity will develop what Erikson described as *Fidelity*, which is described as the ability to sustain loyalties in spite of the inevitable confusions of value systems.

Establishing an identity (ethnic, gender, political, etc.) is not necessarily easy and may lead famously to an *identity crisis*. Not all aspects of identity may go through this crisis, but after the crisis has been resolved (e.g., not getting good enough grades to get into the nursing program, but then deciding to study to be a radiology technician), the identity is more secure.

Adolescents who do not develop an identity become confused about their role: *I do not know what I want to be when I grow up*. This can exhibit itself in what Erikson (190) described as *diffusion*, or wanting to be everything; it can show itself in a *psychosocial moratorium*, which is a return to exploration of making a commitment.

Linda Gottfredson

Returning to the narrative we interrupted, the last of the traditional theories is that of Linda Gottfredson. She is the first to propose a theory specific to childhood and early adolescence. In 1981, she turned the ideas of school counsellors on their heads by proposing that the main task of this period was not to experience ever-widening opportunities for career exploration. She proposed that self-concept and occupational preference develop in a four-stage process from age three on so that, as children have a better understanding of themselves and the world of work, they *restrict* occupational preferences and choices, which is a process Gottfredson refers to as *circumscription*. The process of restriction of occupations is seen as relatively permanent and therefore not completely benign. Children could eliminate from further consideration the vast majority of occupations. The theory also differs from the others we have considered in that it views early career development as an attempt to implement a social self-concept rather than a psychological one.

In the first stage of *orientation to size and power*, children from 3 through 5 years of age recognise size and power distinctions between themselves and adults, and they recognise that adults hold occupational roles. During the second stage of *orientation-to-sex role*, 6- to 8-year-olds categorise jobs by sex appropriateness and eliminate occupations that are perceived as inappropriate for their sex. The crux of the theory can be seen here: most children are aware of their sex. They also can observe such concrete things as what the sex composition of an occupation is, what kinds of clothes they wear to work, etc. Children are also attentive to what they hear about occupations from the adults in their sphere and, they hear that certain occupations are 'good for a mother' or are 'better suited for a man.' Children do not find an occupation attractive because they are boys and they perceive it as a 'man's' job, but they will say they are not interested in an occupation, sometimes very enthusiastically, because they are boys and they perceive the occupation as a 'woman's' job (Gottfredson, 1981).

The third stage of *orientation to social valuation* (Gottfredson, 1981) occurs when children between the ages of 9 and 12 become aware that social class and intelligence constitute critical distinctions between themselves and others. During this stage, occupations that are viewed as too difficult to obtain, given the children's perception of their abilities, or which have unacceptably low prestige, are eliminated. Gottfredson notes that this is the stage at which we first see what has been traditionally called vocational maturity. Gottfredson proposes that the process of circumscription sets tolerable boundaries: for the *tolerable-sex-type boundary*, there would be some kinds of jobs that an individual child would find too cross-sex typed; for the *tolerable-level boundary*, there would be jobs that were below acceptable status; and for the *tolerable-effort boundary*, there would be jobs that were too difficult.

It is only in the final stage, *orientation to internal, unique self*, beginning after age 14, that adolescents eliminate occupations incompatible with their interests, values, and competencies and choose those that maximise their psychological self. Gottfredson's (1981) theory is not without controversy within the counselling community. For instance, Luke and Redekop as recently as 2014 have complained that there is too much emphasis on ability and the idea that some occupations are restricted to many on that basis.

Contemporary approaches to early career development

The previous seven theories are all associated with a person. They are theories in the main in line with Kuhn's (1970) idea of a theoretical 'revolution': the work of a single person upon finding gaps in the predictive ability of previous theory, often abetted by a measurement or methodological innovation (e.g., creating developmental norms, Roe's Map of the World of Work (Roe, 1957), and the Self-Directed Search (Holland, 1985)). Theory today is less tied to the work of a single person and more aligned with an idea. For example, in the last 15 years, we have experienced an explosion of career perspectives such as Happenstance Learning Theory (Krumboltz, Foley, & Cotter, 2013), Action Theory (Young & Valach, 2008), Social Cognitive Career Theory (Lent, 2013), and a number of qualitative/constructivist approaches (Schultheiss, 2005). What these seem to all have in common is a realisation that there has been a profound change in the work environment.

Many writers in developmental psychology have noted the decline of the 'grand' theory (e.g., Clarke-Stewart & Parke, 2014), and this trend is reflected in career theory. It is less 'grand' in one sense. It does not insist on describing everyone's entire work life as a single course; in fact, it insists that there are different paths for different children: not only are there different starting places and different obstacles based on sex, race, culture, social class, economic status, language, parenthood, immigrant status, and disability, but there are also different goals, some of which are not *ultimate*. Children today know that the world of work as we know it may not exist for them in middle age. They know fathers who are working from home for a time to raise toddlers. They read about people who have taken unappealing temporary work to support aspirations as different as becoming an actor to an Olympic athlete. But theory is now even grander in that it would like career theory to be less culture bound and as applicable to refugees from Somalia living in the Ukraine as it is to affluent Upper East Side boys (Nota, Soresi, Ferrari, & Ginevra, 2014).

Here are four qualities that seem to define current theoretical efforts in the career development of elementary- and middle school–aged children:

1   Personality is not seen as the primary intraindividual force in career development. Motivation, ability, flexibility, special skills – all those things Anne Roe (1956) grazed over – now seem more important and personality somewhat less so. There is certainly more of an emphasis in the schools on developing 'marketable skills' than there is on finding oneself.
2   There is much attention on the changing world of work. Nearly every article of recent vintage on career theory carries the following tag: *in a changing workplace*. There is less consensus about how it is changing and what the endpoint might be. But who might have imagined five years ago that taxi driver might not be a job in a few more years or that librarian would become an applied IT profession.
3   Technology will play some role in the changing workplace. Whether it will be the creator of a vast new landscape of work possibilities or the crusher of whole sectors of the economy depends on one's perspective.
4   Bright, white, able-bodied suburban males without mental health issues are not the norm. The grand theories portrayed career development as a wide boulevard down which all were destined to walk, with some perhaps lingering for quite a while in places called career immaturity or moratorium. Today, some are taking different roads to get to the same place, and some are going to different places.

Conclusion

So is it worth revisiting the theories of the mid-twentieth century? We think so. While grand, stage-based developmental theories are no longer in vogue, the mechanisms of change that were proposed – imitation, identification, fantasising, compromising, crystallising, conscripting – still seem to describe what children are doing when they think about the future and their place in it. All of these mechanisms can be constructivist processes; all can be understood in today's context as guides down an individual path, rather than a universal highway; and all can be pushed out into later ages by the necessity of a more rapidly changing workplace.

References

Bordin, E. S. (1959). Comment. *Journal of Counseling Psychology, 6*, 44–45.

Clarke-Stewart, A., & Parke, R. D. (2014). *Social development* (2nd ed.). Hoboken, NJ: Wiley & Sons.

Erikson, E. (1950). *Childhood and society.* New York, NY: Norton.

Ginzberg, E. (1952). Toward a theory of occupational choice. *Occupations, 30*, 491–494.

Ginzberg, E. (1971). *Career guidance: Who needs it, who provides it, who can improve it.* New York, NY: McGraw-Hill.

Ginzberg, E., Ginsburg, S. W., Axelrad, S., & Herma, J. L. (1951). *Occupational choice: An approach to a general theory.* New York, NY: Columbia University Press.

Gottfredson, L. S. (1981). Circumscription and compromise: A developmental theory of occupational aspirations. *Journal of Counseling Psychology, 28*, 545–579.

Havighurst, R. J. (1964). Youth in exploration and man emergent. In H. Borow (Ed.), *Man in a world of work* (pp. 215–235). Boston: Houghton Mifflin.

Holland, J. L. (1959). A theory of vocational choice. *Journal of Counseling Psychology, 6*, 35–44.

Holland, J. L. (1960). The relation of the vocational preference inventory to the sixteen personality factor questionnaire. *Journal of Applied Psychology, 44*, 291–296.

Holland, J. L. (1985). *The self-directed search: A guide to educational and vocational planning.* Odessa, FL: Psychological Assessment Resources.

Holland, J. L. (1997). *Making vocational choices: A theory of vocational personalities and work environments* (3rd ed.). Odessa, FL: Psychological Assessment Resources.

Krumboltz, J. D., Foley, P. F., & Cotter, E. W. (2013). Applying the happenstance learning theory to involuntary career planning and adjustment in the new workplace. *The Career Development Quarterly, 61*, 15–26.

Kuhn, T. S. (1970). *The structure of scientific revolutions.* Chicago, IL: University of Chicago Press.

Lent, R. W. (2013). Career-life preparedness: Revisiting career planning and adjustment in the new workplace. *The Career Development Quarterly, 61*, 2–14.

Luke, C., & Redekop, F. (2014). Gottfredson's theory of career circumscription and compromise. In G. T. Eliason, T. Eliason, J. Samide, & J. Patrick (Eds.), *Career development across the lifespan: Counseling for community, schools, higher education, and beyond* (pp. 65–84). Charlotte, NC: IAP Information Age.

Lunneborg, P. W. (1997). Putting Roe in perspective. *Journal of Vocational Behavior, 51*, 301–305.

Meadow, L. (1955). Toward a theory of vocational choice. *Journal of Counseling Psychology, 2*, 108–112.

Nota, L., Soresi, S., Ferrari, L., & Ginevra, M. C. (2014). Vocational designing and career counseling in Europe: Challenges and new horizons. *European Psychologist, 19*, 248–259.

Roe, A. (1953). *The making of a scientist.* New York, NY: Dodd, Mead.

Roe, A. (1956). *The psychology of occupations.* New York, NY: Wiley.

Roe, A. (1957). Early determinants of vocational choice. *Journal of Counseling Psychology, 4*, 212–217.

Roe, A. (1959). Childhood experience with parental attitudes: A test of Roe's hypotheses: Comment. *Journal of Counseling Psychology, 6*, 155–156.

Roe, A. (1964). Personality structure and occupational behavior. In H. Borow (Ed.), *Man in a world of work* (pp. 196–214). Boston, MA: Houghton Mifflin.

Savickas, M. L. (1995). Donald E. Super. *American Psychologist, 50*, 794–795.

Schultheiss, D. E. P. (2005). Qualitative relational career assessment: A constructivist paradigm. *Journal of Career Assessment, 13*, 381–394.

Strong, E. K. (1927). Differentiation of certified public accountants from other occupational groups. *Journal of Educational Psychology, 18*, 227–238.

Super, D. E. (1953). A theory of vocational development. *American Psychologist, 8*, 185–190.

Super, D. E., & Overstreet, P. (1960). *The vocational maturity of ninth-grade boys*. New York, NY: Columbia Teachers College.

Trice, A. D. (1991). Stability of children' career aspirations. *Journal of Genetic Psychology, 152*, 137–139.

Trice, A. D., Hughes, M. A., Odom, C., Woods, K., & McClellan, N. C. (1995). The origins of children's career aspirations: IV. Testing hypotheses from four theories. *The Career Development Quarterly, 43*, 307–322.

Young, R. A., & Valach, L. (2008). Action theory: An integrative paradigm for research and evaluation in career. In J. Athanasou & R. van Esbroeck (Eds.), *International handbook of career guidance* (pp. 643–658). New York, NY: Springer.

Chapter 3

Childhood

Career construction's opening act

Paul J. Hartung

> All the world's a stage and all the men and women merely players.
> (William Shakespeare, *As You Like It*, 1623)

Childhood forms the opening act for constructing a career (Hartung, 2015; Savickas, 2013); it is a warm-up, of sorts, for the acts to follow during adolescence and the subsequent periods of emerging and full-fledged adulthood. As in Shakespeare's seven ages of man, childhood represents one of many developmental acts in which human life-careers form and play out. Spanning ages 3 to 14 years (Hartung, Porfeli, & Vondracek, 2005), childhood begins career construction's lifelong processes of making the self into the person one wishes to become, adapting to changes in self and situation, and endeavouring to use work to be oneself more fully and in ways that benefit society.

As evidenced by the present book and underscored in prior works (e.g., Hartung *et al.*, 2005; Watson & McMahon, 2005), childhood entails the foundational formative developmental context in which humans construct their work careers. Fully aligned with and advancing this view, career construction theory and practice consider childhood as a vital age period rich in antecedent events, endeavours, and experiences of tremendous consequence for lifelong career growth, development, and work adjustment (Hartung, 2015; Savickas, 2013). As a theory or, preferably and consistent with its constructionist base, a discourse about vocational behaviour, career construction integrates three psychological principles: individual differences in the psychology of occupations (Holland, 1997; Parsons, 1909), lifespan development in the psychology of careers (Super, 1990), and constructivism-social constructionism in the psychology of life design (Savickas, 2012; Savickas *et al.*, 2009). Of these principles, career construction theory takes social constructionism as its guiding convention. As a system of counselling, career construction integrates three corresponding career intervention practices: vocational guidance for matching self to occupations, career education for managing career tasks and transitions, and life design for meaningfully constructing a life-career (Savickas, 2015). Of these practices, career construction counselling takes life design and narrative as its guiding scheme. Combined, these principle and practice integrations permit viewing and fostering the evolving human self in three ways (McAdams, 2013; Savickas, 2013). First, the self may be viewed as an actor resembling a social script that fits corresponding work environments (à la vocational personality types; Holland, 1997). Second, the self may be viewed as an agent who develops readiness to fit work into life (à la career maturity/adaptability; Super, 1990). Third, the self may be viewed as an author who reflexively shapes and realises an identity through work roles (à la life portraits; Savickas, 2011).

As with most career theories and intervention practices, career construction can benefit by amplifying its explanation of and practical applications to child career development. That is because career theory, research, and practice typically attend mostly to adolescence and adulthood with significantly less attention to childhood (Vondracek, 2001). Yet sizeable conceptual and empirical literatures also support the centrality of the childhood years in shaping principal career construction processes of self-making, adaptation, and narration (Hartung *et al.*, 2005; Watson & McMahon, 2005). Recognising these facts, the present chapter specifically considers the foundations and core constructs of career construction theory with respect to the childhood years. Interested readers may find a chapter located elsewhere (Hartung, 2015) and others within the present book useful for considering some practical applications of career construction principles to career intervention with children. The following review and consideration of the foundations and fundamental principles of the theory aim to underscore childhood as the opening act of a lifelong career construction play.

Cornerstones of child career construction

Career construction theory stands as an original statement about how from early childhood individuals construct themselves through language and social interaction, direct their vocational behaviour, and give their work careers meaning (Savickas, 2013). Yet no theory emerges from a vacuum. Career construction thus finds its intellectual roots embedded deeply within constructivism (Kelly, 1955) and social constructionism (Gergen, 1999), and its fundamental constructs are a synergistic blend of vocational psychology's three grand traditions of individual differences (Holland, 1997), lifespan development (Super, 1990), and life design (Savickas *et al.*, 2009). Career construction assembles from these three traditions corresponding views on self as actor, agent, and author. These intellectual forebears, guiding paradigms, and self-views inform comprehending child career construction processes.

Constructivism and social constructionism

Aligned with psychological constructivism (Kelly, 1955), career construction discourse asserts that the developing child, much like Kelly's person-as-scientist, uses personal cognitive structures to make meaning of experiences. Through meaning-making, children form views on self and orientations to the world and to work. Career construction understands the child's nascent self-view and work orientation as a result of the unique language-based constructs they use to organise and make sense of their experiences and the world. Personal constructs represent idiosyncratic hypotheses, ideas, and abstractions children form about themselves, others, and their experiences. They use these constructs to anticipate and give meaning to events, activities, people, and experiences. Work orientations, particularly in the form of vicarious learning through parents' transmission of their own work experiences to children (Porfeli, Wang, & Hartung, 2008), begin to form through which children anticipate, interpret, and shape their work aspirations and expectations (Rojewski, 2005).

Using social constructionism, career construction views the child as a storyteller who uses narrative and relationships to co-construct meaning (Gergen, 1999). In their narratives, children project self in the past and the future in a way that preserves some sense of coherence and meaning (Ahn, 2011). Comprehending the child's career as a story under construction recognises the child as a holistic, self-organising, and active constructor and shaper of a personal life narrative and script played out in family, play, household work, and other elements of their experience. Through the stories they tell, children link past, present, and future and imbue their lives with unity, purpose, and a budding sense of identity (McAdams, 1985). For the child, work in the form of growing vocational aspirations, expectations, interests, abilities, and work values begins to offer a vehicle for advancing a future life project (Savickas, 2011).

Differences, development, and design

Rooted, then, in constructivist and social constructionist principles, career construction discourse proceeds to meld vocational psychology's three grand paradigms of individual differences (Holland, 1997), lifespan development (Super, 1990), and life design (Savickas, 2012) in a singular unified view on human life-careers (Savickas, 2013). Accordingly, career construction asserts that children distinguish social reputations with manifest traits formed by self-making through identification with role models who characterise them as they interact with and adapt to the social and, eventually, occupational world. Career construction recognises, too, that children face imminent societal expectations they must meet to develop initial readiness for managing tasks, transitions, and traumas over the life course. Career construction locates adult careers in life themes traced to pains, preoccupations, and problems experienced in early childhood. Career construction thus combines vocational psychology's language and discourse of traits, tasks, and themes in a comprehensive and synergistic view on lifelong vocational behaviour and processes anchored in the childhood years.

Traits: Differentiating a reputation

Children repeat and rehearse interests, skills, abilities, and other traits in home-, school-, and play-based activities. These behaviours gain consistency and stability to eventually form the child's recognisable personality or, in the language of career construction, the child's emerging socially situated *reputation* (Savickas, 2013). The child's reputation further contains personal strengths, limitations, interests, values, abilities, talents, and personality characteristics by which they begin fashioning themselves into the persons they wish to become.

In the process of self-making, children consciously look to others outside the family to provide a way of solving problems with which life presents them. Children select role models in the form of heroes and heroines who they believe can provide them with effective templates for constructing a self and determining how to live life successfully. By imitating their role models, children develop coping strategies relevant to solving their problems and forming values and interests. If asked, children will describe themselves when describing the admired characteristics of their role models (Savickas, 2011). Through this process of identifying with valued models, children construct a self to be enacted in favoured settings that will provide them with a stage to most fully be themselves.

Tasks: Developing career adaptability

Elaborating on and advancing the career stage of growth (Super, 1990), career construction theory names *orientation* as a central period of child career construction. Through career orientation, children concentrate on the goal of forming an initial and realistic vocational self-concept in part by identifying with significant others. The budding self reflects the child's formative answer to the question 'Who am I?' in a mental representation of the child's growing reputation. This reputation contains the child's public picture and private purpose concerning the future role of work in her or his life. Society expects that opportunities and experiences afforded at home, play, and school will arouse the child's curiosities, fantasies, interests, and capacities to begin constructing a viable self to be enacted in roles within work, family, community, leisure, and other life domains.

Through career orientation, children launch an enduring process of adapting self to situation. By accruing an array of experiences, children hone core attitudes, beliefs, and competencies (ABCs) for planning a future, making career decisions, exploring self and occupations, and building confidence to shape a career. These ABCs comprise core dimensions of *career adaptability*, which is a cardinal construct of career construction (Hartung, Porfeli, & Vondracek, 2008; Savickas, 2013). To begin building career adaptability, children use their activities and experiences to form initial (a) concern about the future, (b) control over their lives, (c) curiosity about work and careers, and (d) confidence to construct a future and deal with barriers (Savickas, 2013). Career concern means envisioning possible futures, control means owning the future, curiosity fuels exploration of possible selves and occupations, and confidence involves feeling empowered to construct a preferred future and to deal with obstacles. Children must learn to imagine, to be self-responsible, and to problem solve in order to construct a viable future consistent with cultural imperatives of work, love, play, and friendship (Dawis, 1995; Hartung, 2002) conveyed in family and community contexts. The orientation task of building career adaptability compels the child to begin to look ahead, to look around, to self-regulate, and to proceed with self-efficacy.

Principal in childhood is the development of a future orientation. Career construction uses the individual development perspective to comprehend career growth and change in the context of the child's whole life. Career context concerns how the child begins to manage life roles, navigate transitions, and meet social expectations. When children deal effectively with developmental tasks, they succeed as agents in managing their careers and fitting work into their lives. Children who adapt to career orientation concerns ready themselves for the future with a planning orientation through which they can more effectively manage the role of work in their lives (Savickas, 2013).

Themes: Designing intentionality

Children participate in goal-directed action and in so doing begin to meaningfully perform their own life stories. In so doing, they build *intentionality* – meaningful engagement in activities embedded within psychosocial roles. From an early age, children purposefully select activities in play and school through which they perform and explore roles (Sutton-Smith, 1997). As an example, a young child "frequently pretends that she is a cheerleader. She dances, jumps, and twirls in youthful imitation of her older heroines" (Vandenberg cited in Sutton-Smith, 1997, p. 187). The child's behaviour perhaps reflects simple role rehearsal and skill development. Yet her behaviour may also reflect intentional action involving her choice of cheerleading from among a host of possible roles because her mother was a cheerleader and encouraged her daughter in this activity. As intentional action, the daughter attempts "to construct a possible future for herself as she plays with the meanings of maturity and adulthood that have been presented to her by her mother" (Vandenberg cited in Sutton-Smith, 1997, p. 187). Envisioning possible selves and future life-careers requires action combined with meaning. Social contexts of family, school, and community typically foster children's gradually burgeoning intentionality.

Childhood also sets the stage for the emergence of a life theme that shapes the adult career, giving it meaning, purpose, and direction (Savickas, 2011). Children begin constructing narrative identities that hint at their life themes and include their views on self in work, family, community, and other psychosocial roles (McAdams, 2008; Savickas, 2002). Childhood thus figures prominently in shaping the rich context and narratives that comprise life histories and career patterns. This basic principle of career construction may best be conveyed in the book *The Power and the Glory*, where Graham Greene (1940) asserted, "There is always one moment in childhood when the door opens and lets the future in" (p. 15). Through play and exploration, children begin envisioning their futures. Play promotes self-construction, as children imagine themselves in work and other social roles. Childhood play also contains the essential theme of the whole life that gets constructed through each ensuing developmental-age period (Mabie, 1898). Self-construction processes and enactment of the life theme continue as childhood gives way to navigating transitions during adolescence and adulthood.

Self-making: Actor, agent, author

Aligned with the core career construction constructs of reputation, career adaptability, and intentionality, career construction theory advances three corresponding views on self-emergence in childhood (Savickas, 2013). These views involve construction of self, respectively, as actor, agent, and author (McAdams, 2013; Savickas, 2011; 2013). Childhood provides the initial stage upon which self as actor, self as agent, and self as author initially get constructed, enacted, and engaged antecedent to an adult work career (Hartung, 2015; Savickas, 2013). Absorbed by fantasy, curiosity, and aspiration, it is constructing self as actor and agent that most occupy the child. In time, children eventually come to match self to adult jobs and occupations, like an actor in a role; manage self in work and career over the lifespan, like an agent who directs a career; and make self through constructing a personally meaningful and socially useful life-career, like an author who writes a script. Accordingly, childhood involves initial and rudimentary orientation to these lifelong career construction self-making processes considered here in turn.

Actor

Emerging during early childhood, the self may be viewed as a social actor with characteristic traits, playing social roles, and resembling social scripts that fit corresponding future work environments. By using various self-constructing strategies, such as role playing, introjecting familial guides like parents and grandparents, and incorporating role models in fantasy and play activities, children perform as social actors (Savickas, 2013). Childhood as lived primarily within the family of origin as well as within educational, community, and other social contexts launches the core career construction processes of self-making. In turn, children initially learn about themselves and occupations that befit their reputations. Much like socially scripted and situationally cued actors, children begin to shape interests, abilities, skills, and talents and prepare to perform roles and play parts that eventually can be played out on corresponding work stages (Tracey, 2001; Tracey & Sodano, 2015). Activity engagement builds experiences through rehearsing traits such as interests, abilities, and skills that will become recognised by the child's social network as her or his reputation. In purposefully selected settings, children nurture interests that fit with their emerging social reputations. These settings can be conceptualised according to vocational personality types (Holland, 1997). Children's extracurricular activities and hobbies indicate what they are training themselves for and on what stage they prefer to enact the self that they are making.

Agent

Emerging during mid to late childhood, the self mirrors a motivational agent with career aspirations exploring possible future life-career plans and projects and developing readiness to fit work into life. They also first deal with developmental tasks, much like self-determined and goal-directed agents making future career plans (Hartung et al., 2008). Through fantasy, curiosity, and aspiration, children play with possibilities for making a future self in work roles. Active occupational engagement through enrichment and exploration processes promotes eventual adaptive career decision making (Krieshok, Black, & McKay, 2009) as well as intentional expression of future selves (Savickas, 2013). Adaptability, as we have seen, involves coping with changes in self and circumstances so that the developing child can begin to handle life's responsibilities, passages, and strains. In this way, the child becomes much like an agent who must formulate goals and projects that ultimately shape a career. A sense of agency – first emerging by middle childhood (Savickas, 2013) – equips and emboldens the child, and later the adolescent and adult, to deal with typical developmental tasks (e.g., complete chores and school work), successfully navigate transitions (e.g., from home to school and school to work), and cope with traumatic crises (e.g., death, divorce, or serious illness in self or a family member). Skills of career adaptability initially take shape in childhood (Hartung et al., 2008; Savickas, 2013). Career adaptability must then be cultivated throughout the life course across its four skill sets or dimensions of concern (looking ahead), control (owning the future), curiosity (looking around), and confidence (problem solving).

Author

Arising during adolescence and emerging adulthood, the self represents an autobiographical author with a life narrative telling an integrative personal life story about how to shape oneself through work. During this age period, too, however, children, like adolescents, begin to tell self-defining stories portraying nascent life themes, much like budding authors who initially reflect on and narrate their own clear and enduring life-career autobiographies (McAdams, 2013; Savickas, 2011; Shweder et al., 1998). It is during childhood that a central life theme comprising one's predominant problem in need of an effective solution first emerges. As Savickas (2011) noted, "Life themes originate in early childhood as unfinished situations and incompletely formed gestalt" (p. 32). Children initially learn to reflect on and explore the selves they are making in relation to where they may best like to be themselves with regard to work and career situations. Doing so helps children begin early the process that will become more pressing by late adolescence of authoring career stories that connect their self-concepts (i.e., who they are and who they are becoming) to their educational plans and future work roles. It also assists them in understanding how they can use school and work to design their lives and become more complete. Narratability means being able to tell one's story clearly and coherently. Children are encouraged to tell stories about themselves and often do so from an early age (Ahn, 2011). Central to their stories are developing life themes that emerge from their personal experiences. These early experiences prove formative in that children use them to understand themselves and the world. And these stories contain lifelong lessons that children will carry with them into adolescence and adulthood.

Children tell and retell their own personal experiences through playful and structured interactions with the social world (Ahn, 2011). By narrating their experiences and participating in a host of activities, children initially express their emotions and thoughts, rehearse behaviours, and exert their will. In so doing, they progress developmentally toward the goal of forming a realistic and viable vocational self-concept in part by identifying with significant others and incorporating role models (Savickas, 2011). An emerging vocational self-concept in childhood prompts formative answers to questions of identity in children's budding mental representations of their perceived strengths, limitations, vocational interests, work values, abilities, talents, and personality traits. This growing self-concept comprises both a public portrayal and a private goal that portends a future role for work and career in the whole of one's life (Super, Savickas, & Super, 1996). This role is continually questioned, shaped, and refined throughout the life course.

Conclusion

Childhood provides the stage for career construction's opening act. Work as a cultural imperative, along with love and friendship (Dreikurs, 1953), sows its seeds in childhood as children play with possibilities for their future careers to be harvested during the adult years. Children's play engages them in self-determined exploration (Deci & Ryan, 1985). By making meaning of their explorations and experiences of the world through self-reflection and social interaction, children construct foundational stories about who they are and who they are becoming (Ahn, 2011). These early and simple self-constructed stories foreshadow the child's narrative identity (Ricoeur, 1986), which grows more complex and rich in expression with the coming of adolescence and emerging adulthood (McAdams, Josselson, & Lieblich, 2006). Through the stories they tell, children portend where in the world – that is, on what occupational stages – they aspire and expect (Rojewski, 2005) to meet work's imperative. In so doing,

32 Paul J. Hartung

they build and reflect on their emerging reputations formed by identifying with significant others, performing socially situated activities, and incorporating role models at an early age (Savickas, 2013).

Career construction recognises that children make themselves and their worlds through the stories they tell. To best achieve life-career success, children can be encouraged to begin to create stories about themselves that express very clearly who they are becoming, where they may most like to be in the work world, and how they may want to use work in a way that best allows them to fully be themselves.

References

Ahn, J. (2011). Review of children's identity construction via narratives. *Creative Education, 2*, 415–417.

Dawis, R. V. (1995). For the love of working on play: Comment on Tinsley and Eldredge (1995). *Journal of Counseling Psychology, 42*, 136–137.

Deci, E. L., & Ryan, R. M. (1985). *Intrinsic motivation and self-determination in human behavior.* New York, NY: Plenum.

Dreikurs, R. (1953). *Fundamentals of Adlerian psychology.* Chicago: Alfred Adler Institute.

Gergen, K. (1999). *An invitation to social construction.* Thousand Oaks, CA: Sage.

Greene, G. (1940). *The power and the glory.* New York, NY: The Viking Press.

Hartung, P. J. (2002). Development through work and play. *Journal of Vocational Behavior, 61*, 424–438.

Hartung, P. J. (2015). Life design in childhood: Antecedents and advancement. In L. Nota & J. Rossier (Eds.), *Handbook of the life design paradigm: From practice to theory, from theory to practice* (pp. 89–102). Boston, MA: Hogrefe Publishing.

Hartung, P. J., Porfeli, E. J., & Vondracek, F. W. (2005). Child vocational development: A review and reconsideration. *Journal of Vocational Behavior, 66*, 385–419.

Hartung, P. J., Porfeli, E. J., & Vondracek, F. W. (2008). Career adaptability in childhood. *The Career Development Quarterly, 57*, 63–74.

Holland, J. L. (1997). *Making vocational choices: A theory of vocational personalities and work environments* (3rd ed.). Odessa, FL: Psychological Assessment Resources.

Kelly, G. A. (1955). *The psychology of personal constructs.* New York, NY: Norton.

Krieshok, T. S., Black, M. D., & McKay, R. A. (2009). Career decision making: The limits of rationality and the abundance of non-conscious processes. *Journal of Vocational Behavior, 75*, 275–290.

Mabie, H. W. (1898). *Essays on work and culture.* New York, NY: Dodd, Mead, and Company.

McAdams, D. P. (1985). *Power, intimacy, and the life story: Personological inquiries into identity.* New York, NY: Guilford Press.

McAdams, D. P. (2008). Personal narratives and the life story. In O. P. John, R. W. Robins, & L. A. Pervin (Eds.), *Handbook of personality: Theory and research* (3rd ed., pp. 242–262). New York, NY: Guilford Press.

McAdams, D. P. (2013). The psychological self as actor, agent, and author. *Perspectives of Psychological Science, 8*, 272–295.

McAdams, D. P., Josselson, R., & Lieblich, A. (2006). *Identity and story: Creating self in narrative.* Washington, DC: APA Books.

Parsons, F. (1909). *Choosing a vocation.* Boston: Houghton Mifflin.

Porfeli, E. J., Wang, C., & Hartung, P. J. (2008). Family transmission of work affectivity and experiences to children. *Journal of Vocational Behavior, 73*, 278–286.

Ricoeur, P. (1986). Life: A story in search of a narrator. In M. Doeser & J. Kray (Eds.), *Facts and values: Philosophical reflections from western and non-western perspectives* (pp. 34–68). Dordrecht: Nijhoff.

Rojewski, J. W. (2005). Occupational aspirations: Constructs, meanings, and application. In S. D. Brown & R. W. Lent (Eds.), *Career development and counseling: Putting theory and research to work* (pp. 131–154). Hoboken, NJ: John Wiley & Sons.

Savickas, M. L. (2002). Career construction: A developmental theory of vocational behavior. In D. Brown (Ed.), *Career choice and development* (4th ed., pp. 149–205). San Francisco, CA: Jossey-Bass.

Savickas, M. L. (2011). *Career counseling*. Washington, DC: American Psychological Association Books.

Savickas, M. L. (2012). Life design: A paradigm for career intervention in the 21st century. *Journal of Counseling and Development, 90*, 13–19.

Savickas, M. L. (2013). Career construction theory and practice. In S. D. Brown & R. W. Lent (Eds.), *Career development and counseling: Putting theory and research to work* (2nd ed., pp. 147–183). Hoboken, NJ: John Wiley & Sons.

Savickas, M. L. (2015). Career counseling paradigms: Guiding, developing, and designing. In P. J. Hartung, M. L. Savickas, & W. B. Walsh (Eds.), *Handbook of career intervention* (Vol. 1, pp. 129–145). Washington, DC: APA Books.

Savickas, M. L., Nota, L., Rossier, J., Dauwalder, J., Duarte, M. E., Guichard, . . . & van Vianen, A. E. M. (2009). Life designing: A paradigm for career construction in the 21st century. *Journal of Vocational Behavior, 75*, 239–250.

Shakespeare, W. (1623). *Mr William Shakespeare's comedies, histories and tragedies*. London: Blount & Jaggard.

Shweder, R. A., Goodnow, J., Hatano, G., Levine, R. A., Markus, H., & Miller, P. (1998). The cultural psychology of development: One mind, many mentalities. In W. Damon (Ed.-in-Chief) & R. M. Lerner (Volume Ed.), *Handbook of child psychology* (5th ed., pp. 865–937). New York, NY: John Wiley & Sons.

Super, D. E. (1990). A life-span, life-space approach to career development. In D. Brown & L. Brooks (Eds.), *Career choice and development: Applying contemporary theories to practice* (2nd ed., pp. 197–261). San Francisco, CA: Jossey-Bass.

Super, D. E., Savickas, M. L., & Super, C. M. (1996). The life-span, life-space approach to careers. In D. Brown & L. Brooks (Eds.), *Career choice and development: Applying contemporary theories to practice* (3rd ed., pp. 121–178). San Francisco, CA: Jossey-Bass.

Sutton-Smith, B. (1997). *The ambiguity of play*. Cambridge, MA: Harvard University Press.

Tracey, T. J. G. (2001). The development of structure of interests in children: Setting the stage. *Journal of Vocational Behavior, 59*, 89–104.

Tracey, T. J. G., & Sodano, S. M. (2015). Assessing children: Interests and personality. In P. J. Hartung, M. L. Savickas, & W. B. Walsh (Eds.), *APA handbook of career intervention* (Vol. 2, pp. 113–124). Washington, DC: American Psychological Association.

Vondracek, F. W. (2001). The childhood antecedents of adult careers: Theoretical and empirical considerations. In R. K. Silbereisen & M. Reitzle (Eds.), *Bericht ueberden 42. Kongress der Deutschen Gesellschaft fuer Psychologie in Jena 2000* (pp. 265–276). Lengerich, Germany: Pabst Science Publishers.

Watson, M., & McMahon, M. (2005). Children's career development: A research review from a learning perspective. *Journal of Vocational Behavior, 67*, 119–132.

Chapter 4

Systems and relational perspectives in understanding children's career development

Wendy Patton

This chapter is dedicated to Merle Jeanette Grech (nee Patton)

The present chapter will describe relational and systemic perspectives of career development, as explained in a number of theories and metatheoretical frameworks. It will then provide discussion on the potential contributions of these perspectives to our understanding of children's career development. Where available, the chapter will reference empirical work derived from these perspectives which has contributed to our understanding. However, as acknowledged by a number of authors (McMahon & Watson, 2008; Skorikov & Patton, 2007; Watson & McMahon, 2008; Watson, Nota, & McMahon, 2015), there remains a dearth of work which adequately explains theoretical bases for children's career development. These authors have also noted the lack of an organising theoretical framework that informs both theory and practice.

In focusing on these two perspectives in career theory, the current chapter will describe systems theory and draw specifically from the work of developmental systems theories (Ford, 1987; D. H. Ford & Lerner, 1992) and their precursor, developmental-contextualism (Vondracek, Lerner, & Schulenberg, 1986), in addition to the Systems Theory Framework (Patton & McMahon, 1999, 2006, 2014). In examining relational perspectives, the chapter will draw from the work of Blustein (2001, 2006, 2011), Richardson (2000, 2012), Schultheiss (2007a, b, 2013), and Contextual Action Theory (Young & Valach, 2004; Young, Valach, & Collin, 1996, 2002). However, as both the systems and relational perspectives are derived from the worldview of contextualism, the chapter will first briefly examine this worldview.

The developing worldview of contextualism, and the development of constructivism and social constructionism in cognitive psychology, have been important influences in career theorising. In explaining their 'future of career', Collin and Young (2000) emphasised the importance of the construction of individual identity and the individual's context, both spatial and temporal, as a crucible for understanding individual career development. The need for theories of career to recognise the importance of the context beyond intraindividual developmental factors in children's career development has been emphasised in key reviews (Hartung, Porfeli, & Vondracek, 2005; Watson & McMahon, 2005) and more recently by Watson *et al.* (2015).

A contextual worldview emphasises that how events are viewed is linked to the perspective of each individual. Furthermore, it conceives development as an ongoing recursive process of interaction between the individual and his/her person-environment context. Within this process, random or chance events contribute to an open-ended unpredictable state of being. An outcome of these elements of the contextualist worldview is the active nature of the individual as a self-building and self-renewing 'self-organizing system' (D. H. Ford, 1987), as opposed to a passive organism at the whim of maturational and developmental stages and/or environmental forces. Career development is not viewed as an intraindividual developmental process.

Constructivism is directly derived from the contextualist worldview in that the 'reality' of world events is seen as constructed from the inside out by the individual (that is, through the individual's own thinking and processing). These constructions are based on individual cognitions in relation to perspectives formed from person-environment interactions. Constructivism therefore views the person as an open system constantly interacting with the environment and seeking stability through ongoing change. The emphasis is on the process, not on an outcome; there is no completion of a stage and arrival at the next stage as in stage-based views of human development. There are significant commonalities between constructivism and social constructionism (Young & Collin, 2004); however, a number of authors have emphasised their inherent complexity (see McIlveen & Schultheiss, 2012). Young and Collin (2004) distinguished the two epistemologies as follows: constructivism assumes the individual mind as the basis for the construction of knowledge, while social constructionism assumes the construction of knowledge as being the basis of social processes. Guichard (2009) distinguished these perspectives by referring to them as psychological constructivism and social constructionism. Young and Popadiuk (2012) commented that "At one level it appears to be a matter of emphasis because for both the constructivists and the social constructionists individual and social processes are important" (p. 10). Young and Popadiuk identified five approaches which they identified as being derived from constructivist/social constructionist and provided a discussion about differences/similarities between them. These approaches included narrative, relational, systems theory, cultural, and contextual action theory. We will feature four of them in the present chapter.

Systems theory perspectives

The work on living systems by D. H. Ford (1987) has furthered the advancement of an integrated framework of human development and the evolution and understanding of systems theory. A number of perspectives have illustrated the applicability of systems theory principles to human behaviour. These include developmental-contextualism (Vondracek *et al.*, 1986), Developmental Systems Theory (DST; D. H. Ford, 1987), the recently formulated living systems theory of vocational behaviour and development (Vondracek,

D. H. Ford, & Porfeli, 2014), and the Systems Theory Framework (Patton & McMahon, 1999, 2006, 2014).

Before focusing on these theoretical perspectives, it is important to emphasise the emerging importance of systems thinking in the developmental sciences. This perspective has moved developmental psychology from limited stage-based thinking "from a field framed by a unidisciplinary, developmental psychological conception of change to one that is framed by a developmental science model, that is, a multidisciplinary integrative approach to understanding the breadth of the course of human life" (Lerner, 2008, p. 71). In addition, Lerner (2008) emphasised the application of systems theory principles to new developmental science, a field which "uses dynamic, developmental systems models to describe, explain, and optimize the course of human life" (p. 71), and noted that developmental systems models "stress that mutually influential relations among the multiple, biological through sociocultural, physical, ecological, and historical levels of organization within the ecology of human life should be the focus of the developmental analysis" (p. 71).

Developmental-contextualism

Vondracek *et al.* (1986) asserted that the developmental-contextual framework synthesises two key ideas from contextualism and developmental organicism: "that contextual change is probabilistic in nature, and that development proceeds according to the organism's activity" (p. 32). Developmental-contextualism, therefore, emphasises ongoing interactive change within the organism and within the environment, emphasising change and dynamic interaction. Further, it acknowledges the internal stability of the organism and the dual nature of influence between the organism and the context: "Dynamic interaction of the developing individual with various context was presented as the paradigm that could, for the first time, adequately account for the complexity of occupational careers, their antecedents, their unfolding, and their consequences" (Vondracek & Porfeli, 2008, p. 211). Further to the interaction between the individual and the environment, Vondracek *et al.* (1986) emphasised the self-determination and agency of the individual. The developmental-contextual approach holds that the environment engenders chaotic and reflexive changes in an individual's behaviour; however, it also emphasises that the environment is facilitated or constrained by the unique characteristics of the individual. Within the model, the individual is an active organism operating in a constantly changing environment, hence the concept of dynamic interaction. An individual's career development is a reflection of the continuous interplay of person and context at all possible levels. Thus this approach has the capacity to include elements of content and process.

Vondracek and Porfeli (2002b) emphasised the potential for an integration of lifespan psychological and sociological life-course approaches to our understanding of career development in children (Hartung, Porfeli, & Vondracek,

2005) and adults (Vondracek & Porfeli, 2002a). In a precursor to further theory development, Vondracek and Porfeli (2008) noted that theoretical formulations of systems theory have added to developmental-contextualism's capacity to address processes of development.

Developmental systems theory

Developmental Systems Theory (DST; D. H. Ford & Lerner, 1992) was formulated to extend developmental-contextualism and to further synthesise this model with the living systems framework. The DST furthers our understanding from the description of human behaviour to an understanding of the underlying processes and attempts to answer the how and why of career decisions of individuals. Vondracek and Porfeli (2008) noted that the DST is a significant advance over the developmental-contextual framework, as it presents a process model that includes content, organisation, and dynamics of the developing person, which addresses the how of development "by describing and explaining the basic change processes and dynamics that are capable of producing the incredible diversity of developmental outcomes in humans" (p. 215). As such, these authors asserted, "The framework is capable, in principle, of accounting for every aspect of human functioning" (p. 216). The DST aims to extend the focus of the individual to all relevant aspects of human development and to the processes by which individuals function. For example, Lerner, Theokas, and Jelicic (2005) explored developmental systems theory's potential to understand the agentic behaviour of adolescents. As such, it can be applicable to an understanding of children's career exploration behaviour.

More recently, Vondracek, Ford, and Porfeli (2014) have developed an advanced theoretical framework: a Living Systems Theory of Vocational Behaviour and Development. This metatheory incorporates the Living Systems Framework (LSF; D. H. Ford, 1987), Developmental Systems Theory (D. H. Ford & Lerner, 1992), and Motivational Systems Theory (M. E. Ford, 1992) as basic theoretical foundations. These authors have purposely included development in their theory to acknowledge the lifespan nature of career development and decision making, although they disagree with the traditional stimulus-response perspective about vocational behaviour and development. As such, they included systems theory principles into their framework as "systems theoretical perspectives, like the living systems framework (D. H. Ford, 1987), eschew simple mechanistic, linear cause and effect, stimulus-response relationships in favour of more dynamic relationships involving causal fields and behavioural/developmental patterns" (Vondracek et al., 2014, p. 4). These authors quite intentionally acknowledge that including development in their framework acknowledges the importance of children's career development and note that children's preparation for work begins in early childhood. Their theoretical formulation includes the importance of person-context interactions in all career development. The authors state, "Theories of vocational behavior and development need not emphasize all of the complexity of human development, but they must be embedded in the larger framework of a person's life" (p. 10). While there is limited scope for expanding discussion in the present chapter, this theoretical framework promises to significantly advance the field, particularly as it incorporates both a conceptual and a propositional model.

Systems theory

A number of authors have acknowledged the value of systems theory in advancing career theory both in relation to integration of career theories using family systems theory (Blustein, 1994; Bordin, 1994) in addition to providing a meta-framework to integrate all of the determinants of human development and specifically career choice and career development (Osipow, 1983). Its development to date has been in providing a specific focus for the four governing functions in decision making: information processing and storage, and directive, regulatory and control processes which can be used in understanding career decision making in concert with the knowledge of their interrelatedness with other relevant subsystems.

The Systems Theory Framework (McMahon & Patton, 1995; Patton & McMahon, 1999, 2006, 2014) was the first attempt to present a comprehensive metatheoretical framework of career theories constructed using systems theory. The STF is a metatheoretical account of career development that accommodates career theories derived from both the positivist and constructivist worldviews. One of its key contributions is its capacity to demonstrate the contribution of all theories in understanding career development. Clearly illustrated in the STF are the content and process of career development. The content influences are presented as a series of interconnecting systems of influence on career development, specifically the individual system, the social system, and the environmental-societal system, while the process influences include recursiveness, change over time, and chance. With the individual as the central focus, constructing his or her own meaning of career, constructs of existing theories are relevant, as they apply to each individual. As such, the emphasis is placed on the individual and not on theory, and an individual's development processes can be applicable at a macrolevel of theory analysis as well as at a microlevel of individual analysis. As such, career development of individuals of all ages can be facilitated through an understanding of, and work with, the STF. As indicated by Skorikov and Patton (2007), the STF's systemic approach assists in incorporating the changing contextual factors in theories of career development in childhood. Its focus on intraindividual factors also means that it can account for children's lifespan development influences.

Systems perspectives and career development in childhood

Watson and McMahon (2007) used the various components of the STF to explore their existence in extant career theories as explanatory guides for children's career development. They concluded that this existence was variable, as

Systems and perspectives in understanding children's career development 39

such emphasising the failure of career theory as a whole to provide theoretical foundations for understanding childhood career development. However, systems perspectives as outlined here have much to offer in providing these theoretical foundations. These perspectives focus on content and process, and they enable a theoretical and empirical understanding that includes both developmental and contextual factors. The inclusion of the living systems framework principles provides specific approaches that can address the how of development (Vondracek & Porfeli, 2008). In particular, the recent advance of the theoretical framework of Vondracek *et al.* (2014) and the specific propositions which provide a guide for research and theory development provide significant promise for this approach to advance our understanding of children's career development.

Relational perspectives

A number of authors within the career development field have extended our understanding of relationships and career development (Blustein, 2001, 2006, 2011; Blustein, Schultheiss, & Flum, 2004; Schultheiss, 2003, 2007a, 2013); they emphasise that their ideas have been derived from a number of theoretical perspectives (e.g., developmental, cultural, and narrative psychologists' work exploring the person in context). The term *relational* is largely associated with the assumption that humans are relational beings for whom developing and sustaining meaningful connections with others is a core activity. Theorists who adhere to these ideas "typically endorse the view that many aspects of interpersonal and intrapersonal struggles reflect human strivings for connection, affirmation, support, and attachment" (Schultheiss, 2007b, p. 170). Blustein (2001) affirms the view that relationships are central to human functioning and that relational life is intertwined throughout our lives, thus emphasising that a realistic view of the individual embedded within a family (or other) system is fundamental to understanding how people develop and implement their plans for work.

A considerable literature on family of origin influences on career development demonstrates that families do influence individuals' career development in specific and predictable ways (Whiston & Keller, 2004). Research suggests that family relationship factors such as parental attitudes and expectations, identification with parents, open communication, parenting styles, parental attachment, psychological separation, direct parent involvement and assistance, and multidimensional aspects of social support exert an influence on adolescents' vocational identity, vocational interests, career maturity, career decision-making self-efficacy, work values, and vocational exploration and decision making (Whiston & Keller, 2004).

A range of empirical data has identified formal and informal processes which support children's developmental career exploration. Although parents seem to have the most prominent influence on children's career development, other family members – such as siblings and extended family – also have been shown to be an important influence (Schultheiss, Palma, Predragovich, & Glasscock, 2002).

McMahon and Patton (1997a, b) highlighted the relevance of parental influences on career choice, and Schultheiss, Palma, and Manzi's (2005) study with fourth- and fifth-grade students reported that childhood exploration encompassed both self-initiated exploration and exploration introduced by teachers and family members. Bandura, Barbaranelli, Vittorio-Caprara, and Pastorelli (2001) also reported a relationship between parents' self-efficacy and children's aspirations and career trajectories. In a similar vein, Blustein, Prezioso, and Schultheiss (1995) examined the application of attachment theory to understanding how relationships function to facilitate or hinder developmental progress in the career domain. Blustein *et al.* (1995) identified connections between attachment theory and career development in the relationship between attachment and exploration which draw a strong connection relevant to children's career development as children need to negotiate new relationships and contexts.

A focus on relational influences is consistent with the conclusions drawn in a review of the literature on child career development (Watson & McMahon, 2005). Watson and McMahon used learning as a unifying theme to accommodate the dynamic and interactional nature of career development and to highlight the need for a dual focus on both how children learn and what they learn about the world of work and their future in it. The authors suggested that *how* children learn may best be understood as a recursive process between children and a broad array of influences from their social and environmental contexts, including the family.

The importance of relational context in children's career development is further emphasised in the work of Patton and Porfeli (2007). The dominant view in the career literature remains that young people move from diverse to specific career exploration during the adolescent years; however, as discussed previously, literature reviews have suggested that this transition may begin earlier (Hartung *et al.*, 2005; Watson & McMahon, 2005). The human exploration literature suggests that children are capable of specific exploration at an earlier age than is traditionally presumed in the career exploration literature, but children typically have a limited exposure to the work environment, and this social structural constraint, often imposed unintentionally by the family and school context, may hinder and consequently delay the shift, thereby supporting the existing career literature.

Regardless of the timing of the process, the developmental course of diverse and specific career exploration is predicted to yield a set of career pathways that are consistent with a child's emerging interests, needs, aspirations, and values on the one hand and his/her environmental opportunities and social and familial expectations on the other. Patton and Porfeli (2007) emphasised the need to develop intentional exploration opportunities to facilitate career exploration for children. More recently, a number of writers have urged the inclusion of emotion into career development theorising (Vondracek *et al.*, 2014) and into considerations of children's career development given parents' influence in children's emotional self-regulation and careers (Oliveira, Taveira. & Porfeli, 2015).

Systems and perspectives in understanding children's career development 41

Integrative and relational theories

In 2003, Schultheiss proposed an integration of relational theory with career theory "to provide a more holistic integrative conceptual framework, or meta-perspective, that recognises the value of relational connection, and quite simply the realities of people's lives" (p. 304). This was further advanced by Blustein *et al.* (2004), in close alignment with Blustein (2001), who proposed that a realistic view of the individual embedded within a family system is fundamental to understanding how people develop and implement their plans for work. Richardson (2000, 2012) and Richardson and Schaeffer (2013) have extended the relational focus to the notion that work and relationships are both public and private contexts and that there needs to be "a shift to thinking about persons as developing through their work and relationships" (Richardson and Schaeffer, p. 276).

Blustein (2001, 2006, 2011) proposed an inclusive and integrative psychology of working, emphasising that much of our work has been developed in relation to understanding the work lives of a small proportion of the population, those who live in relative affluence. His multidisciplinary framework emphasises that vocational psychology must draw upon theories of sociology as well as "theoretical ideas emerging in other domains of psychology outside of the traditional purview of vocational psychology" (p. 177) through studying work in a range of contexts, including organisations, home, and culture. In particular, Blustein (2006) proposed two alternative meta-perspectives which he viewed as possible organising frameworks – social constructionism and the emancipatory communitarian perspective. More recently, Blustein (2011; Blustein, Coutinho, & Murphy, 2011) advocated incorporating relational theory into this model, thus advancing the self-in-relation construct proposed by Blustein and Fouad (2008). This proposition is designed to more firmly connect the self and familial and social, as well as cultural and historical relationships.

This proposal has been further extended by Schultheiss (2007a, 2013) in her discussion of a relational cultural paradigm which emphasises "the cultural shaping of meaning-making through relationships as central to the understanding of work in people's lives" (2013, p. 51). This understanding of culture as integral to an understanding of context is an important addition to the relational perspective: "By recognising the interwoven nature of culture and relationship, this paradigm provides a lens through which to view the multifaceted webbed connections that construct worklife" (2013, p. 51). I would add career development to worklife.

In describing their contextual explanation of career, Young and Valach (2000, 2004) and Young *et al.* (1996, 2002) acknowledged that the concept of context is understood in various ways. These authors proposed a framework for understanding key aspects of many contextual approaches to career. Further, they proposed action theory as a means of integrating aspects of contextualism, defining the basis of contextualism as "the recognition of a complex whole constituted of many interrelated and interwoven parts, which may be largely submerged in the everyday understanding of events and phenomena" (p. 479). Context consists of multiple complex connections and interrelationships, the significance of which is interpreted according to an individual's perspective. Young *et al.* (1996, 2002) identified several aspects of the contextualist metaphor crucial to their contextual explanation of career. These include the goal-directed nature of acts – acts which are embedded in their context. Change is integral within this perspective "because events take shape as people engage in practical action with a particular purpose, analysis and interpretation are always practical" (Young *et al.*, 1996, p. 480). Finally, these authors maintained that reality is constructed from the present event outwards, thereby rejecting the systems theory notion that reality is only constructed in relationship with an individual's own internal representation – that is, only a contextual truth is possible. Thus these authors draw on key concepts of systems theory and reject others. This theory is included under relational perspectives in this chapter, although it could just as well be included under systems perspectives. It is included under relational perspectives in this chapter because the work of these authors strongly emphasise that career development occurs not only in the context of individual development but also within reciprocal interactions and joint actions, such as between children and parents. Young and Valach (2004) emphasised that "our approach is grounded on cultural/contextual rather than developmental psychology . . . the contextual action theory explicates social perspectives that have the effect of moving it beyond traditional career approaches and linking it directly to constructionism" (p. 501).

Contextualist action theory (Young *et al.*, 1996, 2002) differs from other theoretical perspectives that focus on individual perceptions of relationship variables. Action theory is founded on the notion of action as goal-directed, intentional behaviour or action. The term 'action' refers to a focus on human intention, processes, and change in context instead of context as a setting for action. This approach attends to joint goals as constructed through actions and sequences of actions with common goals, called projects. Hence the association between relationships and career is understood as reciprocal. The focus of this theory is therefore on the intentional action in relationship. Indeed Richardson (2015) noted that the field of vocational psychology is indebted to Young and his colleagues for their attention to action, and she has extended this notion to propose the notion of agentic action: "the basic process through which people co-construct lives of meaning" (p. 51).

The work of Young and colleagues over many years has emphasised the relevance of family as active agents in adolescent career exploration and in particular the methodology of jointly constructing action projects through conversation (Young, Domene, & Valach, 2015; Young, Marshall *et al.*, 2011; Young, Valach, & Marshall, 2007). As such, their work is presented in this chapter as both contextual and relational.

Contribution of relational perspectives for understanding children's career development

There is much that the relational paradigm can offer to understanding theorising and practice in children's career development. It is evident that the key to this perspective is focusing on important relational connections in children's context. Research cited previously in this section emphasises the relevance of children's relational context and individuals therein in their career development understandings. Schultheiss (2007b) and Howard, Flanagan, Castine, and Walsh (2015) have provided summaries of research highlighting influences on children's career development thinking. It is also important to draw from the connections between theorising and practice, in particular the work of Young and colleagues. While their work to date has focused on joint actions between parents and adolescents, there is every reason to believe that similar methodology could be applied to working with children.

Conclusion

Many theories within these broad paradigms have strong commonalities, for example, developmental change, relationships, contexts at multiple levels, agency, and joint action. What is evident through this review of systems and relational paradigms is their strong conceptual interconnection, which is emphasised as follows:

> Children's . . . career related attitudes and behaviour undergo various qualitative and quantitative changes as a result of the epigenetic unfolding of the child's capabilities and learning through self-chosen and socially assigned vocational, educational, and leisure activities. The process of change is guided and mediated by the context of significant relationships and social conditions such as societal norms, economy and technological change, which set developmental career tasks and provide resources for accomplishing them.
>
> (Skorikov & Patton, 2007, p. 326)

Indeed, Patton (2007, 2015) has written explicitly about the convergence and interconnections between relational theory, contextual action theory, and the STF. The quote emphasises relationships in context within broader systems changing over time and highlights the relevance of each of these for the career development journeys of children. The need for a holistic and integrated approach to understanding these concepts and how they operate in career development poses an ongoing challenge for theorists, researchers, and practitioners.

References

Bandura, A., Barbaranelli, C., Vittorio-Caprara, G., & Pastorelli, C. (2001). Self-efficacy beliefs as shapers of children's aspirations and career trajectories. *Child Development, 72*, 187–206.

Blustein, D. L. (1994). "Who am I?": The question of self and identity in career development. In M. L. Savickas & R. W. Lent (Eds.), *Convergence in career development theories* (pp. 130–154). Palo Alto, CA: CPP Books.

Blustein, D. L. (2001). Extending the reach of vocational psychology: Toward an inclusive and integrative psychology of working. *Journal of Vocational Behavior, 59*, 171–182.

Blustein, D. L. (2006). *The psychology of working: A new perspective for career development, counseling, and public policy.* Mahwah, NJ: Erlbaum.

Blustein, D. L. (2011). A relational theory of working. *Journal of Vocational Behavior, 79*, 1–17.

Blustein, D. L., Coutinho, M. T. N., & Murphy, K. A. (2011). Self and social class in career theory and practice. In P. J. Hartung & L. Subich (Eds.), *Developing self in work and career: Concepts, cases and contexts* (pp. 213–229). Washington, DC: American Psychological Association.

Blustein, D. L., & Fouad, N. A. (2008). Changing face of vocational psychology: The transforming world of work. In W. B. Walsh (Ed.), *Biennial review of counseling psychology* (Vol. 1, pp. 129–155). New York, NY: Routledge/Taylor & Francis.

Blustein, D. L., Prezioso, M. S., & Schultheiss, D. P. (1995). Attachment theory and career development: Current status and future directions. *Counseling Psychologist, 23*, 416–432.

Blustein, D. L., Schultheiss, D. E. P., & Flum, H. (2004). Toward a relational perspective of the psychology of career: A social constructionist analysis. *Journal of Vocational Behavior, 64*, 423–440.

Bordin, E. S. (1994). Intrinsic motivation and the active self: Convergence from a psychodynamic perspective. In M. L. Savickas & R. W. Lent (Eds.), *Convergence in career development theories* (pp. 53–62). Palo Alto, CA: CPP Books.

Collin, A., & Young, R. A. (2000). The future of career. In A. Collin & R. A. Young (Eds.), *The future of career* (pp. 276–300). Cambridge, UK: Cambridge University Press.

Ford, D. H. (1987). *Humans as self-constructing living systems.* Hillsdale, NJ: Lawrence Erlbaum.

Ford, D. H., & Lerner, R. (1992). *Developmental systems theory: An integrative approach.* Newbury Park, CA: Sage.

Ford, M. E. (1992). *Motivating humans: Goals, emotions, and personal agency beliefs.* Newbury Park, CA: Sage.

Guichard, J. (2009). Self-constructing. *Journal of Vocational Behavior, 75*, 251–258.

Hartung, P. J., Porfeli, E. J., & Vondracek, F. W. (2005). Child vocational development: A review and reconsideration. *Journal of Vocational Behavior, 66*, 385–419.

Howard, K. A. S., Flanagan, S., Castine, E., & Walsh, M. E. (2015). Perceived influences on the career choices of children and youth: An exploratory study. *International Journal for Educational and Vocational Guidance, 15*, 99–111.

Lerner, R. M. (2008). The contributions of Paul B. Baltes to the transformation of the field of child development: From developmental psychology to developmental science. *Research in Human Development, 5*, 69–79.

Lerner, R. M., Theokas, C., & Jelicic, H. (2005). Youth as active agents in their own positive development: A developmental systems perspective. In W. Greve, K. Rothermund, & D. Wentura (Eds.), *The adaptive self: Personal continuity and intentional self-development* (pp. 31–47). Ashland, OH: Hogrefe & Huber.

McIlveen, P., & Schultheiss, D. E. (Eds.). (2012). *Social constructionism in vocational psychology and career development.* Rotterdam, The Netherlands: Sense Publishers.

McMahon, M., & Patton, W. (1995). Development of a systems theory of career development. *Australian Journal of Career Development, 14*, 15–20.

McMahon, M., & Patton, W. (1997a). School as an influence on the career development of students: Comments by young people and considerations for career educators. *Australian Journal of Career Development, 6*, 23–26.

McMahon, M., & Patton, W. (1997b). Gender differences in influences on the career development of children and adolescents. *The School Counselor, 44*, 368–376.

McMahon, M., & Watson, M. (2008). Children's career development: Status quo and future directions. *The Career Development Quarterly, 57*, 4–6.

Oliveira, I. M., Taveira, M. C., & Porfeli, E. J. (2015). Emotional aspects of childhood career development: Importance and future agenda. *International Journal for Educational and Vocational Guidance, 15*, 163–174.

Osipow, S. H. (1983). *Theories of career development* (2nd ed.). Englewood Cliffs, NJ: Prentice Hall.

Patton, W. (2007). Connecting relational theory and the Systems Theory Framework: Individuals and their systems. *Australian Journal of Career Development, 16*, 38–46.

Patton, W. (2015). Career counselling: Joint contributions of contextual action theory and systems theory framework. In R. A. Young, J. Domene, & L. Valach (Eds.), *Counseling and action: Toward life-enhancing work, relationships and identity* (pp. 33–50). New York, NY: Springer.

Patton, W., & McMahon, M. (1999). *Career development and systems theory: A new relationship.* Pacific Grove, CA: Brooks/Cole.

Patton, W., & McMahon, M. (2006). *Career development and systems theory: Connecting theory and practice* (2nd ed.). Rotterdam, The Netherlands: Sense Publishers.

Patton, W., & McMahon, M. (2014). *Career development and systems theory: Connecting theory and practice* (3rd ed.). Rotterdam, The Netherlands: Sense Publishers.

Patton, W., & Porfeli, E. J. (2007). Career exploration for children and adolescents. In V. B. Skorikov & W. Patton (Eds.), *Career development in childhood and adolescence* (pp. 47–70). Rotterdam, The Netherlands: Sense Publishers.

Richardson, M. S. (2000). A new perspective for counsellors: From career ideologies to empowerment through work and relationship practices. In A. Collin & R. A. Young (Eds.), *The future of career* (pp. 197–211). Cambridge, UK: Cambridge University Press.

Richardson, M. S. (2012). The ongoing social construction of the counseling for work and relationship perspective. *The Counseling Psychologist, 40*, 279–290.

Richardson, M. S. (2015). Agentic action in context. In R. A. Young, J. Domene, & L. Valach (Eds.), *Counseling and action: Toward life-enhancing work, relationships and identity* (pp. 51–68). New York, NY: Springer.

Richardson, M. L., & Schaeffer, C. (2013). Expanding the discourse: A dual model of working for women's (and men's) lives. In W. Patton (Ed.), *Conceptualising women's working lives: Moving the boundaries of discourse* (pp. 23–50). Rotterdam, The Netherlands: Sense Publishers.

Schultheiss, D. (2003). A relational approach to career counseling: Theoretical integration and practical application. *Journal of Counseling and Development, 81*, 301–310.

Schultheiss, D. E. (2007a). The emergence of a relational cultural paradigm for vocational psychology. *International Journal for Educational and Vocational Guidance, 7*, 191–201.

Schultheiss, D. E. (2007b). Career development in the context of children's and adolescents' relationships. In V. B. Skorikov & W. Patton (Eds.), *Career development in childhood and adolescence* (pp. 169–180). Rotterdam, The Netherlands: Sense Publishers.

Schultheiss, D. E. (2013). A relational cultural paradigm as a theoretical backdrop for considering women's work. In W. Patton (Ed.), *Conceptualising women's working lives: Moving the boundaries of discourse* (pp. 51–62). Rotterdam, The Netherlands: Sense Publishers.

Schultheiss, D., Palma, T., & Manzi, A. (2005). Career development in middle childhood: A qualitative inquiry. *The Career Development Quarterly, 53*, 246–262.

Schultheiss, D. E. P., Palma, T., Predragovich, K., & Glasscock, J. (2002). Relational influences on career paths: Siblings in context. *Journal of Counseling Psychology, 49*, 302–310.

Skorikov, V. B., & Patton, W. (2007). Future directions in research on career development during childhood and adolescence. In V. B. Skorikov & W. Patton (Eds.), *Career development in childhood and adolescence* (pp. 325–336). Rotterdam, The Netherlands: Sense Publishers.

Vondracek, F. W., Ford, D. H., & Porfeli, E. J. (2014). *A living systems theory of vocational behavior and development*. Rotterdam, The Netherlands: Sense Publishers.

Vondracek, F. W., Lerner, R. M., & Schulenberg, J. E. (1986). *Career development: A life-span developmental approach*. Hillsdale, NJ: Erlbaum.

Vondracek, F. W., & Porfeli, E. (2002a). Life-span developmental perspectives on adult career development: Recent advances. In S. G. Niles (Ed.), *Adult career development: Concepts, issues and practices* (3rd ed., pp. 20–38). Alexandria, VA: National Career Development Association.

Vondracek, F. W., & Porfeli, E. (2002b). Integrating person- and function-centred approaches to career development. *Journal of Vocational Behavior, 61*, 386–397.

Vondracek, F. W., & Porfeli, E. J. (2008). Social context for career guidance throughout the world: Developmental-contextual perspectives on career across the lifespan. In J. A. Athanasou & R. Van Esbroeck (Eds.), *International handbook of career guidance* (pp. 209–225). New York, NY: Springer.

Watson, M., & McMahon, M. (2005). Children's career development: A research review from a learning perspective. *Journal of Vocational Behavior, 67*, 119–132.

Watson, M., & McMahon, M. (2007). Children's career development learning: A foundation for lifelong career development. In V. B. Skorikov & W. Patton (Eds.), *Career development in childhood and adolescence* (pp. 29–46). Rotterdam, The Netherlands: Sense Publishers.

Watson, M., & McMahon, M. (2008). Children's career development: Metaphorical images of theory, research and practice. *The Career Development Quarterly, 57*, 75–83.

Watson, M., Nota, L., & McMahon, M. (2015). Evolving stories of child career development. *International Journal for Educational and Vocational Guidance, 15*, 175–184.

Whiston, S. C., & Keller, B. K. (2004). The influence of the family of origin on career development: A review and analysis. *Journal of Vocational Behavior, 32*, 493–568.

Young, R. A., & Collin, A. (2004). Introduction: Constructivism and social constructionism in the career field. *Journal of Vocational Behavior, 64*, 373–388.

Young, R. A., Domene, J., & Valach, L. (Eds.). (2015). *Counseling and action: Toward life-enhancing work, relationships and identity*. New York, NY: Springer.

Young, R. A., Marshall, S. K., Valach, L., Domene, J. F., Graham, M. D., & Zaidman-Zait, A. (2011). *Transition to adulthood: Action, projects and counseling*. New York, NY: Springer.

Young, R. A., & Popadiuk, N. E. (2012). Social constructionist theories in vocational psychology. In P. McIlveen & D. E. Schultheiss (Eds.), *Social constructionism in vocational psychology and career development* (pp. 9–28). Rotterdam, The Netherlands: Sense Publishers.

Young, R. A., & Valach, L. (2000). Reconceptualising career psychology: An action theoretical perspective. In A. Collin & R. A. Young (Eds.), *The future of career* (pp. 181–196). Cambridge, UK: Cambridge University Press.

Young, R. A., & Valach, L. (2004). The construction of career through goal-directed action. *Journal of Vocational Behavior, 64*, 499–514.

Young, R. A., Valach, L., & Collin, A. (1996). A contextual explanation of career. In D. Brown & L. Brooks (Eds.), *Career choice and development* (3rd ed., pp. 477–512). San Francisco, CA: Jossey-Bass.

Young, R. A., Valach, L., & Collin, A. (2002). A contextual explanation of career. In D. Brown & Associates (Eds.), *Career choice and development* (4th ed., pp. 206–250). San Francisco, CA: Jossey-Bass.

Young, R. A., Valach, L., & Marshall, S. K. (2007). Parents and adolescents constructing career. In V. B. Skorikov & W. Patton (Eds.), *Career development in childhood and adolescence* (pp. 277–294). Rotterdam, The Netherlands: Sense Publishers.

Chapter 5

Supporting the career development of children
The concepts of career choice and attainment model

Kimberly A. S. Howard, Eleanor Castine, Sean Flanagan, and Yerang Lee

As any parent or teacher can attest, from a very early age, children are interested in the idea of work and excitedly imagine themselves in various occupations. Indeed, no preschool classroom is complete without the 'role-play' station that includes the vestments of doctors, construction workers, police officers, bakers, etc. Despite the obvious fascination with the world of work demonstrated by many children, research on career development during the childhood years has been limited (Watson, Nota, & McMahon, 2015; also see Hartung, Porfeli, & Vondracek, 2005; Watson & McMahon, 2005 for reviews of this literature). Existing research largely underscores the content of children's career knowledge and attitudes towards work (Schultheiss, 2008; Watson & McMahon, 2005), with less attention being paid to the process of childhood career development and children's understanding of this process (Porfeli, Hartung, & Vondracek, 2008; Watson & McMahon, 2005). The Conceptions of Career Choice and Attainment (CCCA) model developed by Howard and Walsh (2010, 2011) addresses this gap in the literature. This model describes the developmental changes in children's reasoning about career development processes. It does not focus on the content of children's career knowledge or interests, but instead concentrates on the nature of how children conceptualise key career development processes. In this chapter, we will described the CCCA model as well as its theoretical foundation. The empirical support for the model will be summarised and implications for intervention will be offered.

Theoretical foundation of the model

The CCCA model is built on the recognition that human development is a complex lifespan process. No aspect of development exists in isolation; rather, each is inextricably embedded in the next with changes in one aspect of development having the potential to influence other areas of development in a reciprocal manner (Lerner, 2002). This principle is clearly understood by career theorists interested in children's career development (Ginzberg, Ginsberg, Axelrad, & Herma, 1951; Gottfredson, 1981, 1996, 2002; Super, 1953, 1990; Super,

Conceptions of Career Choice and Containment model 49

Savickas, & Super, 1996; Tiedeman & O'Hara, 1963). Whether explicitly stated or only implied, these theories recognise that the process of children's career development and the content of their interests are shaped by the child's ongoing development.

In Donald Super's (1953, 1990; Super *et al.*, 1996) theory, we find a potential description of the vocational tasks required of individuals as they mature. According to Super, career development progresses by stages, with each stage requiring different tasks of the individual. Career choice is viewed as an implementation of one's vocational self-concept, which develops through feedback gained from the experiences of the individual (and the meaning s/he assigns to these experiences) as well as feedback received from others. Career choice is also understood to be impacted by cultural and systemic experiences, cultural expectations, physical abilities or disabilities and limitations, and parental occupations (Super; Super *et al.*).

While Super (1953, 1990; Super *et al.*, 1996) identifies vocational tasks across developmental phases, Ginzberg and colleagues (1951) provide a description of the development of occupational preferences through childhood and adolescence. This theory identified both the influences that impact children's occupational preferences as well as the manner in which these influences change with age. Ginzberg *et al.* (1951) explain that children begin by making random, unrealistic career preferences when younger and then beginning around age 10 to12 progressively narrow their vocational options first by interest, then by ability, and finally by the relative value of occupations. Gottfredson (1981, 1996, 2002), too, views career choice as a process. She hypothesises that this process is guided and advanced by children's increasing cognitive sophistication, which allows them to progress from basing occupational dreams solely on size and power characteristics to considering gender-typing, prestige, social status level, and, finally, individual characteristics.

Like Ginzberg *et al.* (1951) and Gottfredson (1981, 1996, 2002), Tiedeman and O'Hara (1963) also advance a theory of occupational choice. Their theory, however, focuses on the steps taken as an individual makes a career choice, rather than the factors one relies upon to choose a career or line of work. Tiedeman and O'Hara also include a description of the process through which an individual goes as (s)he attempts to adjust to the new work setting.

These theories provide potential ways for understanding how children develop vocational preferences and vocational identities, thus allowing us to anticipate changes in their career aspirations as they mature and to identify the activities that allow them to develop the vocational skills essential to successful career development. Career education activities will be most impactful when they are tailored to fit not only the developmental tasks facing the child but also his/her developmental level of understanding, as complex information beyond the child's level of cognitive sophistication will not be understood and assimilated. A cognitive developmental approach describes the processes through which individuals make meaning of their experiences and the world around them. As the individual attempts to regulate the dynamic interactions that occur between him/her and the environment, earlier constructions of self and other are reorganised, leading to more flexible, organised, and integrated thought processes (Feldman, 2004; Lerner, 2002).

CCCA model description

Recognising that complex cognitive processes underlie how children conceptualise career development, Howard and Walsh (2010, 2011) developed the Conceptions of Career Choice and Attainment (CCCA) model to better understand children's reasoning about vocational development. Several steps were taken in the development of this model, including the review of contemporary theories of cognitive development and research exploring children's understanding of various phenomena, such as illness (Bibace & Walsh, 1980), violence (Buckley & Walsh, 1998), and ethnicity (Quintana, 1998). A pilot study involving small group and individual interviews allowed for further refinement and specification of the cognitive developmental approach to the processes of career choice and career attainment (Howard & Walsh, 2010).

The CCCA model provides a cognitive developmental organisation of children's conceptions of career choice by identifying three common approaches to reasoning: Association, Sequence, and Interaction. Each approach is further divided into two levels describing in detail children's reasoning styles.

In the first approach, Association, the child's thinking is marked by imagination and fantasy. Lacking the ability to think abstractly, children select future careers in which they can picture themselves (Tiedeman & O'Hara, 1963). Their choices are based on concrete, observable factors related to the occupation, such as a person's attire or the tools they use in their work. Additionally, children demonstrate minimal understanding of the process involved to obtain a job and believe career attainment to be accomplished simply by dressing in the appropriate clothing for the occupation or completing the associated tasks (Nelson, 1978). Thus young children have no concept of the necessary qualifications for certain occupations, such as the need to attend medical school to become a doctor. There are two levels within Association. Children at the first level of thinking, *Pure Association*, simply recognise that the career exists. They are unable to explain how individuals choose their careers or the process involved to secure a job and believe that work is just something that people do. At Level 2, *Magical Thinking*, children are able to describe a basic method for attaining a job but cannot explain how this method operates and results in the job. The child does not consider skills required for a job but rather believes that a person will be suitable for the job provided he or she has the proper apparel and accessories. For instance, having the uniform and the related accessories, such as handcuffs and a squad car, is sufficient to be a police officer.

In the second approach, Sequence, children begin to identify their interests and move away from basing their career dreams on their imagination. As children become more aware of their individual interests, they also become more aware of their strengths and weaknesses. They become more particular about potential careers and exclude those that do not fit with their schema. At this stage, children's preferences for careers tend to be heavily influenced first by gender appropriateness, followed by prestige and social class (Gottfredson, 1981, 1996, 2002). Children reasoning within this approach are able to discern career choice and career attainment as distinct processes yet can also describe the association between the two. In concrete terms and a linear fashion, children explain the choice and attainment of a career by noting that a particular activity leads to a career. The choice of a job and attaining a job are seen as guaranteed results upon completion of the activity or occurrence of an event. More specifically, at Level 3, *External Activities*, children characterise learning about careers by describing external and observable skills and/or activities that lead to securing a job of interest. Children may recognise certain steps that are necessary to obtain a job, such as graduating from high school, but still struggle to explain how achieving this goal will lead to a job. Therefore, they assume that by taking the necessary steps, they will automatically get the job. In the final level of Sequence, *Internal Processes and Capacities*, children hone in on their interests and abilities and consider jobs that match these qualities. They understand career attainment as being a result of learning the necessary skills and possessing competence to do the work.

In the third approach, Interaction, adolescents are able to think more abstractly, which allows for the consideration of occupational prestige. The incorporation of prestige into career decision making, in conjunction with interests, abilities, traits, and values, causes adolescents to narrow the range of potential occupations that they see as suitable for themselves (Ginzberg *et al.*, 1951). Moreover, context is of greater importance so that adolescents reflect on individual factors as well as the needs of the system such as a community or organisation. In terms of choosing a career, adolescents explain that the process involves personal qualities (e.g., interests, skills, and values) in tandem with environmental influences (e.g., availability of job/career, training opportunities, and the status of the job market). The process of career attainment parallels that of career choice, for it also concerns the interaction of personal attributes, job/career details, and how well these two dimensions align, in addition to job availability. In Level 5, *Interaction*, adolescents are able to describe a complex process of choosing and attaining a job by recognising individual, relational, and immediate environmental levels. Lastly, in Level 6, *Systemic Interaction*, while also considering individual, relational, and immediate environmental factors, individuals incorporate factors at systemic levels such as the current status of the job market when explaining how one chooses and attains a job.

In short, this model describes a developmental progression of cognitive reasoning regarding career choice and attainment processes in which one's ability to consider various aspects of self in relation to environment emerges across time. While the CCCA model emphasises developmental level, not age, it is true that generally, younger elementary school age children tend to be reasoning at the Association level, and upper elementary and middle school age children at the Association and Sequence levels. It would be quite rare for children to be functioning at the interaction levels prior to secondary school. However, it is important to note that even in secondary school or beyond, an individual may not reach the highest levels. As such, the CCCA model provides a valuable framework from which career interventions may be structured so as to promote a more sophisticated understanding of career development amongst children and youth and, therefore, a more informed position from which to navigate their preparation for and entry into the world of work.

Empirical support for the model

Support for the model can be found in direct tests of its tenets as well as related research that is consistent with it. Howard and Walsh (2010) conducted two studies to directly test the ability of the model to capture the nature of children's reasoning about career development processes. The first study included 60 children in grades K–6 (~5 to 12 years old), while the second included 72 students in grades K–8 (~5 to 14 years old). In both studies, children were interviewed individually about their career-related beliefs. It was found that the CCCA model could be used successfully to categorise children's reasoning about career choice and career attainment processes. Younger children were more likely to offer answers that reflected use of fantasy and magical thinking about careers. The older the child interviewed the more likely s/he was to identify factors such as personal interests, abilities, and job requirements as influential in her/his career-related beliefs. The complexity of career reasoning increased as age increased, with the oldest participants being more likely to describe career choice and attainment as a dynamic interaction of person and environmental-level factors (Howard & Walsh, 2010).

Indirect support for the CCCA model can be found in a number of studies that examined age- or grade-related differences in how children described their beliefs about how people choose careers and how they prepare themselves to both find and enter specific jobs. For example, both Phipps (1995) and Seligman and colleagues (Seligman, Weinstock, & Heflin, 1991; Seligman, Weinstock, & Owings, 1988) found that children's ability to identify potential jobs or careers for themselves and to understand the educational and training requirements for specific lines of work increased with age. Further, the studies by Schultheiss and colleagues (Schultheiss, Palma, & Manzi, 2005) and Trice and colleagues (Trice, Hughes, Odom, Woods, & McClellan, 1995) offer support for the shift during the elementary school years from a belief that choice just happens (Association) to one where choice is understood to be based on factors such as interest and ability (Sequence). The CCCA model's description of developmental changes in children's understanding of career attainment is reflected in the results found by a number of researchers (e.g., Borgen & Young, 1982; Nelson, 1978; Phipps, 1995;

Schultheiss *et al.*, 2005). When combined, their research suggests a developmental process by which prekindergarten-/kindergarten-age children describe career attainment as simply donning the accessories or tools used in various lines of work, while older elementary school children identify the specific tasks of various occupations and emphasise the need to develop required skills and gain required knowledge before being able to enter those occupations. Finally, high school–age youth describe career attainment as an ongoing, ever-evolving, and complex process.

Implications for intervention

In order to articulate what we see as the potential implications of this model for career development work with children and youth, we began by examining the career development standards used by the American School Counselor Association (ASCA, 2004) as well as the Blueprint competencies for Canada (Hache, Redekopp, & Jarvis, 2000) and Australia (Ministerial Council for Education, Early Childhood Development, and Youth Affairs, 2010). Collectively, these models identify the following competencies as necessary for positive career development: 1) knowledge of self, skills at self-reflection, building of skills to care for self and to successfully navigate in the world; 2) understanding the world of work and how to access information about it, ability to consider the fit between work conditions and personal factors (e.g., needs, values, interests); and 3) acquiring the information and developing the skills to successfully enter into and remain in the workforce, including the ability to balance the dynamic interactions between work and other life roles.

The objectives listed across the standards and competencies can be organised into four categories. The first type of objective focuses on the *what* or the content knowledge needed in order to prepare for future work, with knowledge of self and familiarity with the world of work being key content areas. The second type of objective is concerned with the *how* of career development – that is, teaching students about the different processes involved in career development. These objectives focus on processes such as exploring the world of work, setting and pursuing goals, and making career decisions. The third objective type found in the career standards and competencies involves *applying* the knowledge students have gained and the career development processes in which they have learned to carry out some action such as setting short- and long-term goals and making developmentally appropriate decisions. The final type of objective can be described as *reflection and refinement*. This set of objectives encourages the critical examination of the knowledge gained, the tasks undertaken, and the outcomes experienced to guide one's career development in the future. In short, this set of objectives focuses on the complexity involved in the career development process.

This categorisation of career education objectives can be used to frame our discussion of the implications for intervention that arise from the CCCA model. We suggest types of interventions that are both consistent with the

Implications at the association levels

In the Association approach, children focus on activities, experiences, and observable objects associated with the imagined career. Children imagine themselves in the occupational role with little understanding of how careers are chosen or the process by which they are secured. For children who are reasoning about careers with the Association levels (*Pure Association* and *Magical Thinking*), we would focus our interventions on the first two types of objectives – namely, expanding their content knowledge and facilitating their understanding of simple career development processes. Content-type interventions would provide children with guided opportunities to discover and explore their individual interests and to become aware of particular skills they may have (or would like to have). Awareness of skills appears to develop after the awareness of one's interests, so interventions should be sequenced appropriately. Content-type interventions would also provide young children the opportunity to gain familiarity with the world of work, with the goal of expanding the number of occupations of which children are aware. As children become aware of a wider range of occupations, interventions should then be introduced that allow them to become familiar with the basic characteristics of this range of occupations as well as the tasks performed by workers in those occupations. Beale (Beale, 2000; Beale & Williams, 2000) describes two such interventions, a hospital field trip and an elementary school career day, that are both designed specifically to assist young students in developing a basic understanding of the world of work.

By definition, children reasoning about careers from an Association approach do not have a conceptualisation of career choice or career attainment as processes, but rather understand these events to just occur. Therefore, any process-oriented intervention used would focus solely on helping children within the Association levels to gain a simple and very rudimentary appreciation that preparation is needed in order to enter an occupation in the future. Preparation should be understood as involving both the accrual of specific knowledge used by workers in a particular job/career and developing the skills used regularly by workers with that job/career.

For children using the Association levels of reasoning, play may be a practical and effective way children can learn about careers. Classrooms may have toys (e.g., stethoscope, cooking utensils, blocks, and LEGOs) that represent the work of certain occupations, such as doctors, chefs, architects, and engineers, and that can be used to explicitly explain the basic characteristics and skills of careers. Simple interventions may be created through explicitly stating or explaining how those toys are related to careers. Learning experiences such as play, therefore, will help to support the development of more sophisticated career reasoning.

Implications at the sequence levels

The Sequence level is characterised by a shift in reasoning in which both career choice and career attainment are viewed as simple, stepwise processes. Children first understand that choice is often based on interests and then begin to appreciate the influences of abilities and skills on career choices. Attaining a job/career is understood as a linear process of gaining the knowledge and experiences needed for the work done in that job/career. According to the model, all four types of objectives would be appropriate for use with children reasoning within the Sequence levels (*External Activities* and *Internal Processes and Capacities*).

Content-type interventions would not only support and facilitate children's exploration and growing awareness of career-related interests, skills, and abilities, but would also expand beyond these three constructs to familiarise students with the role of values and needs in career decision making. Further, world-of-work exploration activities should be expanded to include investigation into the types of skills needed by workers in various occupations as well as the dispositions that make workers successful and satisfied with occupations. Interventions that involve occupation-related field trips, speakers, and shadowing experiences (see, for example, Fouad, 1995) may be particularly useful for children reasoning within the Sequence levels. Interventions focused on process aim to help children develop a sense of *how* career choice and career attainment occur. Process interventions would therefore introduce the importance of goal setting and would teach children the steps involved in both setting and pursuing goals. They would facilitate an appreciation among each child of how the steps taken (e.g., education, training) prepare one for an occupation.

Application-type interventions for children reasoning within the Sequence levels give them the opportunity to practise using both the knowledge they have gained about themselves and the world-of-work as well as goal-setting strategies. For example, after completing a self-reflection activity on interests and skills, children may be encouraged to use what they know about their own interests and skills to choose an elective activity in the classroom. Teachers can use the goal-setting steps to have each child identify a goal, whether that is an academic, career, or social-emotional goal, brainstorm the steps needed to reach it, and then work through those steps. Project-based learning activities, whether the projects are completed by the individual or as a group, can provide excellent opportunities to practise using goal-setting and pursuit strategies.

Reflection and refinement interventions are also appropriate to use with children reasoning within the Sequence levels, as they can facilitate a child's ability to appreciate the complexity of career decision making and career attainment. Career education activities that encourage children to explore and learn about the changing nature of their interests, skills, values, needs, and goals can be particularly helpful. These activities may encourage children to hypothesise what their lives may 'look like' in 5, 10, or 20 years in the future. Where will they be living? What will they be doing? What will their family life be like?

Perspective-taking can be encouraged by helping children explore what their needs and priorities may be in a future context.

Implications at the interaction levels

The third approach to reasoning about career processes is Interaction, in which children demonstrate a complex understanding of the dynamic processes of career choice and attainment. Both choice and attainment are understood as resulting from an interaction of person and context factors, and the influence of time and stage of life is readily acknowledged. For children reasoning in the Interaction levels (*Interaction* and *Systemic Interaction*), content-type interventions would continue to encourage ongoing exploration of interests, skills, abilities, values, and needs, but would expand to include an exploration of the personal, relational, and contextual influences that have shaped these factors. Narrative approaches (McMahon & Watson, 2013; Young, Friesen, & Borycki, 1994) to career exploration can be particularly useful to facilitate such insight. Children in the Interaction levels have the capacity to understand the changing nature of the world-of-work. New occupations emerge as new technologies emerge, and technology has the potential to transform how one does one's work. Process-focused interventions would facilitate not only children's appreciation for the shifting landscape of work, but also the resulting need for personal and professional adaptability. Children would learn that adaptability will likely require ongoing professional development and become familiar with avenues for pursuing such continued professional training.

Interaction levels of reasoning about careers are more common amongst older children, many of whom are increasingly inclined to plan for what comes after their secondary school education as they approach the end of the secondary years. Interventions focused on the application of what they have learned about themselves, the world-of-work, career decision making, goal setting, and career pursuit are particularly useful. Such interventions would, of course, assist children to develop their postsecondary plan, but they should also include a consideration of contingencies and unforeseen opportunities. Children in the Interaction levels not only comprehend but can greatly benefit from opportunities to anticipate the challenges they might face and to plan for the 'what ifs.' The development of career adaptability (Savickas, 1997) can be encouraged, even before children officially enter the adult working world. Finally, reflection and refinement interventions can assist children to explore how future life transitions and larger systemic changes, realities, and inequities may modify, shape, and redirect their career pathways. In this sense, the need to understand the developmental nature of career reasoning among individuals as well as groups of children and adolescents has important social justice implications. Of primary importance is this model's ability to categorise the sophistication of reasoning about careers based on one's understanding of structural and systemic influences. The ability to gauge the extent to which one's aspirations are affected or constrained by real or perceived systemic barriers is an important preliminary step to promoting the implementation of interventions that promote development of critical consciousness (Diemer & Blustein, 2006; Prilleltensky & Stead, 2012) among disadvantaged groups and youth at risk within the context of the world-of-work. As such, these learning opportunities may help children be prepared to respond to changes, whether voluntary or involuntary, in flexible, adaptive, and successful ways to ensure that they are able to both navigate and challenge obstacles en route to meaningful career development opportunities.

The future of CCCA

In order to provide appropriate support for children and adolescents' career development, research on the CCCA model must be expanded to include cultural diversity, generational differences, and the inconsistent availability of occupations. Further empirical testing on the model and potential career interventions is needed to focus on the CCCA model's upper levels and other important outcomes for adolescents who are about to enter the world-of-work. The CCCA model may continuously need to be revised to ensure cross-cultural relevance. For example, Kuwabara and Smith (2012) have found differences by culture in children's sensitivity to both the relational context surrounding a task and the decontextualised information presented in the task. Such differences in attention result in variations in performance on social, perceptual, and reasoning tasks. Future research on the CCCA model should consider how one's culturally influenced attention to context may influence how one reasons about career-related tasks.

Conclusion

The CCCA model detailed in this chapter describes the developmental changes in children's reasoning about the career development processes of choosing and attaining a job or career. It complements, rather than replaces, existing theories of children's career development and provides a valuable framework from which career interventions may be structured. Interventions following the CCCA model would be targeted to the type of reasoning displayed by children within each of the CCCA conceptual approaches, and they would also promote development towards a more sophisticated understanding of career development.

References

American School Counselor Association. (2004). *ASCA national standards for students*. Alexandria, VA: Author.

Beale, A. V. (2000). Elementary school awareness: A visit to the hospital. *Journal of Career Development, 27*, 65–72.

Beale, A. V., & Williams, J. C. (2000). The anatomy of an elementary school career day. *Journal of Career Development, 26*, 205–213.

Bibace, R., & Walsh, M. E. (1980). Development of children's concepts of illness. *Pediatrics, 66*, 913–917.

Borgen, W. A., & Young, R. A. (1982). Career perceptions of children and adolescents. *Journal of Vocational Behavior, 21*, 37–49.

Buckley, M. A., & Walsh, M. E. (1998). Children's understanding of violence: A developmental analysis. *Applied Developmental Science, 2*, 182–193.

Diemer, M. A., & Blustein, D. L. (2006). Critical consciousness and career development among urban youth. *Journal of Vocational Behavior, 68*, 220–232.

Feldman, D. H. (2004). Piaget's stages: The unfinished symphony of cognitive development. *New Ideas in Psychology, 22*, 175–231.

Fouad, N. A. (1995). Career linking: An intervention to promote math and science career awareness. *Journal of Counseling and Development, 73*, 527–534.

Ginzberg, E., Ginsberg, S. W., Axelrad, S., & Herma, J. L. (1951). *Occupational choice: An approach to a general theory*. New York, NY: Columbia University Press.

Gottfredson, L. S. (1981). Circumscription and compromise: A developmental theory of occupational aspirations [Monograph]. *Journal of Counseling Psychology, 28*, 545–579.

Gottfredson, L. S. (1996). Gottfredson's theory of circumscription and compromise. In D. Brown & L. Brooks (Eds.), *Career choice and development* (3rd ed., pp. 179–232). San Francisco, CA: Jossey-Bass.

Gottfredson, L. S. (2002). Gottfredson's theory of circumscription, compromise, and self-creation. In D. Brown (Ed.), *Career choice and development* (4th ed., pp. 85–148). San Francisco, CA: Jossey-Bass.

Hache, L., Redekopp, D. E., & Jarvis, P. S. (2000). *Blueprint from life/work designs*. Memramcook, New Brunswick, Canada: National Life/Work Centre.

Hartung, P. J., Porfeli, E. J., & Vondracek, F. W. (2005). Child vocational development: A review and reconsideration. *Journal of Vocational Behavior, 66*, 385–419

Howard, K. A. S., & Walsh, M. E. (2010). Conceptions of career choice and attainment: Developmental levels in how children think about careers. *Journal of Vocational Behavior, 76*, 143–152.

Howard, K. A. S., & Walsh, M. E. (2011). Children's conceptions of career choice and attainment: Model development. *Journal of Career Development, 38*, 256–271.

Kuwabara, M., & Smith, L. B. (2012). Cross-cultural differences in cognitive development: Attention to relations and objects. *Journal of Experimental Child Psychology, 113*, 20–35.

Lerner, R. M. (2002). *Concepts and theories of human development* (3rd ed.). Mahwah, NJ: Lawrence Erlbaum.

McMahon, M., & Watson, M. (2013). Story telling: Crafting identities. *British Journal of Guidance and Counselling, 41*, 277–286.

Ministerial Council for Education, Early Childhood Development and Youth Affairs. (2010). *Australian Blueprint for Career Development*. Prepared by Miles Morgan Australia. Retrieved from www.blueprint.edu.au

Nelson, J. N. (1978). Age and sex differences in the development of children's occupational reasoning. *Journal of Vocational Behavior, 13*, 287–297.

Phipps, B. J. (1995). Career dreams of preadolescent students. *Journal of Career Development, 22*, 19–32.

Porfeli, E. J., Hartung, P. J., & Vondracek, F. W. (2008). Children's vocational development: A research rationale. *The Career Development Quarterly, 57*, 25–37.

Prilleltensky, I., & Stead, G. B. (2012). Critical psychology and career development: Unpacking the adjust–challenge dilemma. *Journal of Career Development, 39*, 321–340.

Quintana, S. M. (1998). Children's developmental understanding of ethnicity and race. *Applied and Preventive Psychology, 7*, 27–45.

Savickas, M. L. (1997). Career adaptability: An integrative construct for life-span, life-space theory. *The Career Development Quarterly, 45*, 247–259.

Schultheiss, D. E. P. (2008). Current status and future agenda for the theory, research, and practice of childhood career development. *The Career Development Quarterly, 57*, 7–24.

Schultheiss, D. E. P., Palma, T. V., & Manzi, A. J. (2005). Career development in middle childhood: A qualitative inquiry. *The Career Development Quarterly, 53*, 246–262.

Seligman, L., Weinstock, L., & Heflin, E. N. (1991). The career development of 10 year olds. *Elementary School Guidance and Counseling, 25*, 172–181.

Seligman, L., Weinstock, L., & Owings, N. (1988). The role of family dynamics in career development of 5-year-olds. *Elementary School Guidance and Counseling, 22*, 222–230.

Super, D. E. (1953). A theory of vocational development. *American Psychologist, 8*, 185–190.

Super, D. E. (1990). A life-span, life-space approach to career development. In D. Brown & L. Brooks (Eds.), *Career choice and development: Applying contemporary theories to practice* (2nd ed., pp. 197–261). San Francisco, CA: Jossey-Bass.

Super, D. E., Savickas, M. L., & Super, C. M. (1996). The life-span, life-space approach to careers. In D. Brown, L. Brooks & Associates (Eds.), *Career choice and development: Applying contemporary theories to practice* (3rd ed., pp. 121–178). San Francisco, CA: Jossey-Bass.

Tiedeman, D. V., & O'Hara, R. P. (1963). *Career development: Choice and adjustment.* New York, NY: College Entrance Examination Board.

Trice, A. D., Hughes, M. A., Odom, C., Woods, K., & McClellan, N. C. (1995). The origins of children's career aspirations: IV. Testing hypotheses from four theories. *The Career Development Quarterly, 43*, 307–322.

Watson, M., & McMahon, M. (2005). Children's career development: A research review from a learning perspective. *Journal of Vocational Behavior, 67*, 119–132.

Watson, M., Nota, L., & McMahon, M. (2015). Child career development: Present and future trends. *International Journal for Educational and Vocational Guidance, 15*, 95–97.

Young, R., Friesen, J. D., & Borycki, B. (1994). Narrative structure and parental influence in career development. *Journal of Adolescence, 17*, 173–191.

Chapter 6

Children as storytellers
Constructing identity through story

Mary McMahon and Mark Watson

> *Mine's sort of been a real progression too . . . first I wanted to be a policeman until I figured out that I couldn't and had to be a policewoman. And then I wanted to be a prosecutor and then I figured out they didn't make enough money. So then I wanted to become a lawyer and that was like a grade six/seven decision . . . And in between I had about a week I wanted to become a neurologist but that sort of really passed over. Yeh, it was pretty much a progression sort of thing. I know that really, law sort of came through.*

These are the words of a female Australian adolescent upper secondary school student commenting on her career development since early childhood. As reflected in her story, children begin to imagine themselves in adult work roles, tell stories of their experiences, and begin the process of constructing occupational identities at a very young age as career theory tells us (e.g., Gottfredson, 2005; Super, 1990). Identity is constructed through narrative (Gibson, 2004; LaPointe, 2010; Meijers & Lengelle, 2012); individuals construct stories based on their life experiences and, in doing so, construct their identities. Narrative identity has been described as an "internalized and evolving life story that a person constructs to make sense and meaning out of his or her life" (McAdams, 2011, p. 99).

Childhood has been described as the "dawn" and "threshold" of vocational development during which, through play, children begin to construct possible future selves in work and social roles (Hartung, Porfeli, & Vondracek, 2008, p. 63). Indeed, the early seminal work of Goldstein and Oldham (1979) close to four decades ago, reminds us that children begin to extensively orient themselves to work in a process that begins early and progresses quickly. For example, demonstrating some understanding of career development as a process, an infant school (grades one and two) girl explained: "I wanted to be a teacher of kindergarten but I changed my mind so probably now well, when I'm in grade eight or nine I'll probably change my mind then as well" and a primary school boy demonstrated rudimentary knowledge about qualifications when he said, "You've got to qualify or something like that. And like if you're going to be a bus driver you've got to have a licence to drive a bus". Through their stories, children begin to "convey to themselves and to others who they are now, how they came to be, and where they think their lives may be going in the future" (McAdams & McLean, 2013, p. 233); their stories depict their narrative identity.

Despite long-term and widespread recognition of the foundational nature of child career development for subsequent life stages, most attention in career theory, research, and practice has focused to date more on adolescents and adults than on children. Further, recent trends in career theory, research, and practice that recognise the importance of narrative and stories in the lives of individuals have also been applied more to adolescents and adults. These trends have resulted in greater awareness and acceptance of the influence of context on career development and the use of narrative practices in career counselling and career programs. Less attention has been afforded to narrative and story in the career development of children. This chapter considers how children, as storytellers, begin to construct identities that are foundational to career development and the construction of vocational identities in adolescence and adulthood. It discusses implications of the "narrative turn" in career development (Hartung, 2013, p. 33) for child career theory, research, and practice. Where appropriate, the voices of children will be used to provide illustrative quotes.

Identity development

> *And then you have to get a piece of wood and hammer it, and hammer it in the middle.*

As reflected in the words of this male preschool child commenting on being a workman, even very young children begin to construct stories of themselves in adult roles. McAdams (2008) suggests that from the second year of life, children begin to store memories and tell stories of experience, by age three they can converse with adults about their experiences, and by the end of the preschool years, they can tell stories of their experiences without adult guidance. Young children may have basic knowledge about occupations and their status and have developed ideas about the suitability of such occupations for them, even though these may be gender stereotyped (Hartung, 2015) as reflected in the following conversation between two infant school boys discussing what girls can do: "They can't be a cowboy like cowboying everywhere" (boy 1), "Yes they can" (boy 2), "They can be a cowgirl then" (boy 1; McMahon, 2007, p. 8). Such rudimentary knowledge of occupations and work may be reflected in children's play and other social roles. As reflected in the comments of the children, essential tasks of childhood include:

> (a) learning about the world of work and establishing a basic sense of self; (b) imagining the self doing various work tasks, having different jobs, and being a part of different work settings; and (c) projecting the self into the world of work (e.g., a future worker self) to establish a budding worker identity.
> (Porfeli, Lee, & Vondracek, 2013, p. 135)

Towards the end of childhood, children become more motivated and agentic, form goals and plans (McAdams, 2011, 2013), and may have realistic ideas about future work roles (Skorikov & Vondracek, 2011). Stories such as those of the preschooler at the beginning of this section contribute to the construction of occupational identity – a term used interchangeably with vocational, work, professional, and career identity (Skorikov & Vondracek, 2007, 2011). Occupational identity is "the conscious awareness of oneself as a worker" (Skorikov & Vondracek, 2011, p. 693) and is evident in the previous comments of the adolescent and the children and in the comments of a primary school girl: "I used to think I could be a teacher, not a music teacher but a normal teacher, but I thought it would be a lot of hard work because I'm not good at everything". Skorikov and Vodracek claim that occupational identity is a core element of identity, which, broadly speaking, is "our understanding of who we are" (Ahn, 2011, p. 415); for children, knowing who they are is a precursor to the process of "becoming" across the lifespan (Ahn, 2011, p. 415). Establishing a vocational identity is a crucial developmental task of childhood and adolescence (Porfeli, Lee, & Vondracek, 2013). Vocational identity serves a number of functions, including enhancing career decision making, providing a sense of direction and meaning and a foundation for goal setting and self-assessment, and enhancing adjustment, well-being, and life satisfaction (Skorikov & Vondracek, 2007).

Stories are fundamental to identity construction and are seldom "finished works"; they are more akin to "works in progress" (McAdams, 2011, p. 104) that develop over time and are contextually embedded. In essence,

> The stories we construct to make sense of our lives are fundamentally about our struggle to reconcile who we imagine we were, are, and might be in our heads and bodies with who we were, are, and might be in the social contexts of family, community, the workplace, ethnicity, religion, gender, social class, and culture at large. The self comes to terms with society through narrative identity.
>
> (McAdams, 2008, pp. 242–243)

Because lives are complex and individuals have a multiplicity of experiences, no single story represents the whole of an individual's life experience; lives are multistoried (McMahon, Watson, & Bimrose, 2010). Individuals, including children, are active agents in the construction of their stories; stories represent a recursive interaction between experience, meaning-making, learning, and the construction of identity (McMahon et al., 2010). Narratives are both personal and social (McAdams, 2008), and a range of theories provide accounts of how narratives are constructed. In common across this body of theory are key ideas, specifically, (1) "The self is storied", (2) "Stories integrate lives", (3) "Stories are told in social relationships", (4) "Stories change over time", (5) "Stories are cultural texts", and (6) "Some stories are better than others" (McAdams, 2008, pp. 244–247). Such ideas are clearly evident in the stories of children presented in this chapter.

Childhood experiences are foundational in the construction of identity; observations of attitudes towards work within families, cultural stereotypes, and influence of the media may influence children's meaning of work and in turn their occupational identities (Skorikov & Vondracek, 2011). Reflecting the construction of vocational identity as a recursive interplay between children, their families and other environmental influences, a primary school girl explained,

> *Well on Curly Sue* [a children's television show] *I found out that there was such a thing as a lawyer. And then I asked my mum what they did and she said they always help people with their life and I always thought helping people would be a nice thing to do so I thought I might be one if I could help people decide what they wanted to do with their life.*

As evident in this child's story, narratives are constructed in context; history, culture, language, relationships, and society all influence the stories that children construct. The context of family is important, especially in childhood. Indeed, narrative identity originates in conversations between parents and their young children (McAdams & McLean, 2013). Family is widely recognised as an important influence on child career development (see Chapter 9 by Liu and McMahon in this book), but its effect on occupational identity formation is less clear (Skorikov & Vondracek, 2011). In relation to family influence, the concept of identity construction with a view to the goal setting, decision making, and occupational choice of adolescence and adulthood may be culturally bound. For example, in some cultures, occupational identity may be predetermined and ascribed within families or communities (Skorikov & Vondracek, 2011; see Chapter 10 by Bakshi in this book) and may be less individually focused and less about meaning. Awareness of differences between cultures and the contextual origins of stories acutely reminds us of the cultural context in which the dominant theoretical stories about career development in childhood and the construction of occupational identity have been told. Occupational identity in the dominant stories is inherently associated with choice and a quest for meaning, yet work for many people is less about meaning and more about survival, and less about choice and more about taking work that is available. Child career development theorists, researchers, and practitioners would do well to remember the less told, hidden and silenced stories (McMahon, 2006) of child career development that prevail for many children in the world, including many in the countries from where the dominant stories originate.

Children as storytellers

Because stories are constructed in context, children have different experiences and tell different stories. For example, a primary school girl told a story about gender and work in her comment that "we saw this lady doing a man's job. She was painting the walls of the supermarket", whereas another primary school girl told a different story about gender and work when she explained, "There's not really girl's jobs or boy's jobs. You can get whatever job you really want to get". While at one level such stories could be dismissed because of the children's age, at another they warrant deep consideration, because "stories are shaping of life" and "have real, not imagined effects" (White, 1992, p. 123). Narratives are both a product and a process (Botella, Herrero, Pacheco, & Corbella, 2004) because they not only describe identity, they shape it (Gibson, 2004).

Stories are the "construction tools" (Savickas, 2011, p. 38) with which narrative identity is built. In the two simple stories told by the primary school girls, we can see one girl telling a career-limiting story through her gender-stereotyped perceptions of careers and the other telling a story that promises more expansive career opportunities. The circumscription of occupations on the basis of gender and social status has been described theoretically in a series of developmental stages (Gottfredson, 2005). According to Gottfredson (2005), from the age of three, children become aware of the adult world and occupations as part of adulthood, as reflected in these comments by a male preschool student, "I wanted to do what my dad does"; a male infant school (grades one and two) student, "I want to be a lifesaver because you get to drive a boat all the time"; and a female infant school (grades one and two) student about what she wants to be when she grows up: "Doctor, cause my mum and dad are both doctors. I have four doctors in my family".

Identifying with influential adults as these three children have done may influence a child's occupational identity from a very young age, even though little self-assessment has occurred (Skorikov & Vondracek, 2011). Subsequently, from approximately age six, children's growing awareness of sex roles, as reflected in the earlier comments made by the primary school girls, results in the circumscription of occupations they perceive as belonging to the opposite sex (Gottfredson, 2005). During this stage, children also begin to develop a growing awareness about social status and from approximately age nine, circumscribe occupations on the basis of perceived social status; they reject occupations they perceive as "low status" from their consideration, perhaps because "what one does for a living is a primary source of information about social class, education, and values" (Raskin, 1985, p. 26) and because having an occupation is a source of income and a mechanism of social integration and self-expression (Skorikov & Vondracek, 2011). Perceived status is reflected by a female primary school student who commented, "Well being famous. I'd just like the whole world to know about me", and another who explained, "I suddenly realised that you don't really get very much money for it so I said no I didn't want to do it". It is little wonder that children tell stories of who they imagine they will be when they grow up: "one's occupation is a public statement of one's identity" (Raskin, 1985, p. 26) and children are keen to make sense of who they may become as adults.

Considering theory, research, and practice

Childhood is a critical period of lifespan career development where children vicariously learn about occupations and the world of work. Such learning ultimately has a "profound affect on the choices they make as adolescents and young adults, and ultimately, on their occupational careers" (Hartung, Porfeli, & Vondracek, 2005, p. 412). The career learning of children is evident in the stories they tell as reflected throughout this chapter. To date, however, less theoretical, research, and practical attention has been afforded to child career development; even less attention has focused on narrative, storytelling, and construction of identity. There is an English proverb that says "children should be seen and not heard". Fortunately, society has come a long way since this proverb was coined in its original form in the fifteenth century. In career theory, research and practice, however, it seems that the voices of children are still little heard and comprehensive stories of identity construction in childhood have not been told.

At a theoretical level, career construction theory (Savickas, 2013) with its emphasis on narratability is one recent theoretical formulation to provide some account of the construction of vocational identity in childhood, in particular through its practical application of life design (Hartung, 2015; see Chapter 3 by Hartung in this book). To date, this theory, in relation to children, remains more conceptual than informed by the stories of children. By contrast, the voices of children have been used to influence the development of the concepts of career choice and attainment model (Howard & Walsh, 2010; see Chapter 5 by Howard *et al.* in this book). As yet, however, it remains the case that a detailed account of the construction of vocational identity in childhood is still to be theorised, as is a detailed understanding of how narrative and story contribute to vocational identity formation in childhood.

In terms of research, while there is agreement that identity is constructed, there is less agreement on "how, from what, by whom and for what" (Castells, 2004, p. 7). Such questions are reflective of challenges facing the field of child career development with successive research reviews claiming that the 'how' of career development in childhood needs further research (e.g., Hartung *et al.*, 2005; Watson & McMahon, 2005). Investigating such questions could provide fertile ground for career researchers. Children themselves may provide some insight into the process of identity formation through their comments. For example, a primary school boy explained, "Well when I heard about scientist, I forgot about being a policeman and I thought I would be better being a scientist than a working policeman", and another explained why he didn't want to be Superman anymore: "I don't know. Just growing up. If you didn't believe it any more". Further, given the cultural location of identity, opportunities to investigate how children from diverse settings construct career stories and their identities abound.

In recent years, a growing number of career assessment instruments have been developed for use with children, most of which are quantitative, which has led Watson, Nota, and McMahon (2015) to caution about the potential consequences of using such instruments to "categorise or foster deficit thinking" (p. 180). Most reported studies on child career development to date are quantitative, and there are few examples that privilege the voices of children. A more recent exception is the research of Howard and Walsh (2010), who interviewed children and subsequently coded the responses to report primarily quantitative results. This approach is consistent with most psychological research and much narrative research, for example, in the field of personality (McAdams, 2008) where techniques such as coding systems and word counts facilitate quantitative data analysis and reporting.

Despite the growing narrative influence in theory and in practice, there remain few examples of qualitative research in the dominant journals in career development. For example, in a content analysis of 11 journals that published career, vocational, and work-related articles between 1990 and 2009, fewer than 10 per cent were qualitative empirical or mixed-method studies (Stead *et al.*, 2012). Further, these authors reported that qualitative research standards of academic rigour and procedures were either not followed or were not reported. For over a decade, there have been calls to diversify research methodologies and for a balance between qualitative and quantitative methodologies and exploratory and confirmatory research (Savickas, 2001; Stead *et al.*, 2012). It seems that an ongoing challenge for the field, especially in view of its "narrative turn" (Hartung, 2013, p. 33), is to find "ways to weave different theoretical perspectives, and findings obtained with widely different methodologies, into a complementary whole that truly represents all of vocational psychology" (Vondracek, 2001, p. 259). While these comments apply to the field of career development broadly, similar comments could apply to the more specific field of child career development. Reflecting the concerns of Stead *et al.* (2012), traditionally, much less acceptance of qualitative research is evident in the field (McMahon & Watson, 2007), which continues to limit the potential impact of the "narrative turn" (Hartung, 2013, p. 33) by denying opportunities for the voices of research participants, including children, to be heard.

At a practice level, schooling plays a critical and inescapable role in the formation of identities that children will take with them into adulthood (Reay, 2010). This is not unexpected given the amount of time children and adolescents spend in school. Given the potential in schools, through their processes and personnel, to encourage or discourage a child's sense of self, identities are constructed through a sense of "what we are not" as well as through others' perceptions of "who 'we' are" (Reay, 2010, p. 277). During schooling, children may acquire work skills and a sense of industry, be exposed to occupational role models, develop occupational interests, and receive direct and indirect guidance (Skorikov & Vondracek, 2011). Much career learning in childhood, however, occurs in unintentional ways such as observation as reflected in the stories of the children presented in this chapter; most children are not provided with formal learning processes that assist them with making sense of their experiences, nor are they guided in their career exploration (Watson & McMahon, 2007). Career development learning may be intentionally facilitated by schools through career guidance such as career education programs (Patton & McMahon, 2014). To date, however, most intentional career development has been provided to adolescents during their secondary school years through career education and career guidance programs; less attention has been paid to career learning in primary schools.

While career programs to assist in the development of occupational identities in children have been advocated widely, there is less evidence of their implementation and even less of activities or programs that are underpinned by narrative and story. Throughout history, however, telling stories (e.g., fables) has been used as a way of engaging children and helping them to learn. In advocating the use of life design approaches with children, Hartung (2015) claims that the career construction interview and the *My Career Story* autobiographical workbook (Savickas & Hartung, 2012) can be adapted for use by children. Further research could establish the nature of adaptations needed and the efficacy of these resources when used with children.

An example of a narrative resource developed primarily for children was reported in small-scale pilot research using career conversation cards as stimuli for primary school children, parents, and a teacher. Each card features an age-appropriate career scenario (a brief story) based on individual, social, and environmental-societal influences on career development that is followed by "conversation-starter" questions (McMahon & Watson, 2014). These authors found that the upper primary school children derived learning from the cards; parents could see the cards being useful and had conversations with their children based on the stimulus questions on the cards, and the teacher had ideas about how and where the career conversations could be integrated into the curriculum.

In practice, there are pockets of hope. For example, the Australian state of Victoria has recognised both the importance of parental influence and story and has developed a program called Engaging Parents in Career Conversations Framework (EPiCC) that is supported by parent workshops and resources. Paying attention to the career stories of children and providing them with opportunities to tell their stories may provide multifaceted benefits. For example, engaging in conversations with parents around a topic of interest – namely, work and future aspirations – may strengthen family relationships and enable children to feel that their stories are listened to.

Because not all children have parents who are "adequate career role models" (Skorikov & Vondracek, 2011, p. 707), facilitating intentional career development learning may foster a sense of industry in children and, through experiences such as class visits (e.g., Beale, 2000) and guest speakers, provide exposure to a broad range of options and role models in order to foster vocational identity construction. Engaging in career conversations with children in the classroom may provide opportunities to address career-limiting thinking (e.g., gender stereotypical thinking). In addition, engaging in career conversations in classrooms and providing opportunities for children to tell their career stories in intentional career development learning programs may enhance the relevance of what children learn in their school subjects as they come to appreciate the relationship between the school subjects and the world of work.

There is widespread agreement that occupational exploration in childhood and committing to occupations in adolescence and adulthood contribute to the construction of occupational identity across the lifespan (Skorikov & Vondracek, 2011). The narratives of children provide insight into how families, peers, and schools influence their sense of self and their identity construction (Reay, 2010). The nature of school influence on occupational identity construction has to date not been widely researched (Skorikov & Vondracek, 2011). In addition, research on the relationship between school, academic learning, and occupational identity is needed (Skorikov & Vondracek, 2011).

The importance of "conversation and social contexts for learning narrative skills, shaping identity expectations, and formulating a meaningful story for one's life" (McAdams & McLean, 2013, p. 237) cannot be understated. Long term, the ability to tell career stories and engage in career conversations is a skill that serves children well into adolescence and adulthood. Over time, as children tell stories of their experiences, their narrative identities build (McAdams & McLean, 2013). Moreover, narrative identity is important to well-being (McAdams & McLean, 2013; Skorikov & Vondracek, 2007): "establishing a strong, self-chosen, positive, and flexible occupational identity appears to be an important contributor to occupational success, social adaptation, and psychological well-being" (Skorikov & Vondracek, 2011, p. 693).

Conclusion

As reflected in the words of the children portrayed in this chapter, children tell stories to make sense of their vicarious experiences of work and, in doing so, begin to construct occupational identities. While the growing influence of narrative is clearly evident in theory, research, and practice concerning adolescents and adults, this influence has, to date, received cursory attention in child career development. Children's career stories reflect their learning about career development, much of which is unintentional. Extending the use of stories and narrative into child career development through creative practices and research remains an area of great promise, as it could stimulate much-needed new theoretical advances that better account for the formation of occupational identity in childhood.

References

Ahn, J. (2011). Review of children's identity construction via narratives. *Creative Education, 2*, 415–417.

Beale, A. V. (2000). Elementary school career awareness: A visit to a hospital. *Journal of Career Development, 27*, 65–72.

Botella, L., Herrero, O., Pacheco, M., & Corbella, S. (2004). Working with narrative in psychotherapy. In L. E. Angus & J. McLeod (Eds.), *The handbook of narrative and psychotherapy: Practice, theory and research* (pp. 119–136). Thousand Oaks, CA: Sage.

Castells, M. (2004). *The information age. Volume 11: The power of identity.* Oxford: Blackwell.

Gibson, P. (2004). Where to from here? A narrative approach to career counselling. *Career Development International, 9*, 176–189.

Goldstein, B., & Oldham, J. (1979). *Children and work: A study of socialization.* New Brunswick, NJ: Transaction Books.

Gottfredson, L. S. (2005). Applying Gottfredson's theory of circumscription and compromise in career guidance and counseling. In S. D. Brown & R. W. Lent (Eds.), *Career development and counseling: Putting theory and research to work* (pp. 71–100). Hoboken, NJ: John Wiley & Sons.

Hartung, P. J. (2013). Career as story: Making the narrative turn. In P. J. Hartung, W. B. Walsh, & M. L. Savickas (Eds.), *Handbook of vocational psychology* (4th ed., pp. 33–52). New York, NY: Routledge.

Hartung, P. J. (2015). Life design in childhood: Antecedents and advancement. In L. Nota & J. Rossier (Eds.), *Handbook of the life design paradigm: From practice to theory, from theory to practice* (pp. 89–102). Boston, MA: Hogrefe.

Hartung, P. J., Porfeli, E. J., & Vondracek, F. W. (2005). Child vocational development: A review and consideration. *Journal of Vocational Behavior, 66*, 385–419.

Hartung, P. J., Porfeli, E. J., & Vondracek, F. W. (2008). Career adaptability in childhood. *The Career Development Quarterly, 57*, 63–74.

Howard, K. A. S., & Walsh, M. E. (2010). Conceptions of career choice and attainment: Developmental levels in how children think about careers. *Journal of Vocational Behavior, 76*, 143–152.

LaPointe, K. (2010). Narrating career, positioning identity: Career identity as a narrative practice. *Journal of Vocational Behavior, 77*, 1–9.

McAdams, D. P. (2008). Personal narratives and the life story. In O. P. John, R. W. Robins, & L. A. Pervin (Eds.), *Handbook of personality: Theory and research* (3rd ed., pp. 242–262). New York, NY: Guilford.

McAdams, D. P. (2011). Narrative identity. In S. J. Schwartz, K. Luyckx, & V. L. Vignoles (Eds.), *Handbook of identity theory and research* (pp. 99–115). New York, NY: Springer.

McAdams, D. P. (2013). The psychological self as actor, agent and author. *Perspectives on Psychological Science, 8*, 272–295.

McAdams, D. P., & McLean, K. C. (2013). Narrative identity. *Current Directions in Psychological Science, 22*, 233–238.

McMahon, M. (2006). Working with storytellers: A metaphor for career counselling. In M. McMahon & W. Patton (Eds.), *Career counselling: Constructivist approaches* (pp. 16–29). Abingdon, UK: Routledge.

McMahon, M. (2007). What will I be? *EQ Australia*, Winter, 8–9.

McMahon, M., & Watson, M. (2007). An analytical framework for career research in the postmodern era. *International Journal for Educational and Vocational Guidance, 7*, 169–179.

McMahon, M., & Watson, M. (2014, July). *Career conversations with children: Moving from research to practice.* In M. McMahon (Chair), Symposium on children's' career development: Transforming theory and research into practice, Conducted at the Meeting of the International Congress of Applied Psychology, Paris, France.

McMahon, M., Watson, M., & Bimrose, J. (2010). *Stories of careers, learning and identity across the lifespan: Considering the future narrative of career theory.* The Institute of Career Guidance. Retrieved from http://www.agcas.org.uk/assets/download?file=2609&parent=1031

Meijers, F., & Lengelle, R. (2012). Narratives at work: The development of career identity. *British Journal of Guidance and Counselling, 40*, 157–176.

Patton, W., & McMahon, M. (2014). *Career development and systems theory: Connecting theory and practice.* Rotterdam, The Netherlands: Sense Publishers.

Porfeli, E. J., Lee, B., & Vondracek, F. W. (2013). Identity development and careers in adolescents and emerging adults: Content, process and structure. In W. B., Walsh, M. L. Savickas, & P. J. Hartung (Eds.), *Handbook of vocational psychology* (pp. 133–181). New York, NY: Routledge.

Raskin, P. M. (1985). Identity and vocational development. *New Directions for Child Development, 30*, 25–42.

Reay, D. (2010). Identity making in schools and classrooms. In M. Wetherell & C. T. Mohanty (Eds.), *The Sage handbook of identities* (pp. 277–294). London: Sage.

Savickas, M. L. (2001). The next decade in vocational psychology: Mission and objectives. *Journal of Vocational Behavior, 59*, 284–290.

Savickas, M. L. (2011). *Career counseling.* Washington, DC: American Psychological Association.

Savickas, M. L. (2013). Career construction theory and practice. In S. D. Brown & R. W. Lent (Eds.), *Career development and counseling: Putting theory and research to work* (2nd ed., pp. 147–183). Hoboken, NJ: John Wiley & Sons.

Savickas, M. L., & Hartung, P. J. (2012). *My career story: An autobiographical workbook for life-career success.* Kent, OH: Vocopher. Retrieved from http://www.vocopher.com/CSI/CCI_workbook.pdf

Skorikov, V. B., & Vondracek, F. W. (2007). Vocational identity. In V. B. Skorikov & W. Patton (Eds.), *Career development in childhood and adolescence* (pp. 143–168). Rotterdam, The Netherlands: Sense Publishers.

Skorikov, V. B., & Vondracek, F. W. (2011). Occupational identity. In S. J. Schwartz, K. Luyckx, & V. L. Vignoles (Eds.), *Handbook of identity theory and research* (pp. 693–714). New York, NY: Springer.

Stead, G. B., Perry, J. C., Munka, L. M., Bonnett, H. R., Shiban, A. P., & Care, E. (2012). Qualitative research in career development: Content analysis from 1990 to 2009. *International Journal for Educational and Vocational Guidance, 12*, 105–122.

Super, D. E. (1990). A life-span, life-space approach to career development. In D. Brown & L. Brooks (Eds.), *Career choice and development* (2nd ed., pp. 197–261). San Francisco, CA: Jossey-Bass.

Victoria State Government. (nd). *Engaging parents in career conversations framework.* Retrieved from http://www.education.vic.gov.au/school/teachers/teachingresources/careers/parentsframe/Pages/default.aspx

Vondracek, F. W. (2001). The developmental perspective in vocational psychology. *Journal of Vocational Behavior, 59*, 252–261.

Watson, M., & McMahon, M. (2005). Children's career development: A research review from a learning perspective. *Journal of Vocational Behavior, 67*, 119–132.

Watson, M., & McMahon, M., (2007). Children's career development learning: A foundation for lifelong career development. In V. B. Skorikov & W. Patton (Eds.), *Career development in childhood and adolescence* (pp. 29–46). Rotterdam, The Netherlands: Sense Publishers.

Watson, M., Nota, L., & McMahon, M. (2015). Evolving stories of child career development. *International Journal for Educational and Vocational Guidance, 15*, 175–184.

White, M. (1992). Deconstruction and therapy. In M. White & D. Epston (Eds.), *Experience, contradiction, narrative and imagination* (pp. 109–152). Adelaide: Dulwich Centre Publications.

Part 2

Research perspectives

Chapter 7

Children's career exploration and development

Research overview and agenda

Íris M. Oliveira, Erik J. Porfeli, and Maria do Céu Taveira

Children are socialised to work through an ongoing interaction with their communities and life roles. Extant literature reviews (e.g., Hartung, Porfeli, & Vondracek, 2005; Watson & McMahon, 2005) suggested the multidimensionality of childhood career development and its implications for learning as children explore and learn about the working world and its intersection with other life domains.

Prior literature reviews illuminated several important trends. First, the literature lacks a predominant theoretical framework, which includes a recognition of key career constructs during the childhood period (Schultheiss, 2008). Second, the literature includes few longitudinal and contextual studies (Watson & McMahon, 2005) that could demonstrate if and how the childhood period serves as an antecedent to adolescent career development and acknowledges the ecology of children's career development. Third, the field could benefit from studying groups that disproportionately struggle with educational and work outcomes (e.g., impoverished children) (Schultheiss, 2008). Fourth, international collaboration could enrich the field's scientific knowledge through cross-contextual research (Porfeli, Hartung, & Vondracek, 2008). Several studies published in a special issue of the *International Journal of Educational and Vocational Guidance* (Watson, Nota, & McMahon, 2015) affirmed the field's progress toward internationalisation, theory-research articulation, and practical innovations.

This chapter offers a review of the literature published since these landmark reviews – namely, research published from 2008 to 2015. This review is guided by a meta-theoretical framework, which suggests that the establishment of a new scientific field springs from the accumulation of scattered findings that converge around a common theme. This framework offers a newfound, or appreciably extended, understanding of phenomena (Kuhn, 2012), which in this case is the field of children's career development.

Theoretical considerations

Developmental career perspectives (e.g., Gottfredson, 2002; Super, 1990) suggest that children develop career exploration and self-concepts based on identification/differentiation processes and integration of gender and prestige representations of work. They also suggest that children progress in career reasoning from concrete/simplistic/fantasy forms to more abstract/complex/realistic ones as children become aware of personal and contextual supports/barriers (Howard & Walsh, 2010).

Moving from these considerations, developmental-contextual and systems career perspectives (e.g., Patton & McMahon, 2014) suggest that the child-context dynamics account for self-construction and individual variability in vocational behaviour. Vondracek, Ford, and Porfeli (2014) extended the developmental-contextual meta-theory into the Living Systems Theory of Vocational Behaviour and Development (LSVD). The LSVD conceives of career development from a systems-based perspective cast within the lifespan of career development beginning in childhood and extending to the end of life. Behaviour episodes and their accumulation in the form of behaviour schemas are presumed to be the building blocks of career development. Career exploration within this framework connects the person and context through ongoing experience, learning, self-reflection, and integration into elaborations of self in the context of becoming and being a worker. Childhood career development proceeds from an accumulation of more or less organised episodes pertaining to work (e.g., watching TV) to increasingly elaborated episodes, schemas, and person-in-context behavioural and psychosocial patterns contributing to educational and career choices.

Systems-based approaches can serve to integrate disconnected and seemingly disparate scientific camps into a unified whole. We, therefore, employed LSVD (Vondracek *et al.*, 2014) to organise our review given that the childhood career development field continues to exist as a fragmented constellation of scientific camps dispersed across disciplines and lacks a strong consensus on a dominant theoretical paradigm.

Organising the review

LSVD (Vondracek *et al.*, 2014) is rooted in emblematic career development constructs. We employed the childhood career development dimensions identified by Hartung *et al.* (2005), as their review appears to encompass the broadest base of literature in contemporary reviews. We characterised (a) career exploration as being fuelled by curiosity and prompting a search for information, experimentation, and imagination of self in life roles; (b) career awareness as the knowledge of occupations and the working world; (c) vocational aspirations and expectations as educational and occupational intentions varying from hopes and desires absent from the practicalities of life to those rooted in such practicalities; (d) vocational interests as expressed preferences for educational and occupational activities/domains; and (e) career adaptability as attitudes, beliefs, and behaviours signalling a readiness to cope with life transitions.

LSVD (Vondracek *et al.*, 2014) is also rooted in Bronfenbrenner's (1979) ecological systems theory. The person level focuses on individual's biological and psychological features. The microsystem focuses on face-to-face relations experienced in proximal settings. The mesosystem includes microsystems jointly influencing the child. The exosystem includes settings within which the person is not directly involved, but his or her influences indirectly operate. The macrosystem comprises lifestyles. The chronosystem addresses the life course and lifespan of career. Our review crossed childhood career development dimensions and contextual levels to conceive of the field as a system of literatures reflecting the person as a living system operating within nested contexts.

Method

Our review covered articles published between January 2008 and May 2015. The search was performed via ERIC, Academic Search Complete, Scopus, PsychINFO, PsycARTICLES, and Web of Science databases and included keywords such as career development with terms such as child/children/childhood. These keywords were coupled with career exploration, awareness, aspirations, expectations, interests, and adaptability. Publications were classified by contextual levels derived from Vondracek and collaborators' (2014) list of influences on career development to include the person, microsystem, mesosystem, exosystem, macrosystem, and chronosystem. Keyword combinations were used to target these system levels, for example, ability and gender for the person level and family and school for the microsystem.

Seventy-seven unique articles were identified. The articles were examined for inclusion using two criteria. First, articles covering career topics were included. Second, we defined childhood as the period until 14 years old inclusive (Hartung *et al.*, 2005). Works derived from older samples were, therefore, excluded. Employing these criteria, 44 per cent (34) of the population of articles was retained. Each article was read by one of the authors. The content of the articles was synthesised according to each career development dimension and codified into data elements.

It is noteworthy that one article covered only parents (i.e., Cinamon & Dan, 2010) and was considered a study of the microsystem of childhood career development. This study was conducted with Israeli parents of preschool children and suggested that parents from high social economic status (SES) present positive attitudes towards early career interventions. However, some parents were reluctant to do so given a desire to protect children from work. This study illustrates the possibility that a parental motive to shield children from work may cause resistance to embracing this field. It seems important to sensitise society about the significance of childhood career development and to clarify empirical/practical aims of the field.

Results

The results of this review were structured in a descriptive overview of the articles and a synthesis of content. The descriptive overview considered the main journals and countries publishing on the topic, the research methods used as well

76   Íris M. Oliveira et al.

as the theories, and career dimensions and contexts most frequently covered in the reviewed articles.

Descriptive overview

Seventeen articles were published through to 2011 and 17 afterwards. The greatest number of publications appeared in 2010, 2011, 2012, and 2015. The *Journal of Vocational Behavior, International Journal for Educational and Vocational Guidance*, and *Journal of Career Development* were the main publication outlets. The authors' affiliations illustrate the field's presence across disciplines, as authors were affiliated in departments of psychology, education, counselling, and medicine. Research was conducted in 12 countries, with the United States offering the highest number of publications (34 per cent) and with other countries signalling emergence of this research (e.g., Israel, Turkey).

Illustrating the field's lack of a theoretical framework, the articles considered 20 different theories. Gottfredson's (41 per cent) and Super's (24 per cent) theories were the most frequently cited. Our review included three articles (i.e., Araújo & Taveira, 2009; Oliveira, Taveira, & Porfeli, 2015; Wright & Perrone, 2008) that focused on advancing theoretical aspects of the field. Empirical studies mostly used quantitative methods (68 per cent), with a lower percentage employing qualitative (23 per cent) or mixed (9 per cent) methods. There were vastly more cross-sectional (85 per cent) than longitudinal studies (15 per cent), indicating limited progress in employing longitudinal research.

The career development dimensions and contexts were inferred or directly stated within the text of the articles (see Table 7.1). The most frequently addressed dimension was vocational aspirations/expectations (27 per cent), followed by adaptability, interests, awareness (19 per cent each), and exploration (16 per cent). As for contexts, most articles focused on the person level (85 per cent) but only

Table 7.1 Distribution of publications per dimension and contextual level

Dimension	Person Level	Microsystem	Mesosystem	Exosystem	Macrosystem	Chronosystem
Career exploration	7	4	1	1	1	0
Career awareness	9	3	0	1	2	0
Vocational aspirations and expectations	12	8	2	7	4	2
Vocational interests	9	4	2	1	4	1
Career adaptability	7	6	2	3	1	2

Note: One article can cover more than one dimension and/or more than one contextual level.

Children's career exploration and development   77

nine (27 per cent) of the total articles focused only on the person level. The microsystem was the most frequently addressed context level (37 per cent), followed by the exosystem (27 per cent), macrosystem (14 per cent), chronosystem and mesosystem (11 per cent each).

Content

The content of the reviewed articles was synthesised for each career dimension, and the levels of context within which each dimension were addressed. Each dimension will now be discussed in turn.

Career exploration

A cross-sectional study with North American fourth graders suggested that girls are more disposed to explore than boys (Wood & Kaszubowski, 2008). This might be related to girls' concern about the future and academic engagement.

The relational nature of career exploration has been addressed. Attachment seems a precursor of children's career exploration and social cognitive mechanisms (Wright & Perrone, 2008). The literature acknowledges the important role of parental emotional support (e.g., helping to assign meaning to positive/ negative experiences) in children's career exploration (Oliveira *et al.*, 2015). Evidence derived from Chinese 11-year-olds and parents also suggested that parents support children's career exploration (Liu, McMahon, & Watson, 2015a). With respect to culture, Chinese parents intend to help children learn about society and choose an occupation that will bring honour and sustainability within the society. This suggests that parents have the potential to promote children's career exploration.

The consequences of career exploration were examined. Evidence from Italian children aged 11 to 13 suggested that career exploration advances their knowledge of Investigative occupations (e.g., involving scientific and analytical activities) and promotes children's actual knowledge about Realistic (e.g., physical and practical), Investigative, Artistic (e.g., creative and expressive), and Enterprising (e.g., managing and entrepreneurial) occupations (Ferrari *et al.*, 2015). These results support theory suggesting that career exploration promotes the acquisition of occupational knowledge.

Contributions for the assessment of career exploration were offered. Results from South African fourth, fifth, sixth, and seventh graders confirmed the utility of the Childhood Career Development Scale to assess career exploration, among other career dimensions (Stead & Schultheiss, 2010). This study also found positive relations among career exploration, locus of control, career information, self-concept, planning, self-esteem, and a developed sense of industry. The psychometric properties of the Career Exploratory Outcome Expectations to assess Portuguese 10-year-olds' career exploratory outcome expectations were also explored (Oliveira, Taveira, Cadime, & Porfeli, 2016). This study found that children's career exploratory outcome expectations relate to self-efficacy expectations for academic and leisure activities, thus suggesting the inter-relation among social cognitive mechanisms in childhood.

Career exploration has been considered in traditional (i.e., fostering career exploration, person-environment fit, and goal setting) and integrative contextual career interventions (i.e., fostering career exploration, person-environment fit, and social skills) (Turner & Conkel, 2010). Evidence from North American 13-year-olds suggests more favourable outcomes from integrative contextual career interventions than traditional ones, thus supporting a contextualist perspective of career development.

The literature suggests that career exploration is an important process in childhood that occurs in context and is associated with key psychosocial constructs. The field has made progress in addressing the relational nature of career exploration. Still, additional research focusing on the role of school and peers in children's career exploration is needed. The field could advance through devoting systematic attention to career exploration through innovations in career exploration assessments and context-attuned interventions.

Career awareness

Research addressed the impact of SES and school progress on children's career awareness. Evidence suggested that less affluent children tend to consider more occupations than their more affluent peers (Wood & Kaszubowski, 2008). A cross-sectional study with North American children (Howard, Flanagan, Castine, & Walsh, 2015) indicated that kindergarten children identified fewer influences to their career preferences and choices than fourth and eighth graders. These findings indicate that economic resources and grade levels influence children's career awareness.

Differences for gender in children's career awareness were found. Results from Italian children aged 9 to 13 suggested that boys are more aware of job prestige than girls (Rohlfing, Nota, Ferrari, Soresi, & Tracey, 2012). Findings from Turkish children indicated that girls present more knowledge on the nature of occupations than boys (Nazli, 2014), which seems consistent with findings suggesting that girls explore more than boys (e.g., Wood & Kaszubowski, 2008). Girls seem to hold more People-related occupational knowledge than boys, whereas Things-related occupational knowledge is higher for boys (Rohlfing et al., 2012). Girls present higher perceived and actual Social-related occupational knowledge than boys, whereas boys present higher perceived and actual Realistic-related occupational knowledge than girls (Ferrari et al., 2015). These findings suggest that girls and boys differ in their search for knowledge in specific domains and that girls may possess more advanced career awareness than boys during childhood.

Within the macrosystem, research suggests that Chinese children are aware of gender differences in occupations (Liu et al., 2015a), which corroborates related theoretical considerations. Still, results from German and Belgian primary school children indicated that the presentation of feminine and masculine forms of jobs (e.g., policeman and policewoman) facilitates children's expected success of women and men in male- and female-dominated occupations (Vervecken, Hannover, & Wolter, 2013). These findings suggest persistent gender-based socialisation to work that could be mitigated by educational practices.

Microsystem influences in career awareness were identified. Chinese children's occupational knowledge seems related to mothers' jobs and influenced by children's differential contact with parental occupations (Liu *et al.*, 2015a). Research addressed correlates of career awareness. North American rural children's occupational knowledge seemed positively associated with academic achievement and occupational aspirations and expectations (Schmitt-Wilson & Welsh, 2012). This result supports the linkage between careers and academics and the importance of children's career awareness in other career processes.

The literature supports the developmental-contextual nature of career awareness and suggests the interplay among gender, career awareness, and academic and career processes. Longitudinal studies could additionally help investigate the progress of children's career awareness across school grades.

Vocational aspirations and expectations

The fantasy and realism of children's vocational aspirations/expectations were acknowledged during the review period. Evidence suggested a reduction of the aspirations-expectations gap over time (Helwig, 2008) and a positive association between 10- to 13-year-olds' aspirations-expectations gap and ethnic discrimination awareness (Hughes, 2011). These findings corroborate previous literature indicating that children shape aspirations as they become aware of environmental features.

Differences for gender in aspirations/expectations were found. Regarding the content of aspirations, evidence indicated that middle school girls often aspire to Social, Artistic, and Investigative occupations, whereas boys mostly aspire to Realistic and Enterprising occupations (Schuette, Ponton, & Charlton, 2012; Watson, McMahon, Foxcroft, & Els, 2010). Considering the level of aspirations, mixed results by gender were found. On the one hand, there is evidence suggesting that 12-year-olds, regardless of gender and ethnicity, present high educational aspirations relative to educational outcomes achieved at the population level and aspire to high- and middle-prestige occupations (Watson *et al.*, 2010; Watson, McMahon, & Longe, 2011). On the other hand, evidence derived from children aged 7 to 12 indicates that girls present higher educational but lower occupational aspirations than boys (Fulcher, 2011). Future research could examine the differential societal expectations for girls and boys and how early socialisation affects later adolescent aspirations and adult work choices.

Differences across school grades lead us to infer that gender socialisation plays a dynamic role over time. Although no differences in Thai children's expressed preferences from preschool to elementary school were reported (Hung-Chang & Mei-Ju, 2014), North American sixth and seventh graders present higher occupational aspirations than fourth and fifth graders (Schmitt-Wilson & Welsh, 2012). Evidence from Thai children attending preschool and elementary school suggests that boys aspire to male-dominated occupations, whereas girls prefer female-dominated occupations (Hung-Chang & Mei-Ju, 2014). However, evidence from Thai six-year-olds indicated that girls' preferences spread across gender balanced, female- and male-dominated occupations (Lee, 2012). This is affirmed by longitudinal evidence suggesting that second- and fourth-grade boys and girls prefer male- and female-dominated occupations, respectively, but girls develop interests for male-dominated occupations as well as they advance toward the seventh grade (Helwig, 2008). These findings indicate that younger children develop expectations socially aligned with their genders, but as they become older, girls also prefer male-dominated occupations. Girls may be moving toward expanding their career options across gender divisions with advancing age more so than boys.

Influences of ethnicity and SES were reported. Seven-year-old boys from more affluent families and those who are from ethnic minorities report more prestigious occupational aspirations (Flouri, Tsivrikos, Akhtar, & Midouhas, 2015). High parental SES coupled with children's cognitive ability were identified as facilitators of high occupational aspirations, completing studies at an older age, and higher SES in adolescence and adulthood (Schoon & Polek, 2011). These findings support the relevance of acknowledging specific career development needs of children from economically disadvantaged backgrounds.

Associations between parents' occupations and children's aspirations were examined. Evidence presented positive and moderate associations among Thai children's vocational expectations and parents' occupations (Hung-Chang & Mei-Ju, 2014), which also suggests that less than 10 per cent of children aspire to the same-sex parent occupation (Lee, 2012). Despite the central role of parents, the impact of leisure and extracurricular experiences in children's vocational aspirations/expectations should also be considered.

Research examined parents' influence on children's aspirations for female- and male-dominated occupations. Evidence suggested that North American middle school boys' preferences for male-dominated occupations related to fathers' jobs (Schuette et al., 2012). Children's non-traditional gender preferences seemed facilitated by the mothers' high educational level and job prestige, less conservative gender attitudes, and expectations for offspring to pursue non-traditional occupations (Fulcher, 2011). These findings indicate that exposure to parents' occupations and beliefs may shape children's vocational aspirations/expectations.

Parental expectations for offspring were considered. Findings suggest that Chinese children and their parents present high educational and occupational aspirations (Liu, McMahon, & Watson, 2015b). These parents also encourage children to attain high educational levels and occupational status. These results support the notion that the family is a vital context for parents to transmit values and beliefs to offspring, thus influencing children's aspirations/expectations.

The literature suggests that, although children continue to present aspirations less rooted in the reality of population-based educational and career outcomes of adolescents and adults, they increasingly acknowledge personal and environmental features and develop more realistic expectations with age. Such shifts seem aligned with evidence identifying influences in children's aspirations/expectations. Gender differences in aspirations/expectations continue to be a dominant topic in research. A predominant theme here suggests that girls are expanding career aspirations across the gender divide more so than boys. This is an important finding in light of growing concerns over boys lagging behind girls in academic and career development outcomes during adolescence.

Vocational interest

Akin to the research on vocational aspirations/expectations, the interests of boys and girls suggest gender differences. Evidence from Black South African rural 12-year-olds indicated that girls prefer Social and Artistic occupations, whereas boys prefer Investigative and Realistic occupations (Watson *et al.*, 2011). The presentation of feminine and masculine forms of jobs appears to encourage 7- to 12-year-old girls to develop preferences for male-dominated fields (Vervecken *et al.*, 2013). Coupled with the aspiration research suggesting that girls aspire to jobs with varying gender compositions, these findings suggest girls develop preferences for male-dominated fields while boys are less inclined to cross the gender divide in terms of interests.

Being aware of gender differences in vocational interests, the Inventory of Children's Activities (Tracey & Ward, 1998) was revised (e.g., including additional items) to reduce the observed gender differences in the People-Things dimension and the Investigative, Social, and Artistic items (Tracey & Caulum, 2015). This revision suggests that care should be taken to ensure a gender-equal assessment of children's career development.

Research examining parental influence in children's interests was limited to two articles that indicated Chinese parents could initiate or encourage offspring's interests (Liu *et al.*, 2015a, b).

Correlates of children's interests were examined. Evidence suggested that North American middle school children's affiliative interpersonal styles related with Social and Conventional interests and competencies, whereas cold interpersonal styles related to Investigative, Realistic, and Enterprising ones (Sodano, 2011). Findings from Italian children aged 7 to 12 suggested that Person- and Ideas-oriented interests are, respectively, associated with Person- and Ideas-related occupational knowledge (Rohlfing *et al.*, 2012). These results support theoretical considerations indicating relations among personal characteristics and interests.

The literature suggests that children's vocational interests integrate personal characteristics, occupational knowledge, and experiences stimulated by key figures.

Career adaptability

Career adaptability was assessed through constructs such as time perspective, choice readiness, and agency. Among Dutch children aged 12 and 13 followed over a year, girls presented greater time perspective than boys (Peetsma & van der Veen, 2011). Regarding school experiences, Turkish children aged 11 to 14 struggled to associate school subjects with careers (Nazli, 2014). These findings support the need to consider the career development of specific groups and to stimulate children's experiential learning.

Social influences in career adaptability were found. Chinese and Italian parents may instil their offspring with autonomy in career decision making and influence work valences and academic achievement (Liu *et al.*, 2015b; Porfeli, Ferrari, & Nota, 2012). The work motivation of North American 11-year-olds seems facilitated by perceived parents' positive work experiences (Porfeli, Wang, & Hartung, 2008). Evidence also indicated that the agency of Italian 12-year-olds is related to career decidedness and academic achievement and sustained by social support from parents, teachers, and peers (Howard, Ferrari, Nota, Solberg, & Soresi, 2009). The literature supports the importance of children's interactions with and perceived support from key figures in career adaptability.

Correlates of career adaptability were investigated. Evidence from Italian children aged 11 to 13 suggested that future time perspective is negatively associated with career indecision (Ferrari, Nota, & Soresi, 2010). A parallel establishment of future time perspective in school and professional career, in social relations, and in leisure was found while following 12- and 13-year-old Dutch children (Peetsma & van der Veen, 2011). This study also indicated that growth in time perspective related to growth in investment in learning and academic achievement (Peetsma & van der Veen, 2011). Regarding personal features of career adaptability, evidence suggested that children's disinhibited temperament precedes wellbeing at age 40 and career stability at age 50 (Blatný, Millová, Jelínek, & Osecká, 2015). This finding illustrates the possibility of identifying facilitators of healthy career trajectories rooted in childhood.

It seems, therefore, important to promote career adaptability during childhood. This might be informed by integrative contextual interventions which positively impact children's social and work readiness (Turner & Conkel, 2010). Synthesising, the literature acknowledged the roots of career adaptability in childhood and suggested its dynamics and correlates.

The sum of these findings highlights the possibility to study personal and contextual dynamics in childhood career development. This is supported by a theoretical proposal to employ a developmental-contextual perspective to understand childhood career development, children's active roles in shaping development and context, and contextual influences in children's careers

Children's career exploration and development   83

(Araújo & Taveira, 2009). This proposal is consistent with our selection of the LSVD to guide this review.

Conclusion

The children's career development field continues to be in an emerging state. Still, the emergence of LSVD and its incorporation here suggests that our field could benefit from an integrative approach to harmonise disparate theories and findings into a common model and language.

The field also called for the identification of core constructs. Following Hartung and collaborators' (2005) identification of five childhood career development dimensions, this chapter reinforced their relevance, as each construct continues to enjoy attention in the literature. Research also suggests that constructs such as work values and social cognitive constructs might be emerging in importance. The correlates of childhood career development dimensions continue to focus on the effects of gender, school levels, and ethnicities, as well as family, school, and peer influences, which inform the key concepts and propositions of childhood career development.

Turning from the theorisation to the examination of childhood career development dimensions, tools exist to support their assessment. From 2008 to 2015, measures were created, confirmed, or revised to assess children's career exploration, career exploratory outcome expectations, and vocational interests (Oliveira et al., 2016; Stead & Schultheiss, 2010; Tracey & Caulum, 2015). However, much can still be done in this area. Watson and colleagues (2015) found that international collaboration is occurring in this field, which this review corroborates. We suggest that such international partnerships continue and focus on the cross-cultural validation of measures and the creation of mixed-method and ecological assessment protocols aligned with children's age and contexts. Computer-based assessments, such as games and computerised adaptive testing, could also be applied to our field.

Previous reviews called for longitudinal and contextual studies. However, the frequency of longitudinal studies remains lower than cross-sectional studies, which is unsurprising in light of the resource demands of longitudinal research. A high frequency of quantitative studies relative to qualitative/mixed methods was also identified. As for contexts, the field focuses heavily on the person and microsystem levels. Action-research projects could benefit longitudinal, mixed-method assessments and evidence-based practice. These projects could sustain an increased attention to the chronosystem and the ecology of childhood career development. Towards that end, the field could benefit from a unified model of the context to include clearer definitions of context levels pertaining to children's career development and a propositional model explaining their interrelationships and nested nature.

The need to address specific groups was previously credited. Recent research examined children from different countries, ethnicities, social classes, and urban/rural areas. Still, further studies could research children from specific academic groups. For example, the career development of academic overachievers/underachievers or children diagnosed with disabilities could be investigated and inform career interventions.

Two implications derived from this review can be inferred. First, continuing to encourage international collaboration may be a fruitful way to unify the field into a coherent agenda. This work could focus on the translation of existing measures into languages representing the countries studying this topic. Doing so would serve to empower scholars in these countries to continue their lines of inquiry. Further, existing scholars could seek out the 'dark literature' (e.g., doctoral dissertations) within their departments/universities and encourage these students to bring their work to published research. Second, existing scholars could reach out to their peers and new students to encourage collaboration with a focus on children's career development. The field is currently dispersed across several disciplines. While this could be considered a weakness, it might also be an opportunity to define the field as interdisciplinary and to capitalise on this nature in establishing it as a confederation of disciplines devoted to child development with a focus on career.

Acknowledgments

We acknowledge Professor Mark Watson and Dr Mary McMahon for their invitation to write this book chapter. This work was funded by the Portuguese Foundation for Science and Technology through a doctoral grant (SFRH/BD/84162/2012) supported by POPH/FSE and the European Union.

References

Araújo, A. M., & Taveira, M. C. (2009). Study of career development in children from a developmental-contextual perspective. *European Journal of Education and Psychology, 2*, 49–67.

Blatný, M., Millová, K., Jelínek, M., & Osecká, T. (2015). Personality predictors of successful development: Toddler temperament and adolescent personality traits predict well-being and career stability in middle adulthood. *Plos-One, 10*, 1–7.

Bronfenbrenner, U. (1979). *The ecology of human development.* Cambridge, MA: Harvard University Press.

Cinamon, R. G., & Dan, O. (2010). Parental attitudes toward preschoolers' career education: A mixed-method study. *Journal of Career Development, 37*, 519–540.

Ferrari, L., Ginevra, M. C., Santilli, S., Nota, L., Sgaramella, T. M., & Soresi, S. (2015). Career exploration and occupational knowledge in Italian children. *International Journal for Educational and Vocational Guidance, 15*, 113–130.

Ferrari, L., Nota, L., & Soresi, S. (2010). Time perspective and indecision in young and older adolescents. *British Journal of Guidance and Counselling, 38*, 61–82.

Flouri, E., Tsivrikos, D., Akhtar, R., & Midouhas, E. (2015). Neighborhood, school and family determinants of children's aspirations in primary school. *Journal of Vocational Behavior, 87*, 71–79.

Fulcher, M. (2011). Individual differences in children's occupational aspirations as a function of parental traditionality. *Sex Roles, 64*, 117–131.

Gottfredson, L. S. (2002). Gottfredson's theory of circumscription, compromise, and self-creation. In D. Brown (Ed.), *Career choice and development* (4th ed., pp. 85–148). San Francisco, CA: Jossey-Bass.

Hartung, P. J., Porfeli, E. J., & Vondracek, F. W. (2005). Child vocational development: A review and reconsideration. *Journal of Vocational Behavior, 66*, 385–419.

Helwig, A. A. (2008). From childhood to adulthood: A 15-year longitudinal career development study. *The Career Development Quarterly, 57*, 38–50.

Howard, K. A. S., Ferrari, L., Nota, L., Solberg, V. S. H., & Soresi, S. (2009). The relation of cultural context and social relationships to career development in middle school. *Journal of Vocational Behavior, 75*, 100–108.

Howard, K. A. S, Flanagan, S., Castine, E., & Walsh, M. E. (2015). Perceived influences on the career choices of children and youth: An exploratory study. *International Journal for Educational and Vocational Guidance, 15*, 99–111.

Howard, K. A. S, & Walsh, M. E. (2010). Conceptions of career choice and attainment: Developmental levels in how children think about careers. *Journal of Vocational Behavior, 76*, 143–152.

Hughes, J. M. (2011). Influence of discrimination awareness on the occupational interests of African American children. *Journal of Applied Developmental Psychology, 32*, 369–378.

Hung-Chang, L., & Mei-Ju, C. (2014). Behind the mask: The differences and stability of children's career expectations. *Procedia – Social and Behavioral Sciences, 116*, 2832–2840.

Kuhn, T. S. (2012). *The structure of scientific revolutions.* Chicago, IL: University of Chicago Press.

Lee, H. C. (2012). "What do you want to do when you grow up?" Occupational aspirations of Taiwanese preschool children. *Social Behavior and Personality: An International Journal, 40*, 115–127.

Liu, J., McMahon, M., & Watson, M. (2015a). Parental influence on child career development in Mainland China: A qualitative study. *The Career Development Quarterly, 63*, 74–87.

Liu, J., McMahon, M., & Watson, M. (2015b). Parental influence on mainland Chinese children's career aspirations: Child and parental perspectives. *International Journal for Educational and Vocational Guidance, 15*, 131–143.

Nazli, S. (2014). Career development of upper primary school students in Turkey. *Australian Journal of Guidance and Counselling, 24*, 49–61.

Oliveira, I. M, Taveira, M. C., Cadime, I., & Porfeli, E. J. (2016). Psychometric properties of a career exploratory outcome expectations measure. *Journal of Career Assessment, 24*, 380–396.

Oliveira, I. M., Taveira, M. C., & Porfeli, E. J. (2015). Emotional aspects of childhood career development: Importance and future agenda. *International Journal for Educational and Vocational Guidance, 15*, 163–174.

Patton, W., & McMahon, M. (2014). *Career development and systems theory: Connecting theory and practice* (3rd ed.). Rotterdam, The Netherlands: Sense Publishers.

Peetsma, T., & van der Veen, I. (2011). Relations between the development of future time perspective in three life domains, investment in learning, and academic achievement. *Learning and Instruction, 21*, 481–494.

Porfeli, E. J., Ferrari, L., & Nota, L. (2012). Work valence as a predictor of academic achievement in the family context. *Journal of Career Development, 40*, 371–389.

Porfeli, E. J., Hartung, P. J., & Vondracek, F. W. (2008). Children's vocational development: A research rationale. *The Career Development Quarterly, 57*, 25–37.

Porfeli, E. J., Wang, C., & Hartung, P. J. (2008). Family transmission of work affectivity and experiences to children. *Journal of Vocational Behavior, 73*, 278–286.

Rohlfing, J. E., Nota, L., Ferrari, L., Soresi, S., & Tracey, T. J. G. (2012). Relation of occupational knowledge to career interests and competence perceptions in Italian children. *Journal of Vocational Behavior, 81*, 330–337.

Schmitt-Wilson, S., & Welsh, M. C. (2012). Vocational knowledge in rural children: A study of individual differences and predictors of occupational aspirations and expectations. *Learning and Individual Differences, 22*, 862–867.

Schoon, I., & Polek, E. (2011). Teenage career aspirations and adult career attainment: The role of gender, social background and general cognitive ability. *International Journal of Behavioral Development, 35*, 210–217.

Schuette, C., Ponton, M., & Charlton, M. (2012). Middle school children's career aspirations: Relationship to adult occupations and gender. *The Career Development Quarterly, 60*, 36–46.

Schultheiss, D. (2008). Current status and future agenda for the theory, research, and practice of childhood career development. *The Career Development Quarterly, 57*, 7–24.

Sodano, S. M. (2011). Integrating vocational interests, competencies, and interpersonal dispositions in middle school children. *Journal of Vocational Behavior, 79*, 110–120.

Stead, G. B., & Schultheiss, D. E. P. (2010). Validity of childhood career development scale scores in South Africa. *International Journal for Educational and Vocational Guidance, 10*, 73–88.

Super, D. (1990). A life-span, life-space approach to career development. In D. Brown, L. Brooks & Associates (Eds.), *Career choice and development: Applying contemporary theories to practice* (2nd ed., pp. 197–261). San Francisco, CA: Jossey-Bass.

Tracey, T., & Caulum, D. (2015). Minimizing gender differences in children's interest assessment: Development of the Inventory of Children's Activities-3 (ICA-3). *Journal of Vocational Behavior, 87*, 154–160.

Tracey, T. J. G., & Ward, C. C. (1998). The structure of children's interests and competence perceptions. *Journal of Counseling Psychology, 45*, 290–303.

Turner, S. L., & Conkel, J. (2010). Evaluation of a career development skills intervention with adolescents living in an inner city. *Journal of Counseling and Development, 88*, 457–466.

Vervecken, D., Hannover, B., & Wolter, I. (2013). Changing (S) expectations: How gender fair job descriptions impact children's perceptions and interest regarding traditionally male occupations. *Journal of Vocational Behavior, 82*, 208–220.

Vondracek, F. W., Ford, D. H., & Porfeli, E. J. (2014). *A living systems theory of vocational behavior and development.* Rotterdam, The Netherlands: Sense Publishers.

Watson, M., & McMahon, M. (2005). Children's career development: A research review from a learning perspective. *Journal of Vocational Behavior, 67*, 119–132.

Watson, M., McMahon, M., Foxcroft, C., & Els, C. (2010). Occupational aspirations of low socioeconomic black South African children. *Journal of Career Development, 37*, 717–734.

Watson, M., McMahon, M., & Longe, P. (2011). Occupational interests and aspirations of rural black South African children: Considerations for theory, research and practice. *Journal of Psychology in Africa, 21*, 413–420.

Watson, M., Nota, L., & McMahon, M. (2015). Evolving stories of child career development. *International Journal for Educational and Vocational Guidance, 15*, 175–184.

Wood, C., & Kaszubowski, Y. (2008). The career development needs of rural elementary school students. *The Elementary School Journal, 108*, 431–444.

Wright, S., & Perrone, K. (2008). The impact of attachment on career-related variables. *Journal of Career Development, 35*, 87–106.

Part 3

Contextual perspectives

Chapter 8

The antecedents of children's aspirations

Eirini Flouri, Heather Joshi, Alice Sullivan, and Vanessa Moulton

Aspirations have been described as personal goals or "possible selves" (Markus & Nurius, 1986, p. 954), distinct from expectations as they reflect what someone would like to achieve rather than what they think they will achieve. Aspirations, especially in adolescence, can be important because they may influence choices, decisions, and activities, which in turn affect subsequent accomplishments (Bandura, Barbaranelli, Caprara, & Pastorelli, 2001; Croll, Attwood, & Fuller, 2010; Gutman, Schoon, & Sabates, 2012; Hill *et al.*, 2004; Schoon, Martin, & Ross, 2007). Although researchers have pointed to the adverse effects of unrealistically high aspirations (Gorard, Huat See, & Davies, 2012), most evidence suggests that high aspirations are, in general, associated with later positive outcomes. But if children's aspirations can determine their outcomes, what predicts aspirations? In the sections that follow, we discuss the individual, family, and contextual antecedents of aspirations. We begin with a brief overview of how aspirations develop.

The development of children's aspirations

In general, children's aspirations develop from vague representations of possible future outcomes to more realistic career preferences. According to Gottfredson's (1981, 2002, 2005) theory of circumscription and compromise, aspirations evolve with age from the fantastical to the concrete, and so, as children grow into adolescents, they revise their aspirations based on their views of their own abilities and interests, as well as on societal and parental expectations. Aspirations typically develop in four stages. In stage 1, which can start as early as three years, children's aspirations are focussed on size and power. In stage 2 (6 to 8 years), children become aware of sex and gender differences and begin to eliminate occupations from further consideration if they are not typical for their own gender. In stage 3 (9 to 13 years), aspirations are based on social valuation and later (ages 14 and older) unique personal characteristics. According to Gottfredson's theory, therefore, in the very early years, aspirations do not reflect how children envisage themselves in the future. As also shown by empirical research on children's episodic future thinking (i.e., the ability to project the self into the future to pre-experience an event), children under the age of five have difficulty representing themselves in future states (Atance & Meltzoff, 2005) and cannot distinguish between near and distant future events (Friedman, 2005).

According to Gottfredson's theory, however, self-concept, not episodic memory, is the basis of aspirations. Self-concept is defined by Gottfredson (1981) as "one's view of oneself, one's view of who one is and who one is not. When projecting oneself into the future, self-concept also includes who one expects or would like to be" (p. 547). Self-concept develops separately across different domains and areas of interest, depends on ability, and is formed on the basis of frames of reference. For example, academic self-concept is dependent on school peers' academic performance and occupational self-concept on knowledge of the world of work (Marsh & Hau, 2003; Super, Savickas, & Super, 1996).

Individual differences in children's aspirations

Perhaps the most important factor in differentiating aspirations is gender. In expressing career aspirations, females tend to endorse intrinsic values, such as helping others, more than males, who tend to favour power and money (Weisgram, Bigler, & Liben, 2010). These gender differences emerge in childhood (Blakemore, Berenbaum, & Liben, 2009) and are reflected in an individual's later aspirations as well (Schoon & Eccles, 2014). Research in the United Kingdom (UK) and United States (US) shows clear differences, whereby girls tend to have 'higher' aspirations than boys as well as greater motivation for school (Schoon, 2001), whereas boys tend to be more adventurous in their dreams, more confident in their abilities, and more likely to aspire to rare jobs (Helwig, 2008). Compared to boys, girls also tend to aspire to a more restricted range of occupations and engage in less career exploration (Hartung, Porfeli, & Vondracek, 2005). Regardless, both boys and girls aspire to gender-typed occupations, with boys, in particular, drawn to jobs predominantly done by men (Croll *et al.*, 2010; Croll, Attwood, Fuller, & Last, 2008). British research using qualitative data from the 1958 British Birth Cohort Study found that as early as the end of primary school (age 11) children showed clear patterns of gendered visions of their imagined futures as adults (Elliott & Morrow, 2007). More recent British evidence from the Millennium Cohort Study suggests that gendered aspirations may well be in place even earlier, at the middle of primary school (Moulton, Flouri, Joshi, & Sullivan, 2015). At the same time, there is evidence for cohort effects, especially in girls' ambitions. It appears that, relative to earlier female cohorts, female cohorts born nearer the end of the twentieth century aspire to occupations that are more prestigious and male dominated, have higher educational requirements, and involve greater competition and selectivity (Hartung *et al.*, 2005; Polavieja & Platt, 2014). Nonetheless, girls' expectations continue to be relatively modest. As a consequence, the gap between the prestige of girls' occupational aspirations and their expectations appears to be getting larger relative to their male peers and earlier female cohorts.

Other individual differences, such as in motivation or temperament, can also explain differences in aspirations in children. Temperament traits are early emerging basic dispositions in the domains of activity, affectivity, attention, and self-regulation, which shape the development of later outcomes (Shiner & Caspi, 2012). The research on the role of temperament is limited but promising. For example, Pulkkinen (2001) found that lower occupational aspirations were a consequence of aggressive behaviour in boys and low emotional control, anxiety, and passivity in girls. Research in adults has certainly shown associations between occupations and temperament, with people tending to choose educational and work experiences whose qualities are concordant with their own personalities (Ackerman & Heggestad, 1997; Gottfredson, Jones, & Holland, 1993).

The association between motivation and aspirations in children has attracted much more research interest than the link between temperament or personality and aspirations, mainly because motivation is thought to explain the relationship between aspirations and achievement. The prevailing view is that aspirations are social-psychological enablers to educational and subsequent occupational (social class) attainment because they are beliefs that outcomes are contingent upon actions (Ross & Broh, 2000; Wang, Kick, Fraser, & Burns, 1999). Of course, having high educational or occupational aspirations (and therefore likely mastery and performance goals) is related to having a desire for control, which, in turn, is an important determinant of several positive outcomes, including achievement (Moffitt *et al.*, 2011). In other words, the link between high aspirations and achievement may be explained by the fact that achievement motivation, mastery over problems, general 'toughness' or 'hardiness', commitment, self-confidence, resilience, optimism, perseverance, self-efficacy, and, in general, personal agency beliefs are all associated with both high aspirations and high achievement. Certainly many motivational constructs, including self-efficacy (Bandura, 2011), locus of control (Lefcourt, 1982), expectancy beliefs (Eccles *et al.*, 1983), confidence beliefs (Dweck & Leggett, 1988), agency beliefs (Ford, 1992), or helplessness (Seligman, 1980) are related to aspirations, and they appear to reflect rather than produce them. For example, Mau, Dominick, and Ellsworth (1995) found that locus of control differentiated eighth-grade girls (about 13 years old) who aspired to homemaking from those who aspired to science or engineering careers. As expected, girls with a more internal locus of control were more likely to aspire to science or engineering careers.

The roles of cognitive ability and academic achievement in predicting children's and adolescents' educational and occupational aspirations have also received attention, not least because ability and achievement can help shape expectations and self-concept. Individuals' imagined future selves are strongly related to their present self-concepts, which are in turn associated with ability and achievement. For example, children who perform well in school find it easier to imagine themselves performing well in the future (Oyserman & Fryberg, 2006). But directly, too, children's aspirations are raised when they are doing well academically (Bond & Saunders, 1999). This, together with the evidence for the predictive role of aspirations in achievement, suggests that academic achievement both predicts educational and occupational aspirations and results from them. As for cognitive ability, lower aspirations, such as for manual occupations, tend to be associated with lower cognitive ability (Creed, Conlon, & Zimmer-Gembeck, 2007). In fact, as early as 1969, Sewell, Haller, and Portes found a positive link between cognitive ability and educational and occupational aspirations, which in turn lead to educational attainment. More recent research also reports associations of aspirations with cognitive ability, but at the same time shows that cognitive ability contributes to the prediction of educational aspirations only modestly and substantially less than prior academic achievement (Guo, Marsh, Morin, Parker, & Kaur, 2015).

The role of parents

Parents are a major influence on children's aspirations (Mau & Bikos, 2000). Several parental characteristics have been associated with children's aspirations, but social class or socioeconomic status (SES) is probably the one most extensively researched. In general, the evidence suggests that children from lower-class backgrounds have lower educational aspirations (Schoon & Parsons, 2002) and aspire to less prestigious occupations than their more advantaged peers (Croll, 2008). One reason is that higher-class, particularly more educated, parents tend to be more involved in their children's learning and more proactive and successful in enabling their children's competencies (Bandura, *et al.*, 2001; Elder, 1995). In turn, parental investment in the child's human capital influences aspirations directly (Hill & Wang, 2015); it also likely influences them indirectly via promoting children's cognitive skills and school engagement (Moreira, Dias, Vaz, & Vaz, 2013), which are related to aspirations (Wang & Eccles, 2012). Parents also influence their children's self-concept and aspirations both via their own aspirations and expectations for – and therefore involvement with – them and via their jobs and networks. Higher-SES parents have higher aspirations and expectations for their children's education (Davis-Kean, 2005; Schoon *et al.*, 2007; Schoon & Parsons, 2002) and foster familiarity with higher-status occupations via their own jobs and those of their social milieu. As will be discussed in the next section about the role of the extra-familial context in aspirations, both children's and parents' social milieu can influence children's aspirations.

As well as what they do, what parents know and think can influence their children's aspirations. Parents transmit cultural capital, values, and gender-role attitudes to their children (Dumais, 2002), and these in turn are associated with aspirations. Parental 'cultural capital' describes family resources such as education, knowledge, and cultural practices that promote success and social mobility beyond economic means (Bourdieu, 1984). Parents' values seem to influence children's aspirations both directly (Jodl, Michael, Malanchuk, Eccles, & Sameroff, 2001) and via increased parental involvement. They may also explain the higher aspirations of ethnic minority children in many countries, including the UK (Croll, 2008; Goodman & Gregg, 2010; Strand, 2007). Ethnic minority children have high aspirations, despite a lack of what would typically be seen as 'cultural capital' (Modood, 2004), arguably because their parents are more likely to want them to stay on at school and attend university, pay for private tuition, supervise them closely, and be involved with their schools (Croll, 2008; Strand, 2011). Parents' gender-role attitudes – related to their values and, more weakly, cultural capital – also appear important. In a recent study, Croft, Schmader, Block, and Baron (2014) examined how parents' behaviours and implicit associations concerning domestic roles, over and above their explicit beliefs, predicted their children's aspirations. As expected, mothers' explicit beliefs about domestic gender roles predicted the beliefs held by their children. Importantly, when fathers enacted or espoused a more egalitarian distribution of household labour, their daughters expressed a greater interest in working outside the home and having a less stereotypical occupation. Fathers' implicit gender-role associations also uniquely predicted daughters' (but not sons') occupational preferences.

The role of the broader context

The family is probably the most important developmental context for children's aspirations, but it is not the only one. The broader (e.g., school and neighbourhood) context can also influence children's aspirations. Research has shown evidence for both neighbourhood (Leventhal & Brooks-Gunn, 2000) and school 'effects' (Sellström & Bremberg, 2006) on a range of child outcomes, even after allowing for families' selective sorting into neighbourhoods and schools. The majority of these studies look at the role of the composition of these two extra-familial contexts in individual children's outcomes. School-composition and neighbourhood-composition effects refer to the collective, rather than the individual, influence of pupils' and residents' characteristics. Composition is the aggregation – at the school and the neighbourhood level, respectively – of pupils' and residents' characteristics. In essence, composition effects capture the influence of peer groups. Although the composition of both these contexts has been related to children's outcomes, when studies examine them simultaneously they find that neighbourhood effects are, at least partially, school effects (Heilmann, Kelly, Stafford, & Watt, 2013; Owens, 2010; Wicht & Ludwig-Mayerhofer, 2014). This suggests that schools are the main pathway through which the influence of the neighbourhood may be transmitted to children (Leckie, 2009).

School-level achievement is the school compositional characteristic most frequently explored in relation to children's aspirations, but also other outcomes related to aspirations such as achievement or academic self-concept. School-level achievement tends to be related positively to individual children's achievement. However, because it enables unfavourable social comparison processes (Marsh & Hau, 2003), it is related negatively to their academic self-concept – the 'big-fish-little-pond' effect. Nagengast and Marsh (2012), who tested the relationship between aspirations, academic self-concept, and school-level achievement in adolescence, showed that attending a school with high-achieving peers lowered academic self-concept, in turn lowering career aspirations. A more recent study showed that school-level achievement may be related not only to aspirations but also to gender differences in aspirations. Mann, Legewie, and DiPrete (2015) found that, as expected, attending a high-performing school had a negative impact on student aspirations for science, technology, engineering, and mathematics (STEM) jobs. Also as expected, girls were less likely than boys to aspire to STEM occupations, even when they had comparable abilities. But attending a high-performing school lowered the aspirations of high-achieving boys more than it did those of high-achieving girls. In girls, aspirations were strongly related to their own performance in both high-achieving and low-achieving schools. This suggests that the gender gap in STEM aspirations narrows among high-achieving students in high-achieving schools.

By and large, however, studies exploring school-composition effects on gender differences in children's aspirations tend to look at the gender, rather than the academic, composition of the school. Proponents of single-sex education believe that separating boys and girls, by classrooms or schools, raises students', particularly girls', achievement, academic interest, and aspirations. Some research appears to show support for this. For example, Watson, Quatman, and Edler (2002) showed that in the US girls in single-sex schools exhibited strong beliefs in their talent and potential and had higher aspirations than both girls and boys in mixed-sex schools. An important concern, however, with much of this research is that it does not always control sufficiently for selection (that is, the pre-existing characteristics of the children attending single-sex schools). Mael, Alonso, Gibson, Rogers, and Smith's (2005) influential review of the literature points out how few high-quality studies there are in this area and suggests the need for further research, given that few studies contain adequate controls for selection. Signorella, Hayes, and Li (2013) put the studies in Mael *et al.'s* review through a meta-analysis and concluded that single-sex schools may offer no advantage, as any apparent advantages may simply reflect selection into single-sex schools. A further meta-analysis of studies published in English on single-sex versus coeducational schooling at any time up to 2013 (Pahlke, Hyde, & Allison, 2014) found only small advantages for single-sex schooling. That study analysed findings from 21 nations, but with the bulk of studies coming from the US, pooling studies from different cultures, educational systems, and historical periods may be seen as problematic, and the distinctive US context, where single-sex schooling in the public sector has been virtually outlawed, must be taken into account. Also, US research has inevitably focused on the usually Catholic private schools. This has been seen as raising difficulties of interpretation, as it is unclear to what extent any findings can be generalised to non-Catholic schools. Finally, neither of these meta-analyses was able to examine self-concept in gendered subject areas (as opposed to overall self-concept), educational choices and qualifications, or occupational outcomes. Some UK studies have shown that single-sex schooling reduces the influence of gender on subject-specific self-concept and subject choice. Sullivan (2009) and Sullivan, Joshi, and Leonard (2010) found, using data from the 1958 and 1970 British Cohort Studies, that, as expected, boys had higher self-concepts in mathematics and science and girls in English, controlling for prior test scores. But single-sex schooling was linked to smaller gender gaps in self-concept. Girls who attended single-sex schools were also more likely to pursue stereotypically male subject options such as maths and science than girls at coeducational schools, while boys in single-sex schools had an increased likelihood of pursuing English and modern languages. More studies are needed to test the influence of the gender composition of contemporary schools on self-concept in gendered subject areas.

It appears, however, that compositional, not contextual, effects on aspirations may be null or mixed. As explained, composition relates to the characteristics of the individuals in one's community (e.g., school, neighbourhood). Context refers to the characteristics of the community itself. Perhaps the strongest evidence for contextual effects on aspirations comes from studies looking at the influence of positive role models. Positive role models, individuals who have achieved outstanding success, are widely expected, and frequently found (Lockwood, Jordan, & Kunda, 2002), to inspire others to pursue similar excellence. The lion's share of the policy-relevant research on the effects of role models comes from studies about the influence of positive female role models in shaping girls' aspirations. The basic idea is simple but contentious. Women in leadership positions have long been thought to have the potential to pave the way for long-term changes by influencing aspirations, in turn shaping educational and career choices. Policymakers hope that gender quotas will have long-term effects on women's labour-market outcomes over and above the immediate impact on leaders' gender balance, because women who become leaders may shape both parents' and children's beliefs about what women can achieve through their policies and/or through a direct role-model effect. In a recent, much-cited study, Beaman, Duflo, Pande, and Topalova (2012) tested this directly by exploiting a randomised natural experiment in India (a 1993 law reserved leadership positions for women in randomly selected village councils). They found that in villages assigned to a female leader, the male advantage in educational aspirations closed by 25 per cent in parents and 32 per cent in adolescents, compared to villages that were never reserved. There was no evidence of changes in young women's labour-market opportunities, suggesting that the impact of women leaders primarily reflected a role-model effect.

Role models are not only found in one's immediate locality, however. In fact, in the West, many efforts to recruit more girls into STEM fields commonly rely on the use of female role models from further afield. In the US, for example, female engineers are sent to high school classrooms (e.g., MIT's Women's Initiative), and websites targeted at girls praise the careers of female scientists and engineers (e.g., http://www.engineergirl.org). The assumption is that STEM female role models can help rebalance the gender disparity in both STEM careers and STEM career aspirations. Women enter STEM careers at lower rates than would be predicted by their abilities in these fields (Ceci, Williams, & Barnett, 2009) and, similarly, gender differences in performance in STEM do not explain the dramatic male preponderance in STEM aspirations in adolescence (Sadler, Sonnert, Hazari, & Tai, 2012). Empirical data, however, suggest that although female role models may be effective in the retention of women in STEM fields, female and male role models can be equally effective in recruitment efforts (Drury, Siy, & Cheryan, 2011). Recent experimental work with adolescents has shown that even the positive effect of female role models on girls' aspirations to enter STEM careers may be more nuanced than initially thought. In two experiments, Betz and Sekaquaptewa (2012) tested their hypothesis that feminine STEM role models may not be effective because their counter stereotypic-yet-feminine success may be demotivating, particularly to young girls. As they expected, female STEM role models that were feminine reduced girls' interest in maths, self-rated ability, and success expectations relative to female STEM role models that were less feminine. These results did not extend to feminine role models displaying general (not STEM-specific) success, indicating that feminine cues were not driving negative outcomes. Also in confirming their expectations, they showed that feminine STEM role models' combination of femininity and success seemed particularly unattainable to girls not interested in, or disliking, STEM.

Conclusion

Gender, ethnicity, and parental SES appear, both directly and in combination with other characteristics or contexts, to be powerful predictors of children's and adolescents' aspirations. Nevertheless, the emerging evidence for cohort effects also suggests that their predictive power can change over time, in turn indicating that characteristics of time periods may also be important 'causes' of children's aspirations. Aspirations are associated with later outcomes but, because of the correlational nature of the empirical studies on aspirations, it is unclear if they predict one's trajectories, or simply reflect one's origins or, more broadly, the historical and societal context one finds oneself in. To our knowledge, there is no published experimental research showing that changing aspirations can change behaviour – an omission we hope future studies will address.

References

Ackerman, P. L., & Heggestad, E. D. (1997). Intelligence, personality, and interests: Evidence for overlapping traits. *Psychological Bulletin, 121,* 219–245.

Atance, C. M., & Meltzoff, A. N. (2005). My future self: Young children's ability to anticipate and explain future states. *Cognitive Development, 20,* 341–361.

Bandura, A. (2011). Social cognitive theory. In P. A. M. van Lange, A. W. Kruglanski, & E. T. Higgins (Eds.), *Handbook of social psychological theories* (pp. 349–373). London: Sage.

Bandura, A., Barbaranelli, C., Caprara, G. V., & Pastorelli, C. (2001). Self-efficacy beliefs as shapers of children's aspirations and career trajectories. *Child Development, 72,* 18–206.

Beaman, L., Duflo, E., Pande, R., & Topalova, P. (2012). Female leadership raises aspirations and educational attainment for girls: A policy experiment in India. *Science, 335*, 582–586.

Betz, D. E., & Sekaquaptewa, D. (2012). My fair physicist? Feminine math and science role models demotivate young girls. *Social Psychological and Personality Science, 3*, 738–746.

Blakemore, J. E. O., Berenbaum, S. A., & Liben, L. S. (2009). *Gender development.* New York: Psychology Press.

Bond, R., & Saunders, P. (1999). Routes of success: Influences on the occupational attainment of young British males. *British Journal of Sociology, 50*, 217–249.

Bourdieu, P. (1984). *Distinction: A social critique of the judgement of taste.* Cambridge, MA: Harvard University Press.

Ceci, S. J., Williams, W. M., & Barnett, S. M. (2009). Women's underrepresentation in science: Sociocultural and biological considerations. *Psychological Bulletin, 135*, 218–261.

Creed, P. A., Conlon, E. G., & Zimmer-Gembeck, M. J. (2007). Career barriers and reading ability as correlates of career aspirations and expectations of parents and their children. *Journal of Vocational Behavior, 70*, 242–258.

Croft, A., Schmader, T., Block, K., & Baron, A. S. (2014). The second shift reflected in the second generation: Do parents' gender roles at home predict children's aspirations? *Psychological Science, 25*, 1418–1428.

Croll, P. (2008). Occupational choice, socio-economic status and educational attainment: A study of the occupational choices and destinations of young people in the British Household Panel Survey. *Research Papers in Education, 23*, 243–268.

Croll, P., Attwood, G., & Fuller, C. (2010). *Children's lives, children's futures.* London: Continuum.

Croll, P., Attwood, G., Fuller, C., & Last, K. (2008). The structure and implications of children's attitudes to school. *British Journal of Educational Studies, 56*, 382–399.

Davis-Kean, P. E. (2005). The influence of parent education and family income on child achievement: The indirect role of parental expectations and the home environment. *Journal of Family Psychology, 19*, 294–304.

Drury, B. J., Siy, J. O., & Cheryan, S. (2011). When do female role models benefit women? The importance of differentiating recruitment from retention in STEM. *Psychological Inquiry, 22*, 265–269.

Dumais, S. A. (2002). Cultural capital, gender, and school success: The role of habitus. *Sociology of Education, 75*, 44–68.

Dweck, C. S., & Leggett, E. L. (1988). A social-cognitive approach to motivation and personality. *Psychological Review, 95*, 256–273.

Eccles, J. S., Adler, T. F., Futterman, R., Coff, S. B., Kaczala, C. M., Meece, J. L., & Midgley, C. (1983). Expectancies, values and academic behaviors. In J. T. Spence (Ed.), *Achievement and academic motivation* (pp. 75–146). San Francisco, CA: Freeman.

Elder, G. H., Jr. (1995). The life course paradigm: Social change and individual development. In P. Moen, G. H. Elder, Jr., & K. Liischer (Eds.), *Examining lives in context: Perspectives on the ecology of human development* (pp. 101–139). Washington, DC: APA Press.

Elliott, J., & Morrow, V. (2007). *Imagining the future: Preliminary analysis of NCDS essays written by NCDS children at age 11.* CLS Working Paper 2007/1. London: Centre for Longitudinal Studies.

Ford, M. E. (1992). *Motivating humans: Goals, emotions, and personal agency beliefs.* London: Sage Publications.

Friedman, W. J. (2005). Developmental and cognitive perspectives on humans' sense of the times of past and future events. *Learning and Motivation, 36*, 145–158.

Goodman, A., & Gregg, P. (2010). *Poorer children's educational attainment: How important are attitudes and behaviour?* York, UK: Joseph Rowntree Foundation.

Gorard, S., Huat See, B., & Davies, P. (2012). *The impact of attitudes and aspirations on educational attainment and participation.* York, UK: Joseph Rowntree Foundation.

Gottfredson, G. D., Jones, E. M., & Holland, J. L. (1993). Personality and vocational interests: The relation of Holland's six interest dimensions to five robust dimensions of personality. *Journal of Counseling Psychology, 40,* 518–524.

Gottfredson, L. S. (1981). Circumspection and compromise: A developmental theory of occupational aspirations. Monographs. *Journal of Counseling Psychology, 28,* 545–579.

Gottfredson, L. S. (2002). Gottfredson's theory of circumscription, compromise, and self-creation. In D. Brown & Associates (Eds.), *Career choice and development* (4th ed., pp. 85–148). San Francisco, CA: Jossey-Bass.

Gottfredson, L. S. (2005). Applying Gottfredson's theory of circumscription and compromise in career guidance and counseling. In S. D. Brown & R. W. Lent (Eds.), *Career development and counseling: Putting theory and research to work* (pp. 71–100). Hoboken, NJ: John Wiley & Sons.

Guo, J., Marsh, H. W., Morin, A. J., Parker, P. D., & Kaur, G. (2015). Directionality of the associations of high school expectancy-value, aspirations, and attainment: A longitudinal study. *American Educational Research Journal, 52,* 371–402.

Gutman, L. M., Schoon, I., & Sabates, R. (2012). Uncertain aspirations for continuing in education: Antecedents and associated outcomes. *Developmental Psychology, 48,* 1707–1718.

Hartung, P. J., Porfeli, E. J., & Vondracek, F. W. (2005). Child vocational development: A review and reconsideration. *Journal of Vocational Behavior, 66,* 385–419.

Heilmann, A., Kelly, Y., Stafford, M., & Watt, R. G. (2013). The contribution of neighbourhoods and schools to cognitive test performance at age seven: Findings from the UK Millennium Cohort Study. *Journal of Epidemiology and Community Health, 67,* A28.

Helwig, A. A. (2008). From childhood to adulthood: A 15-year longitudinal career development study. *The Career Development Quarterly, 57,* 38–50.

Hill, N. E., Castellino, D. R., Lansford, J. E., Nowlin, P., Dodge, K. A., Bates, J. E., & Pettit, G. S. (2004). Parent academic involvement as related to school behaviour, achievement, and aspirations: Demographic variations across adolescence. *Child Development, 75,* 1491–1515.

Hill, N. E., & Wang, M. T. (2015). From middle school to college: Developing aspirations, promoting engagement, and indirect pathways from parenting to post high school enrollment. *Developmental Psychology, 51,* 224–235.

Jodl, K. M., Michael, A., Malanchuk, O., Eccles, J. S., & Sameroff, A. S. (2001). Parents' roles in shaping early adolescents' occupational aspirations. *Child Development, 72,* 1247–1266.

Leckie, G. (2009). The complexity of school and neighbourhood effects and movements of pupils on school differences in models of educational achievement. *Journal of the Royal Statistical Society: Series A, 172,* 537–554.

Lefcourt, H. (1982). *Locus of control: Current trends in theory and research* (2nd ed.). Hillsdale, NJ: Erlbaum.

Leventhal, T., & Brooks-Gunn, J. (2000). The neighborhoods they live in: The effects of neighborhood residence on child and adolescent outcomes. *Psychological Bulletin, 126,* 309–337.

Lockwood, P., Jordan, C. H., & Kunda, Z. (2002). Motivation by positive or negative role models: Regulatory focus determines who will best inspire us. *Journal of Personality and Social Psychology, 83,* 854–864.

Mael, F., Alonso, A., Gibson, D., Rogers, K., & Smith, M. (2005). *Single-sex versus coeducational schooling: A systematic review.* Doc# 2005–01. US Department of Education, Washington, D.C.

Mann, A., Legewie, J., & DiPrete, T. A. (2015). The role of school performance in narrowing gender gaps in the formation of STEM aspirations: A cross-national study. *Frontiers in Psychology, 6*, 171.

Markus, H., & Nurius, P. (1986). Possible selves. *American Psychologist, 41*, 954–969.

Marsh, H. W., & Hau, K. T. (2003). Big-fish-little-pond effect on academic self-concept: A cross-cultural (26-country) test of the negative effects of academically selective schools. *American Psychologist, 58*, 364–376.

Mau, W. C., & Bikos, L. H. (2000). Educational and vocational aspirations of minority and female students: A longitudinal study. *Journal of Counseling and Development, 78*, 186–194.

Mau, W. C., Dominick, M., & Ellsworth, R. A. (1995). Characteristics of female students who aspire to science and engineering or homemaking occupations. *The Career Development Quarterly, 43*, 323–337.

Modood, T. (2004). Capitals, ethnic identity and educational qualifications. *Cultural Trends, 13*, 87–105.

Moffitt, T. E., Arseneault, L., Belsky, D., Dickson, N., Hancox, R. J., Harrington, H., & Caspi, A. (2011). A gradient of childhood self-control predicts health, wealth, and public safety. *Proceedings of the National Academy of Sciences, 108*, 2693–2698.

Moreira, P. A., Dias, P., Vaz, F. M., & Vaz, J. M. (2013). Predictors of academic performance and school engagement-integrating persistence, motivation and study skills perspectives using person-centered and variable-centered approaches. *Learning and Individual Differences, 24*, 117–125.

Moulton, V., Flouri, E., Joshi, H., & Sullivan, A. (2015). The role of aspirations in young children's emotional and behavioural problems. *British Educational Research Journal, 41*, 925–946. Advance online publication.

Nagengast, B., & Marsh, H. W. (2012). Big fish in little ponds aspire more: Mediation and cross-cultural generalizability of school-average ability effects on self-concept and career aspirations in science. *Journal of Educational Psychology, 104*, 1033–1053.

Owens, A. (2010). Neighborhoods and schools as competing and reinforcing contexts for educational attainment. *Sociology of Education, 83*, 287–311.

Oyserman, D., & Fryberg, S. A. (2006). The possible selves of diverse adolescents: Content and function across gender, race and national origin. In C. Dunkel & J. Kerpelman (Eds.), *Possible selves: Theory, research, and applications* (pp. 17–39). Huntington, NY: Nova Science.

Pahlke, E., Hyde, J. S., & Allison, C. M. (2014). The effects of single-sex compared with coeducational schooling on students' performance and attitudes: A meta-analysis. *Psychological Bulletin, 140*, 1042–1072.

Polavieja, J. G., & Platt, L. (2014). Nurse or mechanic? The role of parental socialization and children's personality in the formation of sex-typed occupational aspirations. *Social Forces, 93*, 31–61.

Pulkkinen, L. (2001). Reveller or striver? How childhood self-control predicts adult behavior. In A. C. Bohart & D. J. Stipek (Eds.), *Constructive and destructive behavior: Implications for family, school, and society* (pp. 167–185). Washington, DC: American Psychological Association.

Ross, C. E., & Broh, B. A. (2000). The roles of self-esteem and the sense of personal control in the academic achievement process. *Sociology of Education, 73*, 270–284.

Sadler, P. M., Sonnert, G., Hazari, Z., & Tai, R. (2012). Stability and volatility of STEM career interest in high school: A gender study. *Science Education, 96*, 411–427.

Schoon, I. (2001). Teenage job aspirations and career attainment in adulthood: A 17-year follow-up study of teenagers who aspire to become scientists, health professionals, or engineers. *International Journal of Behavioral Development, 25*, 124–132.

Schoon, I., & Eccles, J. S. (2014). *Gender differences in aspirations and attainment: A life course perspective.* Cambridge, UK: Cambridge University Press.

Schoon, I., Martin, P., & Ross, A. (2007). Career transitions in times of social change: His and her story. *Journal of Vocational Behavior, 70,* 78–96.

Schoon, I., & Parsons, S. (2002). Teenage aspirations for future careers and occupational outcomes. *Journal of Vocational Behavior, 60,* 262–288.

Seligman, M. E. P. (1980). *Helplessness: Theory and application.* New York, NY: Academic Press.

Sellström, E., & Bremberg, S. (2006). Is there a "school effect" on pupil outcomes? A review of multilevel studies. *Journal of Epidemiology and Community Health, 60,* 149–155.

Sewell, W. H., Haller, A. O., & Portes, A. (1969). The educational and early occupational attainment process. *American Sociological Review, 34,* 82–92.

Shiner, R. L., & Caspi, A. (2012). Temperament and the development of personality traits, adaptations, and narratives. In M. Zentner & R. L. Shiner (Eds.), *Handbook of temperament* (pp. 497–516). New York, NY: Guilford Press.

Signorella, M. L., Hayes, A. R., & Li, Y. (2013). A meta-analytic critique of Mael *et al.'s* (2005) review of single-sex schooling. *Sex Roles, 69,* 423–441.

Strand, S. (2007). *Minority ethnic pupils in the longitudinal study of young people in England* (LSYPE). Department of Children, Schools, and Families: Research Report 002. Centre for Educational Development Appraisal and Research, University of Warwick, Coventry, UK.

Strand, S. (2011). The limits of social class in explaining ethnic gaps in educational attainment. *British Educational Research Journal, 37,* 197–229.

Sullivan, A. (2009). Academic self-concept, gender and single-sex schooling. *British Educational Research Journal, 35,* 259–288.

Sullivan, A., Joshi, H., & Leonard, D. (2010). Single-sex schooling and academic attainment at school and through the life course. *American Educational Research Journal, 47,* 6–36.

Super, D. E., Savickas, M. L., & Super, C. M. (1996). The life-span, life-space approach to careers. In D. Brown, L. Brooks & Associates (Eds.), *Career choice and development: Applying contemporary theories to practice* (3rd ed., pp. 121–178). San Francisco, CA: Jossey-Bass.

Wang, L., Kick, E., Fraser, J., & Burns, T. J. (1999). Status attainment in America: The roles of locus of control and self-esteem in educational and occupational outcomes. *Sociological Spectrum, 19,* 281–298.

Wang, M. T., & Eccles, J. S. (2012). Adolescent behavioral, emotional, and cognitive engagement trajectories in school and their differential relations to educational success. *Journal of Research on Adolescence, 22,* 31–39.

Watson, C. M., Quatman, T., & Edler, E. (2002). Career aspirations of adolescent girls: Effects of achievement level, grade, and single-sex school environment. *Sex Roles, 46,* 323–335.

Weisgram, E. S., Bigler, R. S., & Liben, L. S. (2010). Gender, values, and occupational interests among children, adolescents, and adults. *Child Development, 81,* 778–796.

Wicht, A., & Ludwig-Mayerhofer, W. (2014). The impact of neighborhoods and schools on young people's occupational aspirations. *Journal of Vocational Behavior, 85,* 298–308.

Chapter 9

Child career development in family contexts

Jianwei Liu and Mary McMahon

Family is widely regarded as one of the most important influences on child career development. From an early age, children begin to construct career identities based on their experiences of the world around them, many of which occur in family contexts. Families are hierarchically organised social systems consisting of smaller subsystems such as the parental and sibling subsystems (Cox & Paley, 1997). Family systems interact with other social systems such as schools and workplaces and exist within larger systems (e.g., the environmental-societal system; Patton & McMahon, 2014) from which influences such as socioeconomic status, geographical location, and political decisions inevitably impact them and, in turn, the career development of children. Children are embedded in family systems and their career development may be best understood with reference to the family context in which they live (Whiston & Keller, 2004).

This chapter focuses on child career development in family contexts. It considers career theory and career research that offer insight into the nature of family influence on child career development. At the outset, it must be recognised that career theory and research have afforded relatively little attention to child career development (Sharf, 2013; Whiston & Keller, 2004), even though it is widely acknowledged as foundational to career development in later life stages, which have been more widely researched and theorised. Even less attention has been given to the influence of families on child career development despite widespread acceptance that family context is where children begin to learn about and make sense of the world of work (Hartung, 2015; Porfeli, Wang, & Hartung, 2008; Soresi, Nota, Ferrari, & Ginevra, 2014; Whiston & Keller, 2004) and develop career awareness (McMahon & Rixon, 2007), aspirations, and expectations (Rojewski, 2005). First, the chapter considers how career theory has accounted for child career development in the context of families. Second, research examining family influence on child career development will be overviewed. The chapter concludes by considering implications for career theory, research, and practice.

Career theory, child career development, and family context

Career theory has not provided detailed accounts of child career development in family contexts even though family is regarded as the most influential factor (Whiston & Keller, 2004). Such oversight reflects the western nature of most career theory and its individualistic emphasis, its primary focus on adolescents and adults, and its limited attention to the contexts in which career development occurs. Some theories, however, offer insight into the influence of families if not detailed explanatory accounts. Examples include Roe's (1956, 1957; Roe & Lunneborg, 1990) theory of personality development and career choice; Bordin's (1990) psychodynamic model of career choice; Super's (1980, 1990; Super, Savickas, & Super, 1996) lifespan, life-space model; Mitchell and Krumboltz's (1996) social learning theory; Savickas's (2013) career construction theory; Social Cognitive Career Theory (Lent, 2013); and relational theory (Palladino Schultheiss, 2007).

Theoretical recognition of childhood as a life stage of career development has long been present in developmental career theories (e.g., Ginzberg, Ginsburg, Axelrad, & Herma, 1951; Gottfredson, 1981, 2005; Super, 1953, 1957, 1980, 1990; Super, *et al.*, 1996). In terms of child career development, the contribution of these theories cannot be understated because, unlike theories founded in differential psychology (e.g., Holland's [1959, 1997] theory of vocational personalities and work environments), they promoted career development as a process beginning in childhood. Developmental career theories depict career development in childhood as a period where children, through observation of the adults and world around them, begin to recognise that work is a part of life, develop work habits and a future focus, and imagine themselves in adult and work roles. Fantasy and play feature strongly in child career development – much of which occurs in family settings (Hartung, 2015). These theories, in general, did not place emphasis, however, on the context of career development until Super (1980), in his lifespan, life-space theory, specifically acknowledged the home as a context (i.e., a theatre) in which career development occurred and specifically named family as a situational determinant (influence). Home and family life vary, resulting in children from different family backgrounds (e.g., working class, middle class) having different experiences and developing different perspectives of work (Gottfredson, 2005). No detailed attention, however, was given to the process of career development in the home or in families.

Of historical interest in the context of this chapter is Roe's (1956, 1957) theory of personality development and career choice, as it was one of the first career theories to specifically consider the nature of family influence as well as other influences such as culture, socioeconomic background, and gender. Roe considered genetics as an influence on the development of personal characteristics and emphasised parent-child relationships as an influence on later career choice. She posited that a relationship potentially existed between occupational choice and career behaviour and childhood experiences and environments. Although Roe's theory has not been progressed, it raised awareness of the importance of childhood family context. Also of historical interest in this chapter is Bordin's (1990) psychodynamic model of career choice, which proposed that play and work are fused, and that at a young age individuals unconsciously begin to develop a unique identity that draws on the influence of their parents. Similar to Roe's theory, Bordin's work has not been progressed.

Some theories, although not specifically focused on child career development, provide insight into the processes by which career development occurs. Learning is one such process which occurs intentionally (e.g., through career education) or unintentionally (e.g., through observation of family work habits) (Watson & McMahon, 2005, 2007). Mitchell and Krumboltz's (1996) social learning theory describes instrumental and associative learning experiences. For example, children learning through experience that they have particular talents or abilities for which they receive positive feedback constitutes an instrumental or direct learning experience. Associative learning experiences, such as children observing gendered roles or social attitudes about particular occupations, are less direct but nevertheless influential in child career development. Extending from social learning theory, Social Cognitive Career Theory (SCCT; Lent, 2013) emphasises learning in contexts such as home environments. Parents' roles in providing experiences for their children, encouraging the development of abilities, and providing support or barriers contributes to the development of children's self-efficacy, outcome expectations, and interests, all of which influence career choice and decision making. SCCT emphasises the centrality of families, especially in collectivist cultures, in later career decision making (Lent, 2013). Family is also regarded as central in understanding the complex process of vocational development in Palladino Schultheiss's (2007) relational cultural paradigm. In particular, parents play a pivotal role in children's career development and may influence features such as their self-efficacy, work values, career maturity, career decision making, and vocational interests. The role of parents and family context is also emphasised in Savickas's (2013) career construction theory, which proposes that parents act as early role models for children who take on some of the characteristics of their role models as they begin to construct their career identities.

As this brief overview of career theory evidences, career theory agrees that career development is a lifelong process beginning in childhood. Moreover, career theory confirms that career development and the construction of career identity is a social process that begins in families in childhood. While career theory, to date, has failed to provide detailed accounts of the process of career development in family contexts, a body of research has begun to provide insight into the nature of child career development in family contexts.

Career research, child career development, and family contexts

In a previous research review on the influence of family of origin on career development, Whiston and Keller (2004) lamented that "so few researchers have examined family influences on children's career development when, theoretically, that influence may be especially strong" (p. 523). Career research reveals a disparate range of studies on child career development in family contexts with topics ranging from factors within family systems to others that consider the interface between family systems and other social systems such as schools and the environmental-societal system such as geographic location. Just as Whiston and Keller used an existing theoretical framework – the developmental-contextual framework of Vondracek and his colleagues (1986) – to provide a structure for their review, the present chapter draws on the Systems Theory Framework (Patton & McMahon, 2014) of career development to provide a structure because it has previously been found useful for this purpose (Watson & McMahon, 2004) and also because it can accommodate the "multidimensional and interactional" (Whiston & Keller, 2004, p. 561) nature of family influences on children's career development; family influence cannot be considered in isolation from other factors such as socioeconomic status, gender, and culture (Whiston & Keller, 2004). This systemic overview of career research is presented in three parts: first, research on factors within family systems; second, research on the interface between family systems and other social systems; and, finally, research on the interface between family systems and the environmental-societal system.

Research on factors within family systems

This section will focus on research that investigated the influence of factors within family systems on child career development. These factors include family structure/composition, family attitudes and expectation/aspiration, family behaviours, and family relationships.

Children's career aspirations are more likely to originate from family than from other sources (Trice, Hughes, Odom, Woods, & McClellan, 1995). The structure and composition of family systems may vary and may comprise, for example, parents, siblings, grandparents, and other relatives, all of whom may influence child career development. Parents, however, are predominately reported by children as their most important influences (Hartung, Porfeli, & Vondracek, 2005; McMahon & Rixon, 2007). Parental absence may influence children's career expectations. For example, inner-city American boys tended to have low career expectations because they were less likely to have their biological fathers present at home (Cook et al., 1996).

The gender development of children in association with parental sexual orientation, gender-related attitudes, and division of paid and unpaid labour has been investigated. Preschoolers, regardless of parental sexual orientation, were better able to picture a future with fewer gender-related stereotypes if their parents divided labour evenly (Fulcher, Sutfin, & Patterson, 2008). By contrast, children whose parents were more unequal in their sharing of paid and unpaid labour held more traditional career aspirations. Parents who de-emphasise sex-typing in their values and social practices tend to have children who are less stereotyped in their career preferences and about whether boys and girls can engage in non-traditional occupations (Weisner & Wilson-Mitchell, 1990). More studies have focused on the influence of mothers', rather than fathers', gender-role attitudes. Children of mothers who hold non-traditional attitudes are more likely to have non-traditional occupational aspirations (Fulcher, 2011). Further, mothers who perceive their children as more competent in gender-traditional occupations and skills were more inclined to have children who have more traditional career aspirations and more confidence in traditional occupations (Fulcher, 2011). Mothers' gender-role attitudes towards women's roles and rights in society contribute to girls' gender-role attitudes in occupational (as well as educational and intellectual) domains and their career aspirations (e.g., traditional, non-traditional, and neutral) (Fiebig, 2003).

Parents' aspirations for their children's future could affect their children's stereotyped career attitudes, efficacy, and aspirations (Meyer, 1980). Contrasting evidence exists about parental aspirations for boys and girls. For example, Brook, Whiteman, Peisach, and Deutsch (1974) found that parents have higher educational and occupational aspirations for boys than for girls, while no such difference was found in a more recent study (Creed, Conlon, & Zimmer-Gembeck, 2007). Children, especially those in the upper grades of primary school are likely to perceive what their parents expect them to do and are likely to hold career aspirations (usually of high status) similar to those held by their parents for them (Creed et al., 2007; Helwig, 1998; Samiee, Baghban, Abedi, & Hosseinian, 2011). Children's aspirations are more similar to their perceptions of their mothers' expectations (Helwig, 1998). Parents' expectations of their children may be influenced by reading and general ability, whereas children may be more influenced by psychosocial barriers (Creed et al., 2007). Children who detect more positive parental attitudes towards work are likely to develop positive feelings about work and thus are more likely to aspire to their parents' occupations (Hartung et al., 2005).

Parents are likely to socialise their children on the basis of their own aspirations, especially in terms of gender and social class, which in turn influences children's career aspirations. Girls are likely to aspire to traditionally female occupations when their parents encourage feminine behaviour (Ehrhardt, Ince, & Meyer-Bahlburg, 1981). Family's social class socialisation plays a role in children's development of career aspirations. Socially advantaged families are more likely to align their children's careers and their family-class background (Archer, DeWitt, & Wong, 2014). They tend to talk more often about family members' careers and thus form the basis of children's personal identities and their ideas of future careers, and they are more likely to not only support but also actively nurture children's career ideas by using family resources such as social networks.

Parents not only talk about their careers in front of children, but may also take children to their workplaces, through which children develop conceptions of work, career aspirations, and career self-efficacy (Alliman-Brissett, Turner, & Skovholt, 2004; Hutchings, 1996; Mauthner, Maclean, & McKee, 2000). Children observing their parents engaged in their occupations, or parents explaining to their children how they pursued their education and career development, was the primary predictor of boys' (but not girls') career self-efficacy (Alliman-Brissett *et al.*, 2004). Parents may not only provide direct and indirect career messages to children, they may also provide "ambient" messages, which means children could make sense of their parents' actions, feelings, and words (Buzzanell, Berkelaar, & Kisselburgh, 2011, p. 149). Parents are more likely to transmit negative, rather than positive, work emotions to their children, which in turn may have a negative influence on their children's anticipated work emotions and experiences (Porfeli *et al.*, 2008). Parents also influence children's career development by showing support for their career ideas. In socially advantaged families, parents are more likely to not only show supportive attitudes towards children's career ideas but also to actively nurture them (Archer *et al.*, 2014). Children who perceive parental support for their career aspirations towards particular occupational types tend to be more confident in performing tasks related to those occupational types, which in turn influences their interest in such careers (Turner & Lapan, 2002; Turner, Steward, & Lapan, 2004). Parents' provision of career-related support influences children's career development, as does their general emotional support or supportive parenting. When parents show supportive parenting, emotionally or instrumentally, their children tend to report more clearly defined career goals and fewer career barriers to achieving these goals (Alliman-Brissett *et al.*, 2004; Hill, Ramirez, & Dumka, 2003).

Children's perception of the parent-child relationship also influences their career development. For example, American five-year-old children were more likely to articulate their future goals when they perceived their fathers as powerful, important, and attractive, as well as approachable and warm (Seligman, Weinstock, & Owings, 1988). This influence on children's career aspirations, however, declined for 10-year-olds (Seligman, Weinstock, & Heflin, 1991). The mother-daughter relationship of German (but not American) children aged from 11 to 14 was related to girls' traditionality of career aspirations; the mother-child relationship could predict American girls' aspirations for advanced positions in a chosen field (Fiebig, 2003).

In addition, children's perception of the father-mother relationship also influences children's career development. Girls who perceive greater father dominance at home are more likely to aspire to traditionally female-occupied occupations, while their perception of increased maternal dominance was related to greater aspirations towards traditionally male-occupied occupations (Lavine, 1982).

Research on the interface between family systems and other social systems

This section focuses on research that investigated the influence factors within other social systems with which families interact have on child career development. These factors include schools, media, and members of the community.

School is a setting where children, especially primary school children, spend most of their time and develop their career knowledge and aspirations (Archer *et al.*, 2014). Children with secure attachment to their mothers are more curious and more likely to explore the school environment and develop positive relationships with teachers, which allow them, in the process of career exploration, to seek help from teachers in a comfortable manner (Bryant, Zvonkovic, & Reynolds, 2006). Importantly, since school quality closely relates to children's career development, parents (especially middle-class parents) tend to place their children in schools with better teachers and facilities (Buzzanell *et al.*, 2011). In this way, the family is creating career socialisation opportunities by selecting and controlling the social context of their children's career development. Parents who believe they can influence their children's academic performance at school are likely to have children with stronger educational and career self-efficacy and higher aspirations (Bandura, Barbaranelli, Vittorio, & Pastorelli, 2001). Usually, these parents have high educational achievement and expectations for their children and assist them to meet college entrance requirements (Bryant *et al.*, 2006). These parents, therefore, not only verbally encourage their children to study hard but also provide material and human capital to help them to improve their school performance or even help them to plan a future career, which in turn influences children's career self-efficacy and aspirations (Archer *et al.*, 2014; Bandura *et al.*, 2001; Liu, McMahon, & Watson, 2015a, b). Related to parents' involvement with school systems is their enrolment of their children in extracurricular activities outside of school where children may develop career interests and aspirations (Archer *et al.*, 2014; Buzzanell *et al.*, 2011).

Media is an important source of career information (Watson & McMahon, 2005), and children from affluent families tend to have more access to diverse networks, including news media and Internet connection (Buzzanell *et al.*, 2011). A strategic and future-oriented family is likely to attend to career information through media (e.g., news broadcasts) and discuss it in front of, or with, their children. For example, a child's family could pay great attention to news about the education and job market and discuss how it may inform the child's future plans (Buzzanell *et al.*, 2011). This in turn could lead to children's active use of media to explore the world of work and to form or modify their career ideas and aspirations influenced by their family (Archer *et al.*, 2014).

Families also interact with other social systems that influence children's career development. Family friends and neighbours may inspire children's career aspirations (Archer *et al.*, 2014; Buzzanell *et al.*, 2011). People working in the community may be used as examples by families in China to educate children, with parents more often discouraging children from undertaking low-status jobs such as cleaners and waitresses (Liu *et al.*, 2015a, b).

Research on the interface between family systems and the environmental-societal system

This section will focus on research that investigated the influence of factors from the broader environmental-societal system on child career development. These factors include socioeconomic status (SES), geographical location, employment market, and political situations.

Family SES usually refers to parental education background, parental occupational status, and parental income levels (Dubow, Boxer, & Huesmann, 2009; Schulenberg, Vondracek, & Crouter, 1984) and has been a topic of research for over 50 years. Family SES impacts children's attitudes and knowledge about the world of work. Children from rich families are more likely to develop positive attitudes towards work (Galinsky, 2000). Children from lower-SES families tend to know less about both the depth and variety of occupations (Jordan, 1976; Nelson, 1963), which may be because low-income parents are less able to inform their children about the variety of career alternatives because of their own limited information and knowledge (Peterson, Stivers, & Peters, 1986) or because parents who are successful as family providers are more likely to share their experience of work (Galinsky, 2000). Children with parents from lower-SES backgrounds and minority groups hold more conservative attitudes towards the work males and females can do and tend to develop beliefs about appropriate jobs that match their perceived social status (Hartung *et al.*, 2005). Children with well-educated parents express more liberal attitudes towards non-traditional sex-role occupations (Zuckerman & Sayre, 1982). Children from families in poverty perceive little possibility of high-status occupations (Weinger, 1998, 2000). African-American children rated jobs performed by African-Americans as lower status (Bigler, Averhart, & Liben, 2003) and, more than Anglo-American children, gender stereotyped the ability of males and females to do certain jobs (Frost & Diamond, 1979).

Children from lower-SES families are less future oriented (Miller & Stanford, 1987; Vondracek & Kirchner, 1974), less diversified in their aspirations (Bobo, Hildreth, & Durodoye, 1998), and more likely to develop stereotyped career aspirations and expectations based on gender, race, and status of careers. Children from higher-SES backgrounds are likely to aspire to high-status jobs (Bigler *et al.*, 2003; Cook *et al.*, 1996; Frost & Diamond, 1979; Kay & Miller, 1982). This could be attributed to the effort made by socially advantaged families to socialise their children so as to align their children's careers and their family SES background (Archer *et al.*, 2014; Hutchings, 1996). These efforts may include families' use of human capital to improve children's future educational possibilities by, for example, helping with children's homework and discussing possible future career paths with children when watching television (Archer *et al.*, 2014); use of financial capital to provide more career exploration opportunities by arranging, for example, outside school classes and activities (Buzzanell *et al.*, 2011); and use of social networks to help children with work experience (Archer *et al.*, 2014).

Family geographical location affects child career development. Rural children showed more stability in their expressed career aspirations than urban children and were likely to report career aspirations similar to those of their parents, which may be due to the limited opportunities for rural children, compared with urban children, to be exposed to a variety of occupations (Trice, 1991). The employment market may also interact with family systems and plays an important role in child career development. For example, Chinese children may learn from their parents that, because of the competitive job market in China, they may not get a job if they do not study hard for a high-level educational qualification (Liu *et al.*, 2015b). Influenced by the political situation of their country, Lebanese children are more likely to talk about their families doing work that helps others such as engineers who rebuild homes destroyed during war and doctors who heal people (Buzzanell *et al.*, 2011).

Implications for career theory, research, and practice

That career development begins in childhood in family contexts and that parents are significant career influences are undeniable. This important topic, however, has received less theoretical attention and more limited research investigation than topics such as career aspirations, which is consistent with claims that the context and process of child career development has been less researched and requires a greater focus (e.g., Hartung, *et al.*, 2005; Watson & McMahon, 2005). Moreover, the present chapter reveals that influences within family systems on child career development have been more researched than other social and environmental-societal influences that interact with family systems and suggests promising new avenues of research. The present chapter reveals a limited relationship between career theory and research in relation to the influence of families and suggests a possible future direction for research and theory building.

Both theory and research suggest that, in practice, intentional career development learning may be facilitated for children (Watson & McMahon, 2007). Moreover, providing opportunities for parents to be involved in such activities and for developing and enhancing parental skills as supporters and facilitators of their children's career development is critical; collaboration between career development practitioners and parents has been advocated (Watson, Nota, & McMahon, 2015). Early intervention, supported by parents, could strengthen career development in the life stage of childhood and ensure that it provides a firm foundation for career decision making in the later life stages of adolescence and adulthood. Further, parents who develop enhanced skills and knowledge about supporting their child's career development while their child is young will be better positioned to support their child through subsequent life stages.

Conclusion

Families, particularly parents, are an important influence on child career development. Directly and indirectly, parents provide experiences and model behaviours from which children begin to construct career identities. To date, however, career theory and research have provided only partial and incomplete accounts of the nature of parental and familial influence. Thus the influence of parents and families in child career development remains fertile ground for future research and theory development.

References

Alliman-Brissett, A., Turner, S., & Skovholt, T. (2004). Parent support and African American aolescents' career self-efficacy. *Professional School Counseling, 7*, 124–132.

Archer, L., DeWitt, J., & Wong, B. (2014). Spheres of influence: What shapes young people's aspirations at age 12/13 and what are the implications for education policy? *Journal of Education Policy, 29*, 58–85.

Bandura, A., Barbaranelli, C., Vittorio, G., & Pastorelli, C. (2001). Self-efficacy beliefs as shapers of children's aspirations and career trajectories. *Child Development, 72*, 187–206.

Bigler, R. S., Averhart, C. J., & Liben, L. S. (2003). Race and the workforce: Occupational status, aspirations, and stereotyping among African American children. *Developmental Psychology, 39*, 572–580.

Bobo, M., Hildreth, B. L., & Durodoye, B. (1998). Changing patterns in career choices among African-American, Hispanic and Anglo children. *Professional School Counseling, 1*, 37–42.

Bordin, E. S. (1990). Psychodynamic model of career choice and satisfaction. In D. Brown & L. Brooks (Eds.), *Career choice and development: Applying contemporary theories to practice* (2nd ed., pp. 102–144). San Francisco, CA: Jossey-Bass.

Brook, J. S., Whiteman, M., Peisach, E., & Deutsch, M. (1974). Aspiration levels of and for children: Age, sex, race, and social economic correlates. *Journal of Genetic Psychology, 124*, 3–16.

Bryant, B. K., Zvonkovic, A. M., & Reynolds, P. (2006). Parenting in relation to child and adolescent vocational development. *Journal of Vocational Behavior, 69*, 149–175.

Buzzanell, P. M., Berkelaar, B. L., & Kisselburgh, L. (2011). From the mouths of babes: Exploring families' career socialization of young children in China, Lebanon, Belgium, and the United States. *Journal of Family Communication, 11*, 148–164.

Cook, T. D., Church, M. B., Ajanaku, S., Shadish, W. R., Kim, J.-R., & Cohen, R. (1996). The development of occupational aspirations and expectations among inner-city boys. *Child Development, 67*, 3368–3385.

Cox, M., & Paley, B. (1997). Families as systems. *Annual Review of Psychology, 48*, 243–267.

Creed, P. A., Conlon, E. G., & Zimmer-Gembeck, M. J. (2007). Career barriers and reading ability as correlates of career aspirations and expectations of parents and their children. *Journal of Vocational Behavior, 70*, 242–258.

Dubow, E. F., Boxer, P., & Huesmann, L. R. (2009). Long-term effects of parents' education on children's educational and occcupational success medication by family interactions, child aggression, and teenage aspirations. *Merrill-Palmer Quarterly, 55*, 224–249.

Ehrhardt, A. A., Ince, S. E., & Meyer-Bahlburg, H. F. L. (1981). Career aspiration and gender role development in young girls. *Archives of Sexual Behavior, 10*, 281–299.

Fiebig, J. N. (2003). Gifted American and German early adolescent girls: Influences on career orientation and aspirations. *High Ability Studies, 14*, 165–183.

Frost, F., & Diamond, E. E. (1979). Ethnic and sex differences in occupational stereotyping by elementary school children. *Journal of Vocational Behavior, 15*, 43–54.

Fulcher, M. (2011). Individual differences in children's occupational aspirations as a function of parental traditionality. *Sex Roles, 64*, 117–131.

Fulcher, M., Sutfin, E. L., & Patterson, C. J. (2008). Individual differences in gender development: Associations with parental sexual orientation, attitudes, and division of labor. *Sex Roles, 58*, 330–341.

Galinsky, E. (2000). *Ask the children: The breakthrough study that reveals how to succeed at work and parenting.* New York, NY: Harper Collins.

Ginzberg, E., Ginsburg, S. W., Axelrad, S., & Herma, J. L. (1951). *Occupational choice: An approach to general theory.* New York, NY: Columbus University Press.

Gottfredson, L. S. (1981). Circumscription and compromise: A developmental theory of occupational aspirations. *Journal of Counseling Psychology, 28*, 545–579.

Gottfredson, L. S. (2005). Applying Gottfredson's theory of circumscription and compromise in career guidance and counseling. In S. D. Brown & R. W. Lent (Eds.), *Career development and counseling: Putting theory and research to work* (pp. 71–100). Hoboken, NJ: John Wiley & Sons.

Hartung, P. J. (2015). Life design in childhood: Antecedents and advancement. In L. Nota & J. Rossier (Eds.), *Handbook of the life design paradigm: From practice to theory, from theory to practice* (pp. 89–102). Boston, MA: Hogrefe Publishing.

Hartung, P. J., Porfeli, E. J., & Vondracek, F. W. (2005). Child vocational development: A review and reconsideration. *Journal of Vocational Behavior, 66*, 385–419.

Helwig, A. A. (1998). Occupational aspirations of a longitudinal sample from second to sixth grade. *Journal of Career Development, 24*, 247–265.

Hill, N. E., Ramirez, C., & Dumka, L. E. (2003). Early adolescents' career aspirations: A qualitative study of perceived barriers and family support among low-income, ethnically diverse adolescents. *Journal of Family Issues, 24*, 934–959.

Holland, J. L. (1959). A theory of vocational choice. *Journal of Counseling Psychology, 6*, 35–44.

Holland, J. L. (1997). *Making vocational choices: A theory of vocational personalities and work environments* (3rd ed.). Odessa, FL: Psychological Assessment Resources.

Hutchings, M. (1996). What will you do when you grow up?: The social construction of children's occupational preferences. *Children's Social and Economics Education, 1*, 15–30.

Jordan, T. E. (1976). Preschool influences on occupational knowledge of seven-year-olds: A prospective study. *Journal of Experimental Education, 44*, 27–37.

Kay, W. R. M., & Miller, C. A. (1982). Relations of socioeconomic status and sex variables to the complexity of worker functions in the occupational choices of elementary school children. *Journal of Vocational Behavior, 20*, 31–39.

Lavine, L. O. (1982). Parental power as a potential influence on girls' career choice. *Child Development, 53*, 658–663.

Lent, R. W. (2013). Social cognitive career theory. In S. D. Brown & R. W. Lent (Eds.), *Career development and counseling: Putting theory and research to work* (2nd ed., pp. 115–146). New York, NY: John Wiley & Sons.

Liu, J., McMahon, M., & Watson, M. (2015a). Parental influence on child career development in mainland China: A qualitative study. *The Career Development Quarterly, 63*, 74–87.

Liu, J., McMahon, M., & Watson, M. (2015b). Parental influence on mainland Chinese children's career aspirations: Child and parental perspectives. *International Journal for Educational and Vocational Guidance, 15*, 131–143.

Mauthner, N. S., Maclean, C., & McKee, L. (2000). 'My dad hangs out of helicopter doors and takes pictures of oil platforms': Children's accounts of parental work in the oil and gas industry. *Community, Work & Family, 3*, 133–162.

McMahon, M., & Rixon, K. (2007). The career development of rural Queensland children. *Australian Journal of Career Development, 16*(2), 39–49.

Meyer, B. (1980). The development of girls' sex-role attitudes. *Child Development, 51*, 508–514.

Miller, M. J., & Stanford, J. T. (1987). Early occupational restriction: An examination of elementary school children's expression of vocational preferences. *Journal of Employment Counseling, 24*, 115–121.

Mitchell, L. K., & Krumboltz, J. D. (1996). Krumboltz's learning theory of career choice and counseling. In D. Brown & L. Brooks (Eds.), *Career choice and development* (3rd ed., pp. 233–280). San Francisco, CA: Jossey-Bass.

Nelson, R. C. (1963). Knowledge and interests concerning 16 occupations among elementary and secondary school students. *Educational and Psychological Measurement, 23*, 741–754.

Palladino Schultheiss, D. E. (2007). The emergence of a relational cultural paradigm for vocational psychology. *International Journal for Educational and Vocational Guidance, 7*, 191–201.

Patton, W., & McMahon, M. (2014). *Career development and systems theory: A new relationship* (3rd ed.). Rotterdam: Sense Publishers.

Peterson, G. W., Stivers, M. E., & Peters, D. F. (1986). Family versus nonfamily significant others for the career decisions of low-income youth. *Family Relations, 35*, 417–424.

Porfeli, E. J., Wang, C., & Hartung, P. J. (2008). Family transmission of work affecticity and experiences to children. *Journal of Vocational Behavior, 73*, 278–286.

Roe, A. (1956). *The psychology of occupations.* New York, NY: John Wiley & Sons.

Roe, A. (1957). Early determinants of vocational choice. *Journal of Counseling Psychology, 4*, 212–217.

Roe, A., & Lunneborg, P. (1990). Personality development and career choice. In D. Brown, L. Brooks & Associates (Eds.), *Career choice and development: Applying contemporary theories to practice* (2nd ed., pp. 68–101). San Francisco, CA: Jossey-Bass.

Rojewski, J. W. (2005). Occupational aspirations: Constructs, meanings, and application. In S. D. Brown & R. W. Lent (Eds.), *Career development and counseling: Putting theory and research to work* (pp. 131–154). Hoboken, NJ: John Wiley & Sons.

Samiee, F., Baghban, I., Abedi, M. R., & Hosseinian, S. (2011). Elementary-aged boys' occupational aspirations and expectations in Iran. *Interdisciplinary Journal of Contemporary Research in Business, 3*, 498–509.

Savickas, M. L. (2013). Career construction theory and practice. In S. D. Brown & R. W. Lent (Eds.), *Career development and counseling: Putting theory and research to work* (2nd ed., pp. 147–183). Hoboken, NJ: John Wiley & Sons.

Schulenberg, J. E., Vondracek, F. W., & Crouter, A. C. (1984). The influence of the family on vocational development. *Journal of Marriage and the Family, 46*, 129–143.

Seligman, L., Weinstock, L., & Heflin, E. N. (1991). The career development of 10 year olds. *Elementary School Guidance and Counseling, 22*, 172–181.

Seligman, L., Weinstock, L., & Owings, N. (1988). The role of family dynamics in career development of 5-year-olds. *Elementary School Guidance and Counseling, 22*, 223–230.

Sharf, R. S. (2013). *Applying career development theory to counseling* (6th ed.). Belmont, CA: Brooks/Cole.

Soresi, S., Nota, L., Ferrari, L., & Ginevra, M. C. (2014). Parental influences on youth's career construction. In G. Arulmani, A. J. Bakshi, F. T. L. Leong, & A. G. Watts (Eds.), *Handbook of career development: International perspectives* (pp. 149–172). New York, NY: Springer.

Super, D. E. (1953). A theory of vocational development. *American Psychologist, 8*, 185–190.

Super, D. E. (1957). *The psychology of careers.* New York, NY: Harper and Row.

Super, D. E. (1980). A life-span, life-space approach to career development. *Journal of Vocational Behavior, 16*, 282–298.

Super, D. E. (1990). A life-span, life-space approach to career development. In D. Brown, L. Brooks & Associates (Eds.), *Career choice and development: Applying contemporary theories to practice* (2nd ed., pp. 197–261). San Francisco, CA: Jossey-Bass.

Super, D. E., Savickas, M. L., & Super, C. M. (1996). The life-span, life-space approach to careers. In D. Brown, L. Brooks & Associates (Eds.), *Career choice and development: Applying contemporary theories to practice* (3rd ed., pp. 121–178). San Francisco, CA: Jossey-Bass.

Trice, A. D. (1991). Stability of children's career aspiration. *Journal of Genetic Psychology, 152*, 137–139.

Trice, A. D., Hughes, M. A., Odom, C., Woods, K., & McClellan, N. C. (1995). The origins of children's career aspirations: IV. Testing hypotheses from four theories. *The Career Development Quarterly, 43*, 307–322.

Turner, S., & Lapan, R. (2002). Career self-efficacy and perceptions of parent support in adolescent career development. *The Career Development Quarterly, 51*, 44–55.

Turner, S., Steward, J., & Lapan, R. (2004). Family factors associated with sixth-grade adolescents' math and science career interest. *The Career Development Quarterly, 53*, 41–52.

Vondracek, F. W., Lerner, R. M., & Schulenberg, J. M. (1986). *Career development: A lifespan approach.* Hillsdale, NJ: Lawrence Erlbaum.

Vondracek, S. I., & Kirchner, E. P. (1974). Vocational development in early childhood: An examination of young children's expression of vocational aspirations. *Journal of Vocational Behavior, 5*, 251–260.

Watson, M., & McMahon, M. (2004). Children's career development: A metatheoretical perspective. *Australian Journal of Career Development, 13*, 7–12.

Watson, M., & McMahon, M. (2005). Children's career development: A research review from a learning perspective. *Journal of Vocational Behavior, 67*, 119–132.

Watson, M., & McMahon, M. (2007). Children's career development learning: A foundation for lifelong career development. In V. B. Skorikov & W. Patton (Eds.), *Career development in childhood and adolescence* (pp. 29–46). Rotterdam, The Netherlands: Sense Publishers.

Watson, M., Nota, L., & McMahon, M. (2015). Evolving stories of child career development. *International Journal for Educational and Vocational Guidance, 15*, 175–184.

Weinger, S. (1998). Children living in poverty: Their perception of career opportunities. *Families in Society: The Journal of Contemporary Human Services, 79*, 320–330.

Weinger, S. (2000). Opportunities for career success: Views of poor and middle-class children. *Children and Youth Services, 22*, 13–35.

Weisner, T. S., & Wilson-Mitchell, J. E. (1990). Nonconventional family life-styles and sex typing in six-year-olds. *Child Development, 61*, 1915–1933.

Whiston, S. C., & Keller, B. K. (2004). The influence of the family of origin on career development: A review and analysis. *Journal of Vocational Behavior, 32*, 493–568.

Zuckerman, D. M., & Sayre, D. H. (1982). Cultural sex-role expectations and children's sex-role concepts. *Sex Roles, 8*, 853–862.

Chapter 10

Child career development in developing world contexts

Anuradha J. Bakshi

There is no one picture of child career development in developing world contexts. Neither can we overlay the picture of child career development obtained from developed world contexts on children in the developing world. I make these assertions using two principal differences in the experiences of children in developing versus developed world contexts. First, developing economies are characterised by considerably higher degrees of heterogeneity and inequities than are developed economies such that experiences relevant to career development in childhood can range from (extremely) suboptimal to (extremely) optimal. Second, as a developing country is "one in which the majority lives on far less money – with far fewer basic public services – than the population in highly industrialized countries" (World Bank, 2012), the proportion of children whose experiences are suboptimal is far greater in developing than in developed economies.

Let me start by contrasting two extremes: In sheer numbers, but not proportionally, many children in developing countries may have access to high-quality experiences that place them at an advantage even over the average child in a developed economy. On the other hand, both in absolute and proportional terms, for other children in developing countries, work and career are synonymous with human rights violations, not just in childhood but through a process of cumulative continuity (see Elder & Shanahan, 2006) across the entire lifespan. During childhood, precocious and forced entry into paid work or unpaid family labour robs these children of a childhood. Next, they are deprived of adolescence. The pivotal concept of adolescence in human development is a psychosocial moratorium (Erikson, 1968) – a sanctioned delay in assuming the roles of an adult (i.e., marriage, parenthood, maintaining a home, family caregiving, earning a livelihood) so that adolescents can engage in the role exploration that is necessary for identity-related decision making. Children in developing countries have responsibilities which are associated with adulthood thrust on them in childhood. Unless their life trajectories are marked by turning points, these child–adults continue into their second decade of life and start their third decade without the privilege of adolescence. Deprivation of childhood and adolescence means, among other things, deprivation of nurturance, play, and educational attainment. These privations in turn translate into a lifetime of work in precarious conditions; decent work is not guaranteed. Their lives are typified by foreclosure into the informal economy and paid work becomes a means of perpetuating poverty.

Philosophically, when we talk of career development from a Western developed country perspective, work and career are vehicles for self-expression with the potential for self-actualisation; they are a means of optimising the self and one's contributions to the community/society/world at large (e.g., Savickas, 2013). A major focus in the Western literature has been on interests and matching interests to work requirements and work environments (e.g., Holland, 1997). Whereas interests are one relevant dimension, an exclusive or dominant focus on interests portrays a simplistically romantic picture. Unstable economic conditions even in so-called developed economies have underscored the hardships and struggles that can characterise one's engagement in the world-of-work. For many (though not all) children in developing countries, the hardships and struggles in the world-of-work are in the foreground. Nor are these work-related adversities experienced only through parents. Unfortunately, they are experienced first-hand in childhood through exploitative paid or unpaid work experiences in the home and/or another workplace. Work and career 'development' then, conversely to the prevailing position in the Western literature, are a means of suboptimising the self, thus leading to reduction of potential and marginalisation. Instead of promoting career development in childhood, for these children, we need action to prevent work from violating their rights as children and (chronologically) later as adults (see International Labour Organization [ILO], 2013b; UNICEF, 2014).

My aim in this chapter is to underscore how contexts in the developing world differ from those in the developed world. Leading from this, I illustrate how childhood experiences that are relevant to career development are markedly different for children in developing versus developed countries. The extent of these differences exposes the limitations of applying Western career theory and research to children in developing countries.

Culture specificity of career guidance theory and research

While claims to universality may be made explicitly or undergird the literature in implicit ways, it stands to reason that scholars situated in particular contexts explain phenomena that are familiar to them. A case in point is that the phenomenon of poverty is sidelined in career development theory and research from developed economies. Poverty is less of a stark reality in these countries and therefore attention in career theory and research is not centred on poverty. Repeated calls for making vocational psychology or career development theory and research more inclusive have led a few scholars to focus attention on *social class* (e.g., Blustein *et al.*, 2002; Heppner & Jung, 2013). However, because there are differences in the extent and character of poverty among developing versus developed countries, descriptions and explanations that derive from theory/research that does address poverty (or rather classism) in developed economies will not necessarily transfer to (all) developing world contexts. Two examples suffice here. Blustein *et al.*, in reviewing the US literature on the impact of social class on career development, indicated that individuals from lower social classes have poorer access to resources and opportunities and are likely to have reduced aspirations and lower educational and occupational attainment. They go on to report the findings from their study. Young employed adults from lower socio-economic status (LSES) shared that financial survival was the main function of work; in contrast, their higher socioeconomic (HSES) counterparts identified personal satisfaction and personal meaning as the most important reasons for working and noted that, "Money just is not that important" (p. 315). Although the two groups of adults had similar internal resources and barriers, they differed conspicuously with regard to external resources and barriers. LSES young adults described lower-quality guidance services at school than did the HSES young adults and more barriers to education such as needing to support the family financially, violence in the neighbourhood, and parents valuing paid work over higher education. In addition, the LSES young adults were less clear about their career goals, less likely to exercise initiative and agency in working towards their goals, and more likely to identify obstacles and reservations such as not having money, opportunity, or a college education.

Though the Blustein *et al.* (2002) study is insightful, it is still context bound. It highlights how LSES young adults differ from HSES young adults in a developed country but does not capture the conditions of poverty in developing countries. The LSES young adults talked about the lack of agentic support from parents, especially because the parents were not college-educated; however, children in poor families in developing countries are frequently first-generation school goers and have inadequate instrumental support from family members from the preschool years. Whereas the quality of a school and the quality of guidance counselling in a school are important, a child in a developing country may not have the privilege of attending school at all, and when the child does have this privilege, it is more likely than not that the school has no guidance counsellor.

The second example is that of Heppner and Jung's (2013) Gender and Social Class Model (GSCM) of career development. The GSCM is a mediational model with one-way paths leading from gender and social class, through mediators, to three career-related outcomes (e.g., career development, which they define as the development of emotions, thoughts, and behaviours related to educational/occupational paths). There are two levels of mediation proposed between gender and social class and career-related outcomes. Gender and social class each directly impact accessibility of resources and early socialisation (first set of mediators), each of which in turn impact construction of self (second mediator). Heppner and Jung's (2013) efforts at developing the GSCM are commendable because this model addresses important gaps in career theory, identifying as it does gender and class differences in accessibility of resources and early socialisation, both of which have a strong influence on self-construction. It is also sensitive to both the direct and indirect influence of accessibility of resources on career-related outcomes. At the same time, this model is not applicable to all contexts in developing economies because it presumes that gender and social class directly impact *only* accessibility of resources and early socialisation. Moreover, examples of resources that Heppner and Jung provide appear to be limited to those that directly benefit career-related outcomes such as opportunities for educational training, financial and emotional support, part-time jobs, and internships. Also, the model provides a poor fit for any context at all, developed or developing, because it exclusively portrays one-way paths.

Macro-contexts of developing countries: Gravity of the situation

Although theory and research from developed economies have been dominant and hegemonic, it is important to note that of the seven billion people in the world, close to six billion reside in developing countries (Population Reference Bureau, 2011). Developing countries are not yet able to guarantee provision of basic public services to all citizens (e.g., potable water, electricity, health and sanitation services, education), have far lower average per capita daily incomes (less than $2), and have an unacceptably large section of the population living in extreme poverty (less than $1.25 per capita daily income) (World Bank, 2012). Transportation, power, and communication infrastructural systems are less well developed or are inequitably accessed. Poverty in developing countries entails hunger and undernourishment. Of the 795 million people who are undernourished in the world, 780 million reside in developing countries (United Nations [UN], 2015).

Developing economies require development assistance from international development agencies and generally have unsustainable government debts (World Bank, 2012). The World Bank further specifies that developing countries could be more rural and agrarian, and less industrialised than developed economies. Moreover, some developing countries have collapsed governments and armed conflict and some are prone to natural disasters.

Filling the gaps in cultural relevance: Child career development in developing economies

The distinctive characteristics of developing economies spell a very different set of circumstances, albeit heterogeneous, for children in developing economies. In this section, I examine the roles of the family, school, and play to illustrate how child career development in developing economies could vary dramatically from that in developed economies.

Role of the family

Three aspects of the role of the family are discussed: parents' work/career, children's premature work experiences, and religious/ethnic identity.

Role of parents' work/career

In examining the role of parents' work/career in the career development of children in developing economies, it is important to ask the following interrelated questions: (a) What is the ratio of success/achievement to struggle/hardship in the parents' work experiences? Does the hardship translate into destitution? Or does it mean that the family has reduced means? (b) Does the parents' work allow the family to meet basic needs? (c) What are children learning about the world-of-work through their parents' work experiences or their own work experiences? How does learning about the world-of-work impact children's understanding of the world in general and their place in it? A substantial number of children in developing economies may understand work as a way of making ends meet, as a struggle for existence in an unfair world.

Children learn about work and careers from their parents' work and careers. This general statement appears to hold true for children across all cultures. So what are some differences between developed and developing economies? First, the informal economy is extensive in developing economies and generally entails exploitative work conditions, unpredictability, impermanence, low-prestige positions, hardship, and marginalisation (ILO, 2013c; Jütting & de Laiglesia, 2009). A parent or both parents of a child in a developing economy may be casual labourers who solicit work on a day-to-day basis without any guarantee of securing employment for the day. They may have to migrate to urban hubs or scour a city/region in search of employment. Thus many children in developing economies do not learn about decent work from their parents; instead, they learn from their parents about work which strips them of many human rights and keeps them on the fringes of society, unable to access the opportunities/resources of a knowledge-and-technology-dependent world. The International Labour Organization (ILO; 2002a) has noted that "decent work deficits are most pronounced in the informal economy" (p. 25). The concept of decent work recognises that work is a means of achieving and securing one's own and one's family's position in society, that work is a way of meeting personal developmental goals, and of supporting the goals of those in our care. The ILO decent work criteria include the worker's experience of safety, equality (e.g., gender equality), justice (e.g., a fair income), liberty (e.g., freedom to have a voice), empowerment, social protection and integration (ILO, 1999).

Second, parents' work and careers make possible the quality of life that family members experience. Each aspect of the quality of life has implications, direct or indirect, to children's career development. Examples of indirect yet powerful influences include the quality of nutrition and health. In the extreme but unfortunately not rare case in developing economies, poor nutrition and health result in child mortality. More generally, inadequate quantity or quality of child nutrition, poor health services, and lack of hygiene (poor access to water) contribute to child morbidity and negatively impact developmental outcomes and learning. Parents' work and career and the resultant quality-of-life features that act as direct influences on child career development include whether the child goes to school at all, the quality of school if the child does go to school, the quality of neighbourhood (e.g., opportunities for the constructive use of time), the types of peer and adult role models (e.g., exposure to deviant role models), and, in some instances, whether the child has a right to childhood or is forced into child labour.

Parents' type of work – that is, whether the parents are participating in the formal or informal economy and whether their work is temporary, sporadic, seasonal, or permanent – makes for glaring differences in the quality of life that children in developing economies experience, which translate as extreme differences in developmental opportunities and constraints. Moreover, absence of paid work in developing economies carries a heavier penalty and threatens basic survival, as there is no recourse to unemployment benefits.

It is also important to note that the quality of life which is made possible by the parents' work roles is not experienced in similar ways by all children in the family. Especially under conditions of a poor quality of life, it is the girl child who is likely to receive the worst care (e.g., poorer nutrition and health care, truncated education) and whose developmental outcomes are most at risk. Girl children are also more likely to have adult female role models in less powerful or disempowered roles both at home and in the parent's workplace (see UN, 2015).

A third relevant point is the work-life balance of parents. In particular, how do the parents' work roles enrich or impede their parenting? In families of poverty in developing economies, livelihood concerns can severely restrict adults in playing their parental roles. Parents may work long hours on all days of the week, or be out of the house in search of work, or be engaged in labour-intensive household work and may have little time or energy to engage in parenting.

In contrast, children who are from more privileged families in developing economies have multiple family role models who are successful in advantaged positions in the world-of-work, have many opportunities to listen to complex yet generally encouraging conversations about the work experiences of parents/ family members, may also have opportunities to visit the parents' workplace or observe and contribute in reasonable ways to home-based occupations, have parents who are more available as parents, and have access to educational experiences that help scaffold their preparedness for entry (later) into advantaged positions in the world-of-work. The quality of nutrition, health care, schooling, and neighbourhood ranges from adequate to high for these children as well. By and large, as they grow up they may consider the world-of-work as comprising challenges, which nonetheless are surmountable; have favourable notions of their own success; and be convinced that the assuredness of success rests on their own efforts and the support of family members/others. In other words, these children learn to believe in their own power and the power of those who care for them. In Bandura's (2001) language, they learn to be self-efficacious and to exercise both personal agency and proxy agency.

Children's premature work experiences: The phenomenon of child labour

In a developing economy, children's most proximal experiences of the world-of-work need not be through their parents' work and career; it can be their own work experiences. Because of destitution, children in developing economies may be forced into paid work. As child labour is illegal, children work in the most unregulated segments of the informal economy (e.g., as domestic workers) (ILO, 2013a). These premature work experiences may be off-putting, damage their health and development, occur at the cost of education, and curtail the quality of their work experiences and quality of life, even later when chronologically they turn into adults.

What qualifies as child labour? The ILO defines child labour as "work that deprives children of their childhood, their potential and their dignity, and that is harmful to physical and mental development" (ILO, 2004, p. 16). Child labour means children working in contravention of (a) ILO Convention No. 138 (along with ILO Recommendation No. 146), which specifies the minimum age for starting non-hazardous work/employment (14 years for developing countries) as well as for starting hazardous work (18 years for all countries) and light work (12–14 years for developing countries) and (b) ILO Convention No. 182 (along with ILO Recommendation No. 190), which specifies the worst forms of child labour (i.e., slavery, bonded labour, child soldiering, sexual exploitation, induction into drug trafficking, and other gravely abusive conditions) (ILO, 2002b; ILO, 2015). Child labour also constitutes a violation of Article 32 of the UN Convention on the Rights of the Child, which stipulates the right of the child (below 18 years) to be safeguarded from economic exploitation and from doing any work which is hazardous or could damage the child's health or harm the child's physical/cognitive/social/moral/spiritual development or hinder the child's education (UN, 1989). Child labour also interferes with several other child rights such as the child's right to education (Article 28) and the child's right to play and recreation, rest and leisure (Article 31).

A substantial number of children in developing countries are "trapped in child labour" (ILO, 2015, p. 1). The ILO Convention No. 138 (which raised the minimum age for work and employment) was adopted in 1973 with the aim of the total abolition of child labour. Noteworthy reductions in child labour notwithstanding, there continue to be 168 million children (5 to 17 years old) engaged in child labour worldwide, with 120 million being younger than 14 years (ILO, 2013b). Almost all of these working children are in developing countries, with the highest incidence in Sub-Saharan Africa where more than one in five children is engaged in child labour (ILO, 2013b). Moreover, the child labour estimates do not account for unpaid household work, and millions of additional children, particularly girls, spend inordinate amounts of time each day completing household chores and have age-inappropriate responsibilities such as surrogate parenting of younger siblings (UN, 2010).

Female children and youth have special vulnerabilities with regard to their right to education and protection from child labour; traditional roles for women, which include early marriage and disproportionately high domestic responsibilities, pull girl children out of school (ILO, 2015): "Girls are also particularly vulnerable to worst forms of child labour such as commercial sexual exploitation and to hidden forms of child labour in domestic work in third party households" (p. 2).

The Statistical Information and Monitoring Programme on Child Labour (SIMPOC) – part of ILO's International Programme on the Elimination of Child Labour (IPEC) – has conducted surveys in 12 developing countries (low-income economies such as Madagascar and Niger; lower-middle-income economies such as Indonesia, Yemen, and Bolivia; upper-middle-income economies such as Ecuador and Brazil) (ILO, 2015). There are three main conclusions that SIMPOC has drawn from these surveys for both female and male children: (a) young persons (15–24 years old) who worked as children have substantially poorer levels of educational attainment compared to other youth, (b) young persons who worked as children are less likely to obtain paid employment and more likely to become unpaid family workers than are other youth, and (c) in the lowest earnings quintile, the proportion of young persons who worked as children is considerably greater than that of other youth, indicating that child labour compromises securing decent work. Thus the ILO (2015) states that "prior involvement in child labour is associated with lower educational attainment and with jobs that fail to meet basic decent work criteria" (p. 15).

Child labour results in human rights violations across the lifespan. Child labour divests children of their childhood, their education, and their health (UNICEF, 2014); it hinders capacity building, preparedness, and eligibility for advantaged positions in the world-of-work (ILO, 2015). Instead, these child-adults grow up marginalised, and "intergenerational cycles of poverty" are strengthened rather than broken (UNICEF, 2014, p. 3).

Role of religious identity, ethnic identity, discrimination, and violence

Because of religious and/or ethnic identity, a child may be witness to and even subjected to discrimination, injustices, and, perhaps, violence, which can have a disruptive influence on developmental outcomes, including those relating to career and work. The child, as he or she grows up, may view the mainstream/ other culture(s) as hostile and reject the social integration that work represents. The older child may already lean towards considering the seemingly benign overtures made by gangs, terrorists, or other armed-conflict groups; at the very least, the child is at risk for developing an oppositional identity (see Bisin, Patacchini, Verdier, & Zenou, 2011; Ogbu & Simon, 1998) or becoming disaffected (see Bandura, 2001). High-quality relationships in the family, school, or neighbourhood become crucial in helping the child balance his/her views about the world and the integration of his/her own community in the larger world. When successful, the child is able to build a positive orientation towards future roles (including the worker role) and is thereby motivated to select and persevere on developmental paths that lead to socially integrative work opportunities. Although this description fits multiple contexts in the world (i.e., both developing and developed), prolonged armed conflict and related political instability are more likely to characterise developing countries (see World Bank, 2012).

Role of school

Literacy rates are far lower in developing than in developed economies (Huebler & Lu, 2013). Children's right to education is not guaranteed in developing economies, and in many families in poverty, formal education remains an option rather than a given. With governments pushing for school enrolment, children may be enrolled in schools, but they do not necessarily remain in school. First-generation school learners may not have attitudinal and academic support from the family. Discrimination against the girl child, illness, malnutrition, poor quality education and related experiences in schools, and competing tasks (such as extensive household chores) in the family or another workplace are other reasons which explain the high drop-out rates among underprivileged children, starting from primary school. Thus, "many children are registered in schools but fail to attend, participate but fail to learn, are enrolled for several years but fail to progress and drop out from school" (Sabates, Akyeampong, Westbrook, & Hunt, 2010, p. 3). Once a child from a family in poverty has dropped out, the child will work in age-inappropriate ways either at home or 'more formally' in the informal economy. Developmental sequelae of reduced educational attainment and child labour have already been noted earlier in this chapter.

Whereas children from privileged homes in developing countries are likely to persist in schools, one of the differences in school-related career development of these children versus children in developed countries is that career guidance and counselling in schools may be absent or of indeterminate or poor quality (e.g., Arulmani & Nag-Arulmani, 2005). Also, in some developing countries such as India and China, among the more privileged, parents and schools have very high expectations for children (Liu, McMahon, & Watson, 2014; Pew Global Attitudes Survey, 2011; Wike & Horowitz, 2006). Children experience academic pressure and are pushed towards a few high-prestige occupations (typically engineering or medicine), which escalates academic stress as the entry into the educational programmes for these professions is highly competitive. Though some children do succumb to academic pressure and take drastic steps such as attempting/committing suicide and others conform to parental and school standards, there are also children who negotiate and cope with the (unreasonable) excellence

Child career development in developing world contexts   123

standards along with exploring and pursuing educational and career options that personally interest them.

Role of play

The critical role of play in human development has been receiving increasing attention with scholars (e.g., Brown, 2009; Pelligrini & Bjorklund, 2004; Pelligrini, Dupuis, & Smith, 2007) identifying vital benefits of play. However, the role of play as a positive influence on career development has been neglected. Play offers opportunities for exploring one's interests, likes, and dislikes. Play allows children to extend their attention, concentration, and engagement for hours in an activity of their liking and choice. This is unlike the fragmented engagement in schoolwork which many children experience because of short teaching-learning periods in school and also the one-size-fits-all approach in education which does not attract every child's interest or wholehearted participation. Solitary and social play each provide valuable instances for learning and rehearsing intrapersonal (i.e., autonomy, initiative) and interpersonal (e.g., teamwork, turn-taking) skills, which are also important for success in the world-of-work. Play may invite more creative responses than a structured academic curriculum does and, possibly, in conjunction with formal education, provide the foundation for innovation and creativity later in the world-of-work.

In many developing economies, children may have reduced opportunities for play either because of involvement in paid/unpaid work or because of an immoderate focus on academics. Either way, optimal career development is undermined when children are forced into activities at the complete cost of play. When I have seen a child vendor in a suburban train in Mumbai, I have reflected that a child of that age could well engage in sociodramatic play and 'sell articles'. But what distinguishes the child vendor and a child playing is that the child vendor unremittingly plays the same role again and again, whereas a child in play, despite some repetitions, spontaneously switches from one role and one play activity to another. The flexibility that play affords is crucial for catalysing positive career developmental outcomes.

Conclusion

There are oft-cited criticisms in the Western career development literature which are particularly relevant to this chapter. One is that the period of childhood has received inadequate attention in Western career development theory, research, and practice (Schultheiss, 2008; Watson & McMahon, 2005). Second, "the influence of social class and poverty in career development continues to be understudied" (Juntunen, Ali, & Pietrantonio, 2013, p. 245). Third, far less is known about the career development of ethnically diverse groups, even within high-research-output countries such as the United States (see Fouad & Kantamneni, 2013). In fact, Fouad and Kantamneni state, "we are just beginning the process of fully understanding how culture affects career development" (p. 234). Moreover, the roles of the family, school, and community in child career development have been inadequately researched (Schultheiss, 2008). In a sense, child career development literature also has tended to be over-specific (focusing as it does almost exclusively on vocational interests/aspirations/expectations/preferences). Instead, as Schultheiss (2008) has pointed out, the field can benefit from theory and research in allied areas such as developmental psychology.

These criticisms constitute one set of reasons why theory and research from developed countries can only have partial utility in explaining child career development in developing countries. An even more valid set of reasons has to do with differences between the developing versus developed world contexts. My focus in this chapter has been on illustrating how child career development in developing economies differs markedly depending on whether the child's family is marginalised or well integrated. Literature from developed economies will best be applicable to children in developing economies whose families are well integrated, although cultural differences will still limit the applicability of such literature. Some concepts from the Western literature are also worthwhile with regard to addressing poverty and its impact on child career development such as social justice (e.g., Blustein, McWhirter, & Perry, 2005), the psychology of working (e.g., Blustein, Kenna, Gill, & DeVoy, 2008), socio-political development/ critical consciousness (Diemer & Blustein, 2006), work/vocational hope (e.g., Diemer & Blustein, 2007), and neighbourhood socioeconomic status (Diemer & Ali, 2009). At the same time, the main contribution of this chapter is in showing that Western literature, if extrapolated to developing world contexts, will not do sufficient justice to children's career development pathways in developing world contexts. There are differences in the character of poverty and its relationship to (general and specific) developmental outcomes in developing versus developed economies. Instead of paid work in *many* of the developing world contexts enabling social integration, it can result in social exclusion, and precocious paid work can suboptimise development generally and career development specifically in enduring ways.

Clearly, *both* child and adult career development in developing world contexts need even more urgent attention than they do in developed world contexts. In order to optimise child career development in developing countries, efforts must also be made to optimise adult career development. Parents' working lives, for the most part, enable those affordances which are facilitative of general and specific (e.g., career-related) developmental outcomes. It is time to be less insular in studying child and adult career development. It is also time to bridge the gaps between developing and developed world contexts.

References

Arulmani, G., & Nag-Arulmani, S. (2005). *Work awareness and responses to career choices: Indian regional survey (WORCC-IRS)*. Bangalore: The Promise Foundation.

Bandura, A. (2001). Social cognitive theory: An agentic perspective. *Annual Review of Psychology, 52*, 1–26.

Bisin, A., Patacchini, E., Verdier, T., & Zenou, Y. (2011). Formation and persistence of oppositional identities. *European Economic Review, 55,* 1046–1071.

Blustein, D. L., Chaves, A. P., Diemer, M. A., Gallagher, L. A., Marshall, K. G., Sirin, S., & Bhati, K. S. (2002). Voices of the forgotten half: The role of social class in the school-to-work transition. *Journal of Counseling Psychology, 49,* 311–323.

Blustein, D. L., Kenna, A. C., Gill, N., & DeVoy, J. E. (2008). The psychology of working: A new framework for counseling practice and public policy. *The Career Development Quarterly, 56,* 294–308.

Blustein, D. L., McWhirter, E. H., & Perry, J. C. (2005). An emancipatory communitarian approach to vocational development theory, research, and practice. *The Counseling Psychologist, 33,* 141–179.

Brown, S. L. (2009). Discovering the importance of play through personal histories and brain images: An interview with Stuart L. Brown. *American Journal of Play, 1,* 399–412.

Diemer, M. A., & Ali, S. R. (2009). Integrating social class into vocational psychology: Theory and practice implications. *Journal of Career Assessment, 17,* 247–265.

Diemer, M. A., & Blustein, D. L. (2006). Critical consciousness and career development among urban youth. *Journal of Vocational Behavior, 68,* 220–232.

Diemer, M. A., & Blustein, D. L. (2007). Vocational hope and vocational identity: Urban adolescents' career development. *Journal of Career Assessment, 15,* 98–118.

Elder, G. H., Jr., & Shanahan, M. J. (2006). The life course and human development. In W. Damon & R. M. Lerner (Series Eds.), and R. M. Lerner (Vol. Ed.), *Handbook of child psychology: Vol 1. Theoretical models of human development* (pp. 665–715). Hoboken, NJ: Wiley.

Erikson, E. H. (1968). *Identity: Youth and crisis.* New York, NY: W. W. Norton.

Fouad, N. A., & Kantamneni, N. (2013). The role of race and ethnicity in career choice, development, and adjustment. In S. D. Brown & R. W. Lent (Eds.), *Career development and counseling: Putting theory and research to work* (2nd ed., pp. 215–243). Hoboken, NJ: John Wiley & Sons.

Heppner, M. J., & Jung, A.-K. (2013). Gender and social class: Powerful predictors of a life journey. In W. B. Walsh, M. L. Savickas, & P. J. Hartung (Eds.), *Handbook of vocational psychology* (pp. 81–103). New York, NY: Routledge.

Holland, J. L. (1997). *Making vocational choices: A theory of vocational personalities and work environments* (3rd ed.). Odessa, FL: Psychological Assessment Resources.

Huebler, F., & Lu, W. (2013). *Adult and youth literacy: National, regional and global trends, 1985–2015* (UIS information paper). Montreal, Quebec: UNESCO Institute for Statistics.

ILO. (1999). *Report of the Director-General: Decent work.* International Labour Conference, 87th Session, Geneva.

ILO. (2002a). *Resolution concerning decent work and the informal economy.* The General Conference of the International Labour Organization, 90th Session, Geneva.

ILO. (2002b). *The international labour organization's fundamental conventions.* Geneva: ILO.

ILO. (2004). *Child labour: A textbook for university students*/International Labour Office. Geneva: ILO.

ILO. (2013a). *Ending child labour in domestic work and protecting young workers from abusive working conditions*/International Labour Office, International Programme on the Elimination of Child Labour (IPEC). Geneva: ILO.

ILO. (2013b). *Marking progress against child labour: Global estimates and trends 2000–2012*/International Labour Office, International Programme on the Elimination of Child Labour (IPEC). Geneva: ILO.

ILO. (2013c). *The informal economy and decent work: A policy resource guide, supporting transitions to formality*/International Labour Office, Employment Policy Department. Geneva: ILO.

ILO. (2015). *World report on child labour 2015: Paving the way to decent work for young people.* Geneva: ILO.

Juntunen, C. L., Ali, S. R., & Pietrantonio, K. R. (2013). Social class, poverty, and career development. In S. D. Brown & R. W. Lent (Eds.), *Career development and counseling: Putting theory and research to work* (2nd ed., pp. 245–274). Hoboken, NJ: Wiley.

Jütting, J. P., & de Laiglesia, J. R. (Eds.). (2009). *Is informal normal? Towards more and better jobs in developing countries.* Issy-les-Moulineaux, France: Development Centre of the Organisation for Economic Co-operation and Development.

Liu, J., McMahon, M., & Watson, M. (2014). Childhood career development in Mainland China: A research and practice agenda. *The Career Development Quarterly, 62,* 268–279.

Ogbu, J. U., & Simon, H. D. (1998). Voluntary and involuntary minorities: A cultural-ecological theory of school performance with some implications for education. *Anthropology & Education Quarterly, 29,* 155–188.

Pelligrini, A. D., & Bjorklund, D. F. (2004). The ontogeny and phylogeny of children's object and fantasy play. *Human Nature, 15,* 23–43.

Pelligrini, A. D., Dupuis, D., & Smith, P. K. (2007). Play in evolution and development. *Developmental Review, 27,* 261–276.

Pew Global Attitudes Survey. (2011). Americans want more pressure on students, the Chinese want less: The parenting gap – U.S. versus China. Survey report. *Pew Research Center Q86.* Retrieved from http://www.pewglobal.org/2011/08/23/americans-want-more-pressure-on-students-the-chinese-want-less/

Population Reference Bureau. (2011). Retrieved from http://www.prb.org/pdf11/2011 population-data-sheet_eng.pdf.

Sabates, R., Akyeampong, K., Westbrook, J., & Hunt, F. (2010). School drop out: Patterns, causes, changes and policies. *Paper commissioned for the EFA global monitoring report 2011, the hidden crisis: Armed conflict and education.* Paris, France: UNESCO.

Savickas, M. L. (2013). Career construction theory and practice. In S. D. Brown & R. W. Lent (Eds.), *Career development and counseling: Putting theory and research to work* (2nd ed., pp. 147–183). Hoboken, NJ: John Wiley & Sons.

Schultheiss, D. E. P. (2008). Current status and future agenda for the theory, research, and practice of childhood career development. *The Career Development Quarterly, 57,* 7–24.

UN. (1989). Convention on the rights of the child. *United Nations Treaty Series, 1577,* 3.

UN. (2010). *The world's women 2010: Trends and statistics.* New York, NY: United Nations.

UN. (2015). *The millennium development goals report 2015.* New York, NY: United Nations.

UNICEF. (2014). *Child labour and UNICEF in action: Children at the centre.* New York, NY: UNICEF.

Watson, M., & McMahon, M. (2005). Children's career development: A research review from a learning perspective. *Journal of Vocational Behavior, 67,* 119–132.

Wike, R., & Horowitz, J. M. (2006). Parental pressure on students. *Pew Research Centre: Global attitudes and trends.* Retrieved from http://www.pewglobal.org/2006/08/24/parental-pressure-on-students/

World Bank. (2012). *FAQs – About development.* Retrieved from http://web.worldbank.org/WBSITE/EXTERNAL/EXTSITETOOLS/0,contentMDK:20147486~menuPK:344190~pagePK:98400~piPK:98424~theSitePK:95474,00.html

Part 4

Assessment perspectives

Chapter 11

Career assessment of children

Terence J. G. Tracey and Sandro M. Sodano

The focus in this chapter is on the assessment of children (i.e., those between the ages of 7 and 14). Obviously, any model of children's development requires quality measures to enable valid examination. However, assessment of children involves different issues than are salient to the assessment of adolescents and adults. A goal of this chapter is to present an explication of the unique characteristics associated with valid assessment of children. Given the career development context of this book, we will focus specifically on the assessment of interests, self-efficacy, general aspects of career development, and personality traits as these are the most salient. These all play central roles in the career development literature, and our focus is on their assessment so as to inform our theories of career development. The issues involved in each, as well as representative measures, will be presented.

Assessing children

Assessing psychological constructs in children is a difficult task. It cannot involve simply administering an instrument to children that is designed and validated on adolescents and adults. Even if such instruments are adapted in a manner so as to make the items more age appropriate, this does not mean that children understand the item in the same manner as adults or that the response will be indicative of the same underlying construct. Indeed the problem of asking children to respond to self-report items has led many researchers to abandon such assessments and move toward using informed others such as parents and teachers to rate children's behaviour (De Los Reyes *et al.*, 2015). Such observer ratings of behaviour are common in the assessment of children and often yield much more valid and reliable information than those obtained from the children themselves (Brinthaupt & Erwin, 1992). Much of these results are due to the difficulty children have with self-report inventories, which require the child to read and understand the item, search memory for instances, and then form aggregate evaluations culminating in a response to the questionnaire. This is a difficult process involving many abstract skills that are less developed in children.

The use of knowledgeable observers is common in ratings of personality (e.g., Tackett, Kushner, DeFruyt, & Mervielde, 2013) and distress (e.g., Achenbach, 2001; De Los Reyes *et al.*, 2015) where outward behaviours are telling, and the adults can perform the requisite abstractions to yield valid ratings. However, there are some constructs that do not lend themselves to this observer rating format. One is self-esteem, or more specifically self-efficacy (assessments of one's value or competence generally or in specific domains). These are constructs that are less observable in behaviour and only the individual is most knowledgeable. Hence self-report is the most appropriate means of assessing such internal constructs. The same issue applies to interests. While parents may be able to make inferences about what a child likes or dislikes based on behaviour, there is little knowledge of the internal construct from the child's view, and also parents' inferences can be coloured by what the parent likes or desires. Further, adults make evaluations using their own models and ideas, which may not correspond highly to those used by children. It is our assumption that the child is the best judge of what he or she likes and dislikes and thus interest measures should be self-report. However, this recommendation raises many issues salient to the use of self-ratings with children.

Children cannot be assumed to respond to items in the same manner as adults, so merely adapting measures to children is often difficult and tends to result in poor assessment. De Leeuw (2005, 2012) has made many recommendations regarding the design of self-report instruments with children. Any self-report is difficult for those under seven years old given the cognitive requirements involved in such responding. However, for children aged 7 to 14, there are several principles that enhance the reliability and validity of self-ratings. The language needs to be simple and concrete such as simple declarative sentences. Conjunctions (e.g., this and that; this or that), and negations (e.g., "I am not interested in dolls") should be avoided. In addition, children are good at reporting current functioning, but are less accurate with respect to the past or future. Questions asking about what they have done in the past week or what they expect to do in the future are thus to be avoided. The content of the instrument needs to be familiar to the child so that an evaluation can be made. Asking children to evaluate something that is abstract or outside of their everyday experience is likely to yield less valid responses. Finally, children differ in their reading levels. Those with higher reading comprehension skills will readily grasp content, while those with lower skills may not. With younger children especially, but also with older children who have less-developed reading skills, it is appropriate to read the instrument (including instructions) to the children so they understand the content, thus enabling them to respond to the item. So reliable and valid self-reports from children are possible, but care must be taken in the design and implementation of any assessments. Although the issues described here may be obvious, they are often overlooked during the development of assessments for children. We now focus on three areas that are especially salient to career development in children: interests, self-efficacy, and personality, with respect to how these issues manifest.

Children's interests

While a good deal is known about the structure of interests, their assessment, and their relation to many important constructs, such as productivity and satisfaction, almost all of this pertains to adolescents and adults (e.g., Rounds & Su, 2014). Very little is known about interests and their development in children (Tracey, 2001). How do interests develop? The most prominent model of interests is that of John Holland (1997) whose theory did not address the development of interests. There are several career theories that expressly include the development of interests (Gottfredson, 1981, 2002; Super, 1990), but the research supporting development from the perspective of these theories is modest at best. Overall, little is known about the development of interests (Hartung, Porfeli, & Vondracek, 2005; Watson & McMahon, 2005). One potential reason for this dearth of research on the development of interests in children is the lack of measures or the use of measures that do not adequately represent the broad range of interests.

Interests are defined in several ways, but the most common is a summary of the likes and dislikes of an individual and these are viewed as being dispositional in nature and serve a motivating function (Savickas, 1999). While there is evidence of a genetic basis of interests in adults (Lykken, Bouchard, McGue, & Tellegen, 1993), there is also evidence that interests are relatively gross and labile during childhood and become much more stable in rank-order stability (Low, Yoon, Roberts, & Rounds, 2005), profile stability (Swanson, 1999), and structural stability (Darcy & Tracey, 2007; Tracey & Rounds, 1993) from the ages of 14 to young adulthood where they plateau.

The research on interests in children generally uses one of two assessment models: aspiration and narrow-band scales. Tracey and Sodano (2014) expressed concern over the use of aspiration measures where children are asked what they wish to be when they grow up. Such assessments reflect mostly familiarity and very primitive occupational knowledge (Rohlfing, Nota, Ferrari, Soresi, & Tracey, 2012). Applying these ratings of occupations as a representation of interest type is dubious. Further, narrow-interest scales (such as interest in mathematics), while focused, only take into account a narrow band of interests, omitting other interest areas that could be more important to the individual. Moreover, drawing conclusions about interest development in children based on such narrow-band assessment assumes that all interests develop in the same manner. Such an assumption is very tenuous. In addition, narrow-band scales confound narrow interests with a general endorsement style (Tracey, 2012). The most appropriate means of assessing interests and for learning how interests develop is to use broad-based interest scales that encompass the entire domain of interests salient to children. However, few such measures exist.

One measure is the Inventory of Children's Activities (ICA; Tracey, 2002; Tracey & Ward, 1998), which is designed to represent Holland's (1997) interest types (Realistic, Investigative, Artistic, Social, Enterprising, and Conventional, collectively referred to as RIASEC). This scale was developed to embody the principles outlined earlier. The content consists of concrete, common everyday activities to which children endorse the extent of their liking and perceived competence (i.e., "how good are you at"). Usage of this instrument with children and adolescents has demonstrated that it has structural validity in that it fits the hexagonal structure and does so increasingly with age (Tracey & Ward, 1998). It can be used with children to assist them in understanding themselves as well as in academic planning.

One of the findings yielded using this measure (Tracey, 2002; Tracey & Ward, 1998) is that children have increasing levels of interests and competence perceptions as they age up to the entry into middle school (typically aged 12–13), where the interest level and competence perceptions uniformly drop in level. Children moving into middle school show a dramatic worsening shift in their perceptions of themselves in terms of what they like and what they are good at. In addition, this drop is the most extreme for girls in Investigative areas. For all children, these declines slowly improve in level over time, but they do not return to the high levels endorsed prior to middle school. Middle school is thus a key time in the development of interests. The data show that the drop in interests could have long-lasting effects, especially for girls since Investigative interests continue to stay much lower for girls in subsequent grade levels relative to boys (Tracey, Robbins, & Hofsess, 2005). Interest tests are helpful in representing how children view their equivalent of work, but also as a means of structuring their decisions. If a child sees that his or her interests are low in certain areas, the child may then avoid such activities.

A key issue in the assessment of interests generally and especially in children are the large differences that exist in the People (Social) versus Things (Realistic) dimension of interests. One of the largest differences between men and women in all psychological measures is on this People-Things interest dimension (Lippa, 1998; Su, Rounds, & Armstrong, 2009). Similar differences exist among children (Tracey, 2002; Tracey & Ward, 1998). Tracey (2002) found that the differences in People-Things interests became exacerbated during the transition into middle school. Given that this is a key time when future plans start becoming established and school curricula are selected, such differences can have dramatic effects. With regard to academic planning, this could mean that a child with relatively low Investigative scores may eschew mathematics and science courses. Avoiding math and science courses early dooms any student to a much narrower set of career options given the salience of this content to many majors and occupations. So a key issue in interest assessment is to adequately measure children's interests, but also to help them use such information in appropriate academic planning.

With regard to interest development, an important issue is to assist children in keeping options open and not reinforcing what may be a premature foreclosure of certain areas. This foreclosure is especially salient with girls. Given this, the ICA was revised (ICA-3, Tracey & Caulum, 2015) such that common gender differences on Realistic and Investigative versus Social are minimised. The instrument is still equally valid with respect to representing the hexagonal structure of interests, but it is designed to minimise gender mean differences in interests, especially for the middle school age group. This minimisation of gender mean differences as a means of preventing premature narrowing of options is crucial with children, though it may be less salient with older students. Clearly more needs to be known about interests in children, and there are very few measures that are valid and appropriate for use.

Self-esteem and self-efficacy

Another area where self-ratings are necessary is that of self-esteem/self-concept. Self-esteem and self-concept are overlapping, but also somewhat separate constructs; both generally refer to a broad positive sense of self and are viewed as important aspects of functioning (e.g., Harter, 1990). The child is really the only person who is able to rate these constructs, as they are internal to the individual. However, obtaining quality self-ratings is still paramount. Several measures exist with respect to the evaluation of self-esteem/self-concept (see Butler & Gasson, 2005 for a review of issues and different assessment instruments). For our purposes here, we will focus on self-efficacy, which is a much more specific measure of self-concept, as it relates specifically to the assessment of one's ability to successfully perform very specific behaviours (Bandura, 1977, 1982). As such, it is far more specific than generalised indicators such as self-esteem and self-concept. Given the prominence of self-efficacy to models of career development (e.g., Social Cognitive Career Theory [SCCT], Lent, Brown, & Hackett, 1994, 2000), we will focus on the assessment of self-efficacy in this chapter.

The literature has demonstrated that self-efficacy assessment has the same circular structure as interests in adults and thus can be examined in a similar manner (Armstrong & Vogel, 2009; Tracey, 1997, 2002). Indeed it is common for both interests and self-efficacy assessment to be used together, as each offers a unique prediction of career outcomes in adolescents and adults (Betz & Rottinghaus, 2006; Donnay & Borgen, 1999; Flores, Spanierman, Armstrong, & Velez, 2006; Tracey, 2010; Tracey & Hopkins, 2001). This equivalence of structure also has been found in children (Tracey, 2002; Tracey & Ward, 1998). This means that RIASEC scales can be developed that are comparable to interest scales, and they can be used in tandem. While interest scores and self-efficacy scores covary highly (Tracey, 1997, 2002), there can still be differences which may be very salient in individual cases (e.g., where an individual very much likes an area but feels inadequate in that domain).

The ICA (Tracey & Caulum, 2015; Tracey & Ward, 1998) is an instrument that assesses both interests and self-efficacy. It thus provides a vehicle for the examination of the different constructs that can prove useful in research (e.g., the relative extent to which interests and self-efficacy predict key career outcomes such as course enrollment or performance), but also in practice where instances of lack of agreement between interests and self-efficacy can serve as key interventions (Betz, 1999; Tracey, 2010).

Examinations of the structure of RIASEC-based self-efficacy assessments with children and adolescents also demonstrate that there is a strong general factor (ACT, 1995; Tracey & Ward, 1998) which represents an endorsement of all the items in the same manner. Some children highly endorse all the items regardless of content and others respond with lower ratings to all. This general factor of undifferentiated responding is generally higher in children and tends to go down in magnitude with older samples. The meaning of this general factor in interests is evolving (see Tracey, 2012 for a discussion), but with respect to self-efficacy, the general factor was related to perceived difficulty with higher scores associated with perceptions of tasks being more difficult. Children who had high general-factor self-efficacy scores saw themselves as being able to succeed with more difficult tasks. In this sense, the general factor (i.e., the mean of all self-efficacy items) represents a more general assessment of competence that is more akin to self-esteem. So the assessment of a broad range of activities as in the ICA enables researchers and practitioners to assess specific interest and competence with respect to RIASEC types, but also to gain a broad indication of general self-esteem.

Aspects of career development

There are several theories of career development in children (e.g., Ginzberg, Ginsburg, Axelrad, & Herma, 1951; Gottfredson, 2002; Super, 1990); however, there is an absence of focused research on the validity of these theories in part attributable to an absence of quality instruments (Stead & Schultheiss, 2003; Stead, Watson, Gallant, & Sauls, 2001). A promising theory of childhood career development is that of Super (1990), where he proposed nine dimensions that are especially salient: curiosity, exploration, information, key figures, interests, locus of control, time perspective, self-concept, and planfulness. Stead *et al.* (2001) developed the Occupational Awareness Inventory (OAI) as an assessment of these dimensions of Super; however, they found that the measure did not represent the theorised model. As noted earlier, one of the potential reasons for this lack of support is the inappropriate content of the items with respect to children. The items were all based on occupational and work environments, and as a result, it is highly likely that children cannot respond given their lack of familiarity. A subsequent measure of Super's dimensions undertaken by Schultheiss and Stead (2004) took care to develop items that were representative of children's experience such that valid responses could be obtained. Their instrument, the Childhood Career Development Scale (CCDS), consisted of 48 items and, in principal component analysis of two samples of US children aged 8–13 was found to represent eight of the nine dimensions posited by Super: curiosity, exploration, information, key figures, locus of control, time perspective, self-concept, and planning. The interest dimension was not supported in the measure, but interest is a multidimensional construct as noted earlier and there are already valid scales available. The CCDS thus appears to have initial evidence of structural validity.

A subsequent study of the CCDS by Stead and Schultheiss (2010) provided an indication of the construct validity of the scales. They administered the CCDS to South African children aged 8–14 along with several scales that would demonstrate convergent validity (i.e., industry, locus of control, and self-esteem). They found good support for the structural validity of the eight scales using confirmatory factor analysis as well as the individual subscales being related to industry, locus of control, and self-esteem as hypothesised. These results support the overall validity of the CCDS with both United States and South African children. Future researchers should now use this instrument to explore how these dimensions develop and change over time. A key issue that does need to be answered in this process is does the structure itself change over time? As demonstrated with interests (Tracey & Ward, 1998), the invariance of any structure over time cannot be assumed. Younger children respond in a more concrete manner than older children, and this could be manifest in how the instrument operates at a structural level across different age groups. So the invariance of the CCDS over the key childhood years of 7–14 needs to be examined before it can really be applied in a longitudinal manner. Similarly, there is no examination of structural invariance across gender, which is needed before one can compare means. So the CCDS is a very promising measure that has undergone careful development, but it still requires some more research with respect to structure prior to extensive use.

Personality dispositions

In this section, we will focus on two prominent models of general and interpersonal personality dispositions as they are assessed in childhood. The Big Five or Five-Factor Model (FFM) (Digman, 1990) is the dominant model of general personality dispositions or traits. Often used interchangeably, the Big Five and the FFM refer to the same five broad dimensions of personality. The labels for the five dimensions can vary in the literature, but those most commonly employed are Extraversion, Agreeableness, Conscientiousness, Neuroticism, and Openness, which we will utilise here. Interpersonal dispositions, also known as interpersonal styles, are related to general personality dispositions. According to Interpersonal Theory (Sullivan, 1953), personality is viewed as developing and being constituted within interpersonal interactions, beginning with caregivers and significant others and continuing through adulthood as a characteristic style of relating to others. The Interpersonal Circumplex (IPC; Wiggins, 1982, 1995) is the prominent model of interpersonal personality, hailing from a strong theoretical and empirical tradition (Leary, 1957; Sullivan, 1953; Wiggins, 1982, 1995). The two main interpersonal dimensions are Dominance and Affiliation, which run from dominance to submission and warm to cold, respectively. These two dimensions are perpendicular to each other and together they anchor eight interpersonal dispositions represented as octants arranged in a circular pattern. The IPC encompasses extraversion and agreeableness as blends of the Dominance and Affiliation dimensions, so the IPC is complementary to the FFM (McCrae & Costa, 1989). From the perspective of the IPC, Extraversion is a blend of warmth and dominance (i.e., friendly dominance), while Agreeableness is a blend of warmth and submission (i.e., warm unassuming).

Assessing children's personality can promote understanding of their developing selves, thereby aiding their academic, career, and social development. Personality is applicable to day-to-day living, whether taking place in academic, work, or home environments and beyond. In adolescence and young adulthood, the work environment becomes increasingly salient, eventually replacing the academic one. Thus the application of personality assessment data to foster self-understanding while viewing the academic environment as a precursor to the work environment aligns with fundamental notions of promoting understanding of self and of the world of work from the Person-Environment fit tradition (Parsons, 1909). Further, it is advantageous to have a common model for assessing personality from childhood through adulthood because it facilitates understanding across developmental periods. The FFM and the IPC thus provide a common language and models for describing personality applicable across settings and development.

Recent meta-analyses have shown that, beyond cognitive ability, the FFM dimensions are the most robust predictors of academic performance in childhood and adolescence (Poropat, 2009, 2014). The FFM is similarly important for predicting work performance in adults (Barrick, Mount, & Judge, 2001). However, it is important to consider who is doing the ratings, especially for children. Although there is moderate agreement generally found between child and adult raters, the magnitude of predictor-criterion relations can vary by rater. For instance, parent and teacher ratings exhibited stronger associations between Conscientious and Openness and academic performance relative to children's own ratings. A marked difference was that Agreeableness was associated with academic success when children rated themselves, but not when parents or teachers did the rating (Poropat, 2014). Apparently, adult raters did not view Agreeableness as relevant to children's grades, but since it is relevant from the viewpoint of children, it is important to be mindful of this with their self-reported assessment data. Of course, personality is also relevant more broadly than academic performance, defined as grade point average in studies that were considered in the aforementioned meta-analysis. For example, the sociability associated with Extraversion may contribute to success in other contexts, but could help or hinder a child in academic contexts. Our position with respect to who should rate children's personality dispositions is consistent with previous sections of this chapter. As such, we believe that children – age 7 to 14 – are the best raters for assessing their own personality dispositions, so long as the assessments are designed specifically for children following the guidelines that were described earlier.

Early studies of the FFM in children generally yielded the five dimensions by adapting measures originally developed for adults based on teacher or parent ratings. Key earlier studies utilised existing Big Five assessments composed of trait descriptive adjectives plus classroom behaviours rated by teachers (Digman, 1990; Digman & Inouye, 1986; Digman & Takemoto-Chock, 1981). Researchers also focused on adapting other personality measures to specifically assess the FFM by parents' ratings (e.g., John, Caspi, Robins, Moffitt, & Stouthamer-Loeber, 1994). Exploring parents' free descriptions of their children also yielded descriptors of the FFM (e.g., Halverson et al., 2003). When employing self-ratings of children's personality, this was often approached by making minor modifications to established adult assessments of the FFM (e.g., Markey, Markey, Tinsley, & Ericksen, 2002). As an example, researchers might discard items from established scales if they observed children not understanding them. Alternatively, researchers and clinicians might answer questions about items when children had difficulty understanding them. Overall, there was little systematic attention paid to finding equivalent language for child self-rated personality assessments and a conceptually equivalent model of personality between children and adults. However, despite the different paths taken to assess the main dimensions of personality in children (e.g., different raters and instruments), along with a variety of measurement issues encountered, the level of convergence in five basic dimensions of children's personality has been described as remarkable (Tackett et al., 2013). Recent calls have been made for increasing the focus on child-specific personality assessments to further investigate instruments that may yield common higher-order dimensions, such as those of the FFM from the perspective of children (Poropat, 2014; Tackett et al., 2013). We agree with these calls and offer the following example for developing a self-report measure of interpersonal personality dispositions designed specifically for children.

Development of the CAIS

Noting the lack of interpersonal personality measures for children, Sodano and Tracey (2006) developed the Child and Adolescent Interpersonal Survey (CAIS) to be a self-report measure of the IPC designed explicitly for children. Specifically, the researchers focused on addressing language differences and establishing a common model between adult and child interpersonal personality assessment by self-report. The presence of the IPC model had been supported in children through parent ratings (Markey et al., 2005), while self-rating of similarity to a prototype yielded the interpersonal dimensions increasingly in first to third grade children (Broughton, Boyes, & Mitchell, 1993). Previous research also made it clear that children's own ratings could be employed to assess global personality dispositions and that the items should consist of simple and concrete statements. To gain access to the language of children,

Sodano and Tracey (2006) employed popular cartoon characters representing corresponding types on the IPC as the stimulus for initial item generation with third and fourth-grade children. This process relied on children's own words to yield interpersonal descriptions in a language that was appropriate to their own reading levels. Initial items were then piloted on another sample of children for refinement. The process included interviewing each child for task difficulty and any words not understood. Consultation with teachers also informed the design of the survey. This approach to item development yielded simple, concrete statements representing global interpersonal dispositions from the perspective of children.

Development of the CAIS also focused on establishing equivalency in its representation of the IPC between boys and girls, children, adolescents, and young adults. The structure of the CAIS octant scales were shown to have a good fit to the circular order model in fourth and sixth grades and in college students (Sodano, 2011; Sodano & Tracey, 2006). Specifically, the structure was shown to be invariant between boys and girls and the child and young adult samples, thus supporting the similar meaning of the CAIS scores across gender and developmental periods. As would be expected, the CAIS Extraversion and Agreeableness octant scales converged with their counterparts in a measure of the FFM with children (Sodano & Tracey, 2006). Furthermore, the CAIS octant scales converged with those of a well-established measure of the IPC for adults – the Interpersonal Adjectives Scale (Wiggins, 1995) – in a sample of college students (Sodano & Tracey, 2006).

Research has supported applications of the CAIS to career development, highlighting the importance of considering children's own perceptions when using personality as well as career assessments. An examination of the interpersonal aspects of specific RIASEC interests showed that middle school children have similar interpersonal perceptions of Realistic, Investigative, and Social interests as adults, but differ from adults in their perceptions of Artistic, Enterprising, and Conventional interests (Sodano, 2011). In addition, academic achievement self-efficacy was found to align more with the Affiliation dimension in a sample of fifth- and sixth-grade students (Sodano, Vosbourgh, Bervoets, & Lander, 2011) – a finding that is less likely to be observed in later years. Furthermore, general competency scores of the ICA-R were associated with the Dominance dimension, not Affiliation, in samples of third- through sixth-grade Italian children (Sodano, Soresi, Nota, & Ferrari, in preparation). This link between general competency estimates (as being akin to self-esteem) and the Dominance dimension is consistent with Interpersonal Theory (Sullivan, 1953). In summary, the findings presented here further underscore the importance of considering children's own views in the assessment of their personalities beyond their interests and self-efficacy. Accordingly, the CAIS has been utilised to promote awareness of middle school children's own interpersonal styles as part of career development activities, which often include exploration of interests and perceived competencies with the ICA assessments.

Conclusion

It is increasingly recognised that many important career and life decisions are being formed earlier than previously thought. Furthermore, it is increasingly important to better understand and assess children in their development as it pertains to academic and vocational choices. Such research can then provide information for appropriate intervention. However, the field currently does not have the research base to enable this set of valid interventions. We propose that an important reason for this lack of research is that there are few measures that are appropriate for valid use with children. We have reviewed the issues that are important in the development of assessments of children using self-ratings. Many of these are obvious, but still rarely implemented. Further, we then presented exemplar assessments in interest, self-efficacy, and personality that are specifically designed for valid use with children. Many of the issues these assessments were designed to address in their development and validation were summarised. We encourage researchers to use these instruments and/or others like them that approach assessment of children as being different from the assessment of adolescents and adults.

References

Achenbach, T. M. (2001). *Child behavior checklist for ages 6–18*. Burlington, VT: University of Vermont, Department of Psychiatry.

ACT. (1995). *UNIACT technical manual*. Iowa City, IA: Act.

Armstrong, P. I., & Vogel, D. L. (2009). Interpreting the interest–efficacy association from a RIASEC perspective. *Journal of Counseling Psychology, 56*, 392–407.

Bandura, A. (1977). Self-efficacy theory: Toward a unifying theory of behavioral change. *Psychological Review, 84*, 191–215.

Bandura, A. (1982). Self-efficacy mechanism in human agency. *American Psychologist, 37*, 122–147.

Barrick, M. R., Mount, M. K., & Judge, T. A. (2001). Personality and performance at the beginning of the new millennium: What do we know and where do we go next. *International Journal of Selection and Assessment, 9*, 9–30.

Betz, N. E. (1999). Getting clients to act on their interests: Self-efficacy as a mediator of the implementation of vocational interests. In M. L. Savickas & A. R. Spokane (Eds.), *Vocational interests: Meaning, measurement, and counseling use* (pp. 327–344). Palo Alto, CA: Davies-Black Publishing.

Betz, N. E., & Rottinghaus, P. J. (2006). Current research on parallel measures of interests and confidence for basic dimensions of vocational activity. *Journal of Career Assessment, 14*, 56–76.

Brinthaupt, J., & Erwin, J. (1992). *The self: Definitional and methodological issues: SUNY series, studying the self*. Buffalo, NY: University of New York at Buffalo Press.

Broughton, R., Boyes, M. C., & Mitchell, J. (1993). Distance from the prototype (DISPRO) personality assessment for children. *Journal of Personality Assessment, 60*, 32–47.

Butler, R. J., & Gasson, S. L. (2005). Self-esteem/self-concept scales for children and adolescents: A review. *Child and Adolescent Mental Health, 10*, 190–201.

Darcy, M. U. A., & Tracey, T. J. G. (2007). Circumplex structure of Holland's RIASEC interests across gender and time. *Journal of Counseling Psychology, 54*, 17–31.

De Leeuw, E. D. (2005). Surveying children. In S. J. Best & B. Radcliff (Eds.), *Polling America: An encyclopedia of public opinion* (pp. 831–835). Westport, CT: Greenwood Press.

De Leeuw, E. D. (2012, May). *Improving data quality when surveying children and adolescents: Cognitive and social development and its role in questionnaire construction and pretesting.* Paper presented at the Annual Meeting of the Advisory Scientific Board of Statistics, Sweden.

De Los Reyes, A., Augenstein, T. M., Wang, M., Thomas, S. A., Drabick, D. A. G., Burgers, D. E., & Rabinowitz, J. (2015). The validity of the multi-informant approach to assessing child and adolescent mental health. *Psychological Bulletin, 141,* 858–900.

Digman, J. M. (1990). Personality structure: Emergence of the five-factor model. *Annual Review of Psychology, 41,* 417–440.

Digman, J. M., & Inouye, J. (1986). Further specification of the five robust factors of personality. *Journal of Personality and Social Psychology, 50,* 116–123.

Digman, J. M., & Takemoto-Chock, K. (1981). Factors in the natural language of personality: Re-analysis, comparison, and interpretation of six major studies. *Multivariate Behavioral Research, 16,* 149–170.

Donnay, D. A. C., & Borgen, F. H. (1999). The incremental validity of vocational self-efficacy: An examination of interest, self-efficacy, and occupation. *Journal of Counseling Psychology, 46,* 432–447.

Flores, L. Y., Spanierman, L. B., Armstrong, P. I., & Velez, A. D. (2006). Validity of the Strong Interest Inventory and Skills Confidence Inventory with Mexican American high school students. *Journal of Career Assessment, 14,* 183–202.

Ginzberg, E., Ginsburg, S. W., Axelrad, S., & Herma, J. L. (1951). *Occupational choice: An approach to a general theory.* New York, NY: Columbia University Press.

Gottfredson, L. S. (1981). Circumscription and compromise: A developmental theory of occupational aspirations [Monograph]. *Journal of Counseling Psychology, 28,* 545–579.

Gottfredson, L. S. (2002). Gottfredson's theory of circumscription, compromise, and self-creation. In D. Brown & Associates (Eds.), *Career choice and development* (4th ed., pp. 85–148). San Francisco, CA: Jossey-Bass.

Halverson, C. F., Havill, V. L., Deal, J., Baker, S. R., Victor, J. B., Pavlopoulos, V., & Wen, L. (2003). Personality structure as derived from parental ratings of free descriptions of children: The Inventory of Child Individual Differences. *Journal of Personality, 71,* 995–1026.

Harter, S. (1990). Issues in the assessment of self-concept of children and adolescents. In A. M. LaGreca (Ed.), *Through the eyes of the child* (pp. 292–325). Needham Heights, MA: Simon and Schuster.

Hartung, P. J., Porfeli, E. J., & Vondracek, F. W. (2005). Child vocational development: A review and reconsideration. *Journal of Vocational Behavior, 66,* 385–419.

Holland, J. L. (1997). *Making vocational choices: A theory of vocational personalities and work environments* (3rd ed.). Odessa, FL: Psychological Assessment Resources.

John, O. P., Caspi, A., Robins, R. W., Moffitt, T. E., & Stouthamer-Loeber, M. (1994). The "little five": Exploring the nomological network of the five-factor model of personality in adolescent boys. *Child Development, 65,* 160–178.

Leary, T. (1957). *Interpersonal diagnosis of personality.* New York, NY: Ronald Press.

Lent, R., Brown, S., & Hackett, G. (1994). Toward a unifying social cognitive theory of career and academic interest, choice, and performance. *Journal of Vocational Behavior, 45,* 79–122.

Lent, R. W., Brown, S. D., & Hackett, G. (2000). Contextual supports and barriers to career choice: A social cognitive analysis. *Journal of Counseling Psychology, 47,* 36–49.

Lippa, R. (1998). Gender-related individual differences and the structure of vocational interests: The importance of the people–things dimension. *Journal of Personality and Social Psychology, 74*, 996–1009.

Low, K. S. D., Yoon, M., Roberts, B. W., & Rounds, J. (2005). The stability of vocational interests from early adolescence to middle adulthood: A quantitative review of longitudinal studies. *Psychological Bulletin, 131*, 713–737.

Lykken, D. T., Bouchard, T. J., Jr., McGue, M., & Tellegen, A. (1993). Heritability of interests: A twin study. *Journal of Applied Psychology, 78*, 649–661.

Markey, P. M., Markey, C. N., & Tinsley, B. J. (2005). Applying the interpersonal circumplex to children's behavior: Parent-child interactions and risk behaviors. *Personality and Social Psychology Bulletin, 31*, 549–559.

Markey, P. M., Markey, C. N., Tinsley, B. J., & Ericksen, A. J. (2002). A preliminary validation of preadolescents' self-reports using the Five-Factor model of personality. *Journal of Research in Personality, 36*, 173–181.

McCrae, R. R., & Costa, P. T. (1989). Rotation to maximize the construct validity of factors in the NEO Personality Inventory. *Multivariate Behavioral Research, 24*, 107–124.

Parsons, F. (1909). *Choosing a vocation*. Boston: Houghton Mifflin.

Poropat, A. E. (2009). A meta-analysis of the five-factor model of personality and academic performance. *Psychological Bulletin, 135*, 322–338.

Poropat, A. E. (2014). A meta-analysis of adult-rated child personality and academic performance in primary education. *British Journal of Educational Psychology, 84*, 239–252.

Rohlfing, J. E., Nota, L., Ferrari, L., Soresi, S., & Tracey, T. J. G. (2012). Relation of occupational knowledge to career interests and competence perceptions in Italian children. *Journal of Vocational Behavior, 81*, 330–337.

Rounds, J., & Su, R. (2014). The nature and power of interests. *Current Directions in Psychological Science, 23*, 98–105.

Savickas, M. L. (1999). The psychology of interests. In M. L. Savickas & A. R. Spokane (Eds.), *Vocational interests: Meaning, measurement, and counseling use* (pp. 19–56). Palo Alto, CA: Black-Davies.

Schultheiss, D., & Stead, G. B. (2004). Childhood career development scale: Scale construction and psychometric properties. *Journal of Career Assessment, 12*, 113–134.

Sodano, S. M. (2011). Integrating vocational interests, competencies, and interpersonal dispositions in middle school children. *Journal of Vocational Behavior, 79*, 110–120.

Sodano, S. M., Soresi, S., Nota, L., & Ferrari, L. (2014, June). *Interpersonal dispositions, vocational interests, and competency perceptions in Italian children*. Paper presented at the annual meeting of the Society for Interpersonal Theory and Research, New Haven, CT.

Sodano, S. M., & Tracey, T. J. G. (2006). Interpersonal traits in childhood and adolescence: Development of the child and adolescent interpersonal survey. *Journal of Personality Assessment, 87*, 317–329.

Sodano, S. M., Vosbourgh, E. D., Bervoets, D., & Lander, G. C. (2011, November). *Interpersonal perceptions of academic self-efficacy: Gender differences in urban youths*. Paper presented at the Biennial Meeting of the Society for Vocational Psychology, Boston, MA.

Stead, G. B., & Schultheiss, D. E. P. (2003). Construction and psychometric properties of the childhood career development scale. *South African Journal of Psychology, 33*, 227–235.

Stead, G. B., & Schultheiss, D. E. P. (2010). Validity of childhood career development scale scores in South Africa. *International Journal for Educational and Vocational Guidance, 10*, 3–88.

Stead, G. B., Watson, M. B., Gallant, E., & Sauls, F. A. (2001, August). *Occupational Awareness Inventory: Psychometric properties among South African students*. Paper presented at the Annual Meeting of the American Psychological Association, San Francisco.

Sullivan, H. S. (1953). *The interpersonal theory of psychiatry*. New York, NY: Norton.

Super, D. E. (1990). A life-span, life-space approach to career development. In D. Brown, L. Brooks & Associates (Eds.), *Career choice and development* (pp. 197–261). San Francisco, CA: Jossey-Bass.

Su, R., Rounds, J., & Armstrong, P. I. (2009). Men and things, women and people: A meta-analysis of sex differences in interests. *Psychological Bulletin, 135*, 859–884.

Swanson, J. L. (1999). Stability and change in vocational interests. In M. L. Savickas & A. R. Spokane (Eds.), *Vocational interests: Meaning, measurement, and counseling use* (pp. 135–158). Palo Alto, CA: Black-Davies.

Tackett, J. L., Kushner, S. C., DeFruyt, F., & Mervielde, I. (2013). Delineating personality traits in childhood and adolescence: Associations across measures, temperament, and behavioral problems. *Assessment, 20*, 738–751.

Tracey, T. J. G. (1997). The structure of interests and self-efficacy expectations: An expanded examination of the spherical model of interests. *Journal of Counseling Psychology, 44*, 32–43.

Tracey, T. J. G. (2001). The development of structure of interests of children: Setting the stage. *Journal of Vocational Behavior, 59*, 89–104.

Tracey, T. J. G. (2002). Development of interests and competency beliefs: A 1-year longitudinal study of fifth- to eighth-grade students using the ICA-R and structural equation modeling. *Journal of Counseling Psychology, 49*, 148–163.

Tracey, T. J. G. (2010). Relation of interest and self-efficacy occupational congruence and career choice certainty. *Journal of Vocational Behavior, 76*, 441–447.

Tracey, T. J. G. (2012). Problems with single interest scales: Implications of the general factor. *Journal of Vocational Behavior, 81*, 378–384.

Tracey, T. J. G., & Caulum, D. (2015). Minimizing gender differences in children's interest assessment: Development of the Inventory of Children's Activities-3 (ICA-3). *Journal of Vocational Behavior, 87*, 154–160.

Tracey, T. J. G., & Hopkins, N. (2001). The correspondence of interests and abilities with occupational choice. *Journal of Counseling Psychology, 48*, 178–189.

Tracey, T. J. G., Robbins, S. B., & Hofsess, C. D. (2005). Stability and change in adolescence: A longitudinal analysis of interests from grades 8 through 12. *Journal of Vocational Behavior, 66*, 1–25.

Tracey, T. J., & Rounds, J. B. (1993). Evaluating Holland's and Gati's vocational interest models: A structural meta-analysis. *Psychological Bulletin, 113*, 229–246.

Tracey, T. J. G., & Sodano, S. M. (2014). Assessing children: Interests and personality. In P. J. Hartung, M. L. Savickas, & W. B. Walsh (Eds.), *APA handbook of career intervention* (Vol. 2, Applications, pp. 113–124). Washington, DC: American Psychological Association.

Tracey, T. J. G., & Ward, C. C. (1998). The structure of children's interests and competence perceptions. *Journal of Counseling Psychology, 45*, 290–303.

Watson, M., & McMahon, M. (2005). Children's career development: A research review from a learning perspective. *Journal of Vocational Behavior, 67*, 119–132.

Wiggins, J. S. (1982). Circumplex models of interpersonal behavior in clinical psychology. In P. C. Kendall & J. N. Butcher (Eds.), *Handbook of research methods in clinical psychology* (pp. 183–221). New York, NY: Wiley.

Wiggins, J. S. (1995). *IAS: Professional manual*. Tampa, FL: Psychological Assessment Resources.

Chapter 12

A review of assessment in child career development

Graham B. Stead, Donna E. P. Schultheiss, and Ashley Oliver

Childhood career assessment provides a means of gaining information about children's developmental progress within the career domain. Although children are not faced with immediate career decisions, theory (e.g., Super, 1990) suggests that childhood antecedents and adult career development are important to assess and nurture. Hence childhood career assessment can play an important role in assessing individual student progress and program effectiveness. Although scholars have emphasised the need for a lifelong perspective on career development to better prepare children for subsequent adaptation and well-being (Ferrari *et al.*, 2015; Hartung, Porfeli, & Vondracek, 2005; Porfeli, Hartung, & Vondracek, 2008; Watson, Nota, & McMahon, 2015a), few established assessment procedures exist to further these efforts (Stead & Schultheiss, 2010). During childhood, individuals explore educational opportunities, begin to develop a career identity, contemplate future careers, and make tentative career decisions (Betz, 2006; Flum & Blustein, 2000; Jantzer, Stalides, & Rottinghaus, 2009). The choices made during late childhood may have a strong effect on one's academic and career future. Thus career research with middle school students (i.e., age 12–13) is essential to facilitate the academic and career decision making faced by many students, but particularly those in educational contexts that demand academic and career choices that impact the rest of their lives (Ferrari, Nota, Schultheiss, Stead, & Davis, under review; Nota & Soresi, 2004).

Currently, most career assessment procedures for children consist of single-question measures to assess complex constructs such as interests, aspirations, barriers, and self-efficacy. This is problematic given that developmental progress occurring during childhood has been thought to lay the foundation for later career progress and adaptability (Hartung, Porfeli, & Vondracek, 2008). The dynamic context of contemporary life and work necessitates the use of both quantitative and qualitative childhood career assessment procedures (Watson, Nota, & McMahon, 2015b). Quantitative measures offer a means of quantifying developmental progress and facilitating comparisons across individuals and groups, while qualitative assessments provide a means of gaining a richer understanding of childhood experiences and behaviours within life contexts. Together, both methodologies offer a means of providing a holistic assessment of childhood career development within a developmental continuum (Schultheiss, 2008).

What follows is a review of the quantitative and qualitative instruments and procedures currently available to assess both childhood career development and the efficacy of career intervention programs.

Quantitative measures

Quantitative career measures among children that have been reported in the literature include Childhood Career Development Scale, Middle School Self-Efficacy Scale, Mapping Vocational Challenges, Career Exploration Scale, Ideas and Attitudes on School/Career Future, Occupational Knowledge Scale, Inventory of Children's Activities, and the Todt Vocational Questionnaire.

Childhood career development scale

The Childhood Career Development Scale was developed for US (CCDS-USA; Schultheiss & Stead, 2004) students in grades 4 through 6 and South African (CCDS-SA; Stead & Schultheiss, 2003) students in grades 4 through 7. Both measures are theoretically driven by Super's (1990) nine dimensions of childhood career development, are in English, have 5-point Likert-type scales ranging from 1 (strongly disagree) to 5 (strongly agree), take approximately 20 minutes to complete, are paper-and-pencil versions, and measure career development and career progress among children. Evidence for the construct validity of both measures was determined using principal components analysis and coefficients of congruence, thus supporting the eight-component structure. Example items include "I wonder about different jobs," "I know what subjects I like in school," and "It is important for me to plan things out before I do them."

The CCDS-USA comprises 52 items and 8 scales, namely Curiosity/Exploration (7 items, $\alpha = 0.66$), Information (6 items, $\alpha = 0.72$), Interests (6 items, $\alpha = 0.68$) Key Figures (5 items, $\alpha = 0.68$), Locus of Control (7 items, $\alpha = 0.79$), Time Perspective (4 items, $\alpha = 0.69$), Self-Concept (6 items, $\alpha = 0.84$), and Planning (11 items, $\alpha = 0.84$ (Schultheiss & Stead, 2004). There was no statistically significant ($p > 0.05$) grade by gender MANOVA interaction for all scales.

The CCDS-USA has been employed among fourth-grade students in a rural school district in a Midwestern state to identify the career development needs across Super's (1990) dimensions of career development growth (Wood & Kaszubowski, 2008). A ranking of prioritised career development needs was determined based on the percentage of the total possible score for each scale and the subscale mean. Findings suggested that the areas of the greatest career development needs of students in the sample were curiosity, information, key figures, and planning.

The CCDS-SA was also developed using principal components analysis and coefficients of congruence. Eight scales emerged comprising 48 items – namely,

Information (4 items, α = 0.67), Curiosity (8 items, α = 0.69), Exploration (3 items, α = 0.54) Locus of Control (8 items, α = 0.77), Key Figures (4 items, α = 0.62), Time Perspective (4 items, α = 0.70), Self-Concept (7 items, α = 0.84), and Planning (10 items, α = 0.85). There was also no statistically significant (p < 0.05) grade x gender MANOVA interaction for all scales. Using a confirmatory factor analysis, Stead and Schultheiss (2010) confirmed the eight-component structure of the CCDS-SA among grade four to seven South African students. Evidence for the concurrent validity of the CCDS-SA was provided by evidence of predictable relationships with a sense of industry or competence, self-esteem, and general locus of control for all subscales except Key Figures and Time Perspective (Stead & Schultheiss, 2010).

Middle school self-efficacy scale

The Middle School Self-Efficacy Scale (MSSES; Fouad & Smith, 1997) comprises 45 items designed for seventh- and eighth-grade students, ages 12–15 years old, to measure self-efficacy, outcome expectancy, and intentions and goals in career decision making and mathematics/science. Part I comprises the following Process subscales – namely, Career Decision-Making Self-Efficacy (CDMSE, 12 items, α = 0.79) and Career Decision-Making Outcome Expectancies (5 items, α = 0.70)/Intentions-Goals (5 items, α = 0.74). Part II comprises Content subscales using a 5-point Likert-type format – namely, Mathematics and Science Self-Efficacy (MSSE, 12 items, α = 0.84) and Mathematics and Science Outcome Expectancies (6 items, α = 0.80)/Intentions-Goals (6 items, α = 0.81). An example item is "If I do well in science, then I will be better prepared to go to college." Evidence for the construct validity of the MSSES scores was provided for the process and content scales using confirmatory factor analyses (Fouad & Smith, 1997). In addition, validity evidence was provided for the math subscales with statistically significant MANOVA interactions for gender x time (pre- and post-tests), but not for Process scales or science subscales. Fouad and Smith conclude that apart from the science content items, there is evidence for the validity and reliability of the MSSES's scores in relation to assessing intervention programs for math and science career awareness, especially for females and minority students.

Mapping vocational challenges

The Mapping Vocational Challenges Career Development Program (MVC; Lapan & Turner, 1999) includes a self-report, computer-assisted career assessment for middle school students (i.e., age 11–14) that measures career interests, efficacy for pursuing various occupations, perceived parental support for pursuing various occupations, and perceived gender-typing of occupations. Students are presented with the titles of 90 occupations, of which 15 are for each Holland type – namely, Realistic, Investigative, Artistic, Social, Enterprising, and

Conventional. For each occupation, participants indicate their interest level on a 3-point Likert-type scale (α range = 0.70 to 0.77), their efficacy expectations using a dichotomous scale (α range = 0.77 to 0.85), their perceptions of the extent to which parents would support each occupation on a dichotomous scale (Cronbach α range = 0.82 to 0.91), and their perception of gender-typing on a 5-point Likert-type scale. The Interpretation Module is a computer-generated report that enables the respondents to understand their results.

Using a sample of 160 middle school students in a treatment and delayed treatment quasi-experimental non-equivalent groups design, Turner and Lapan (2005) found that the MVS career intervention increased students' career exploration efficacy, educational and vocational development efficacy, and interest in careers that are non-traditional. Various additional studies have employed the MVC among middle school children (e.g., Ji, Lapan, & Tate, 2004; Lapan, Adams, Turner, & Hinkelman, 2000; Turner & Lapan, 2002, 2003, 2005).

Career exploration scale

The Career Exploration Scale (CES; Tracey, Lent, Brown, Soresi, & Nota, 2006) was developed among a middle school sample (*M* age = 11.35, *SD* = 0.57) in the United States with the purpose of determining respondents' career exploratory behaviours over the past three months. The measure comprises 13 items on a 5-point Likert-type scale ranging from Never to Lots of Times. An example item is "Read a book about how to choose careers." The internal consistency of the measure was 0.80 and the test-retest correlation over a one-year interval was 0.48. Ferrari *et al.* (2015) found the internal consistency to be 0.63 among elementary school children. There was a predictable relationship between the CES and the correspondence index, which measures the extent to which scores fit a circular order model (Tracey *et al.*, 2006), thus suggesting validity evidence. Ferrari *et al.* reported correlations of the CES with CCDS-USA (Schultheiss & Stead, 2004) subscales – namely, 0.18 (Interests), 0.33 (Locus of Control), 0.27 (Time Perspective), 0.49 (Planning), 0.26 (Self-Concept), and 0.18 (Curiosity / Exploration) among middle school children in Italy, providing some evidence of CES concurrent validity.

Ideas and attitudes on school/career future

The Ideas and Attitudes on School/Career Future measure (IASCF: Ferrari, Nota, & Soresi, 2002; Soresi & Nota, 2001) is based on Savickas and Jarjoura (1991) and measures students aged 11–12 years (Nota & Soresi, 2004) and their future ideas, attitudes, and behaviours related to school and career. The measure comprises 17 Likert-type items ranging from 1 (does not describe me at all) to 5 (describes me very well). There are three subscales – namely, Level of Assurance, Commitment, and Certainty. Level of Assurance has nine items and measures assurance in relation to self-knowledge and academic/vocational information (e.g., "I find it difficult to see clearly what I like and what interests me. This is why I can't decide yet"). Level of Commitment comprises five items measuring the extent of commitment to and involvement in the decision-making process (e.g., "It is useless to think about a future job for myself. One way or another I will certainly find something to do"). Level of Certainty has three items and measures one's future work or professional identity (e.g., "I still can't picture what I will do as an adult").

Nota and Soresi (2004) reported the reliability estimates to be 0.83 (Level of Assurance), 0.64 (Commitment), and 0.65 (Level of Certainty). Among Italian junior high school students, Soresi and Nota (2001) employed confirmatory factor analysis and confirmed the factor structure of the measure. Ferrari *et al.* (2015) found that among middle school Italian children, the IASCF Level of Commitment subscale correlated 0.31 with the Career Exploration Scale (Tracey *et al.*, 2006) and 0.26, 0.27, and 0.16 with the CCDS-USA (Schultheiss & Stead, 2004) Locus of Control, Planning, and Self-Concept subscales, respectively. The IASCF Level of Certainty subscale correlated 0.25, 0.13, and 0.14 with the CCDS Time Perspective, Planning, and Curiosity/ Exploration subscales, respectively. This provided some evidence of the concurrent validity of the Level of Commitment and Level of Certainty IASCF subscales.

Other measures

The Occupational Knowledge Scale (OKS; Rohlfing, Nota, Ferrari, Soresi, & Tracey, 2012) was adapted from the Personal Globe Inventory (Tracey, 2002). The OKS was employed with elementary and middle school children (ages 7 to 12) in Italy. The measure comprises 36 occupational titles and respondents indicate their knowledge of each occupation on a 5-point, Likert-type scale. Four subscales emerged – namely, a Total Knowledge scale ($\alpha = 0.94$), a People/Things Knowledge scale ($\alpha = 0.86$), an Ideas/Data Knowledge scale ($\alpha = 0.82$), and a Prestige Knowledge scale ($\alpha = 0.79$). No validity evidence was provided.

Other measures described elsewhere in this book include the Inventory of Children's Activities (ICA-Revised; Tracey & Ward, 1998) and the Todt Vocational Questionnaire (TVQ; Todt & Mesa, 1988; also see Vondracek & Skorikov, 1997). The ICA-R is an instrument for elementary and middle school (i.e., aged 12–13 years) children that measures the structure of interests and competencies in relation to Holland's RIASEC codes. It comprises 30 activities in which children indicate their liking of each activity on 5-point Likert-type scales. The TVQ (Todt & Mesa, 1988) is a measure of activity preferences and vocational identity characteristics. It has been translated from German into English and employed among US grade 7–12 students (Vondracek & Skorikov, 1997). The TVQ lists 15 activities, such as music, technology, skilled labour, homemaking, and science. Respondents are asked to rate the activities on 5-point Likert-type scales as to whether they engage in these activities, their confidence in working in these areas, and their desirability of working in these areas. Evidence of the measure's psychometric properties has not been provided.

As is evident from the previous review, very few established measures of childhood career assessment are currently available. Of those that are, not all are used regularly in practice, as many are used as research tools. These measures span development, self-efficacy, vocational challenges, career exploration, career knowledge, interests, competencies, attitudes, and behaviours. Psychometric support varies across these measures as does the degree to which they are theory-based.

Qualitative measures

The purpose of this section is to describe qualitative career assessments that can be used with children. The qualitative career assessments that will be described are Career Family Tree, Survey of Interests and Plans, the Life-Career Assessment, Conceptions of Career Choice and Attainment Protocol, My Career Story, the Revised Career Awareness Survey, and the Occupational Knowledge Interview.

Career family tree

The Career Family Tree (Gibson, 2005) is a qualitative instrument that utilises a tree template to enhance a child's career awareness. The purpose of the Career Family Tree is to facilitate children's understanding of their past, to aid in the understanding of their present, and to help them to plan for their work- and career-related future (Gibson, 2005). The tree template can be employed for individual or group use with elementary school age children. Gibson suggests that the instrument be disseminated at school, but recommends that it be completed with the involvement of the child's family to enhance communication about career aspirations between children and their parents. Students are instructed to include their parents' and siblings' names in their tree. After developing the tree, which includes the children's parents and siblings, they are instructed to write the occupation of each family member next to his or her name. The primary goal of this assessment for elementary school students is to enhance career awareness.

Survey of interests and plans

The Survey of Interest and Plans (SIP; Helwig, 2004) involves a 20–30 minute semi-structured interview to assess several career-related domains (i.e., school likes and dislikes, out-of-school activities, work-related goals and expectations, college goals, work-related gender roles, hobbies, chores, and college attendance) of children from age seven. For example, occupational aspirations were measured with the question, "As an adult, if you could have any job you wanted, what job would that be?", while occupational expectations were measured by asking, "As an adult, what job do you really think you will have?" Helwig's longitudinal study comprised 208 (110 boys and 98 girls) second-grade students that attended four elementary schools. The mean age of the children was 7.8 years at the beginning of the study. Children were then tested again at ages 12 (n = 160), 14 (n = 123), 16 (n = 115), and 18 (n = 103). A final sample size of 75 students was used due to participant drop out. Helwig assessed for students aspiring to professional, technical, and managerial occupations compared to "other" occupations (p. 52) and whether or not a participant wanted to attend college and his or her expected yearly salary. As the children aged, additional questions were asked to assess for parental involvement in their career exploration and confidence in their career aspirations. Over the ten-year period, children developed more hobbies and the majority of children chose professional, technical, and managerial occupations over "other." Overall, the Survey of Interest and Plans highlights potential career development issues, such as work-related goals and expectations and can help children gain career awareness.

The life career assessment

The Life Career Assessment (Gysbers & Moore, 1987) is a qualitative instrument that assesses an individual's goals, problems, and career maturity by using a semi-structured interview. Though it was not developed for the sole use of assessing the career exploration of children, Gysbers, Heppner, and Johnson (2003) argue that it can be adapted for use with children. This semi-structured interview takes approximately 20 to 30 minutes to complete and comprises four sections: 1) career assessment, 2) typical day, 3) strengths and obstacles, and 4) summary. The career assessment portion explores work experience, education and training progress and concerns, and leisure. The typical day portion helps individuals to explore their personality types by becoming aware of their typical daily routines. The strengths and obstacles portion may allow children to explore their main strengths and identify potential barriers in the career planning and development process.

Conceptions of career choice and attainment protocol

The Conceptions of Career Choice and Attainment (CCCA) Protocol (Howard & Walsh, 1999) is a semi-structured interview that consists of eight questions to help children who are in kindergarten through sixth grade to explore their conceptualisation of career choice and career attainment. The interview begins with an introductory question: "When people become grown-ups they sometimes get a job. What are all the different kinds of jobs (work) that people can do?" This is followed by three questions that explore the child's perception of how others make career choices, such as "How do people decide what they want to be when they grow up? Of all the jobs they can get, how do people decide which one they want? How do they decide what they want to be?" The remaining four questions explore the child's personal career choices (Howard & Walsh, 2010). For instance, some questions help to facilitate the development of career awareness. An example is "What do you want to be when you grow up?" (Howard & Walsh, 1999).

Howard and Walsh (2010) used the CCCA protocol to determine whether or not reasoning about career choice (i.e., matching one's self to an existing job) and attainment (i.e., how an individual obtained the desired job) differed by grade level and age. Career choice refers to matching one's self to an existing job, while career attainment refers to how an individual obtains the desired job. Participants included 60 children (20 in kindergarten, 20 in third grade, and 20 in sixth grade). Results suggested that younger children (Grade K) were more likely to use reasoning strategies for career choice and attainment associated with pretend and magical thinking, compared to older children (Grade 6) who were more likely to consider personal interests, skills, and job requirements. To minimise the first rater's potential data scoring bias of the interviews, a second rater was employed. Interrater reliability for Conceptions of Career Choice yielded a Spearman r of 0.92 ($p < 0.001$), with a 70 per cent exact agreement rate. For the Concepts of Career Attainment interrater reliability, a Spearman r of 0.98 ($p < .001$) and an 85 per cent agreement between the raters were obtained (Howard & Walsh, 2010).

My career story

My Career Story (MCS; Savickas & Hartung, 2012) is an autobiographical workbook for life-career success, which can be adapted to promote children's development of life design goals, including activity, adaptability, narratability, and intentionality (Hartung, 2015). Exploring the activity component allows children to engage in role playing and incorporate role models in imaginary play to help explore their interests, abilities, and skills. A sample question is "Who did you admire when you were growing up? Who were your heroes or heroines?" (Savickas & Hartung, 2012). Adaptability is related to children's ability to learn and explore appropriate ways to handle typical developmental tasks, life barriers, and stressors. Developing such skills may ultimately help children to shape their careers. Next, narratability provides the child with the opportunity to tell his or her story, ultimately revealing themes. One way a child can begin to explore life themes includes exploring his or her favourite saying:

> What is your favorite saying? Think about a motto you live by or a saying that you have heard and really like. Maybe you've seen some words on a car bumper sticker or have a poster or plaque in your room or house that has words to live by. You might even have more than one saying or motto that you can list here. If you can't think of a saying, you might even create your own and write it down here.
>
> (Savickas & Hartung, 2012, p. 8)

By doing so, children progress toward career exploration and imagine themselves in the world of work. Intentionality refers to the belief that children engage in meaningful and purposeful activities that are rooted within social roles. A sample question is "Look carefully at the words you used to describe your heroes or heroines . . . Now, using the words you wrote down above, tell in two to four sentences who you are and who you are becoming."

Overall, completing the *My Career Story Workbook* helps children to tell, hear, and author their life story, thereby adding meaning to their career plans and choices. The *My Career Story* utilises career counselling principles to help individuals think about their future (Savickas & Hartung, 2012).

The revised career awareness survey

The Revised Career Awareness Survey (RCAS; McMahon & Watson, 2001) is a self-report questionnaire based on the Career Awareness Survey (Gillies, McMahon, & Carroll, 1998). The RCAS gathers information about children's knowledge and understanding of the world of work over five sections. Form 1 of the RCAS consists of a series of open-ended questions about different aspects of children's personal-social knowledge regarding career development, i.e., their career interests, career influences they can identify, and their sources of career information. Children list careers that interest them, nominate their favourite, identify what would make them good at their favourite career, list who or what could influence them towards or away from careers they have listed, report how they found out about the listed careers, and explain how they could find further information. Form 2 uses open-ended questions that focus on career gender stereotypes and asks children what careers they believe are more or less suitable for men and women. While Form 3 also explores career gender stereotypes, children are provided with a prescribed list of careers that they must indicate as being suitable for males, females, or both. Form 4 explores whether children can recognise similarities between different types of careers. Each question lists three careers and asks children to name a common feature for all three careers. In the final Form 5, children describe possible links between a list of careers and what they learn at school. The RCAS has been used successfully in a range of international research studies (e.g., McMahon & Rixon, 2007; McMahon & Watson, 2005; Watson & McMahon, 2004). Evidence has yet to be provided of the measure's trustworthiness and reliability.

The occupational knowledge interview

The Occupational Knowledge Interview (OKI; Soresi & Nota, 2013) was adapted from the Occupational Knowledge Scale (Rohlfing *et al.*, 2012). The OKI was employed with elementary and middle school children (ages 9 to 13) in Italy. The OKI assesses for children's knowledge and perception of knowledge of each occupation. To assess for one's perception of occupational knowledge, the OKI consists of 12 cards that illustrate different occupations in which each respondent is asked, "How much do you think you already know about this job?", which is assessed using a 4-point Likert scale. Notably, there are two cards for every Holland interest category: Realistic (airplane pilot, fireman), Investigative (pharmacist, veterinary), Artistic (actor/actress, journalist), Social (nurse, school teacher), Enterprising (shop assistant, taxi driver) and Conventional (accountant, secretary). The second part of the interview explores actual occupational knowledge – the original 12 cards are presented again and the respondent is asked, "Tell me any action, task, or activity that is carried out by a person working as . . ." For each occupation displayed on the cards, the number of activities provided was summed with higher numbers representing greater occupational knowledge. To minimise the first rater's potential data scoring bias of the interviews, a second rater was used. Agreement was over 95 per cent for each of the analysed occupations.

Incorporating open-ended questions as writing prompts for children can also provide useful qualitative data. Schultheiss, Palma, and Manzi (2005) gave children that were aged 9–12 years old weekly writing assignments as part of a career intervention program to help the children explore their career development process. The participants responded to open-ended writing prompts about themselves, influential others, goals, and decision making. The prompts were developed based on a review of the career development literature (e.g., Super, 1990; Trice *et al.*, 1995). For example, children were asked to

(a) Write about how your family has influenced you in choosing your favorite jobs; (b) Write about how your teachers have influenced you in choosing your favorite jobs; (c) Write about all the things that you are good at. Write about how you got to be good at these things; (d) Describe how you make important decisions; (e) Write about the school and work goals you have for yourself when you grow up. What job do you think that you will have when you grow up? What will you need to do to get a job like this?

(Schultheiss *et al.*, 2005, p. 249)

Though such qualitative assessments can be utilised with children and adolescents, empirical support for their utility in promoting career development is lacking. Qualitative assessments are difficult to evaluate due to the diverse range of qualitative approaches and methodologies (Stead & Davis, 2015). However, utilising such assessments can provide creative outlets (cf., Heppner, O'Brien, Hinkelman, & Humphrey, 1994) for children to explore their career aspirations.

Conclusion

It has been suggested that individual and programmatic assessment of career development must become a crucial component of competent career practice with children (Schultheiss, 2008). In the context of a competitive global workforce, it is of great theoretical and practical importance to study childhood interests, abilities, and skills that ultimately lead to worker behaviours and attitudes (Stead & Schultheiss, 2010).

As is evident in the preceding review, there are few quantitative instruments to assess childhood career development. Those measures that do exist vary in their use, from research to practical applications. In addition, the availability of reliability and validity data varies across the instruments. Qualitative measures provide assessments that do not rely on the individual's reading level. This provides a means of gaining an understanding of the knowledge and experiences of younger children and those with lower reading abilities. Both quantitative and qualitative assessment procedures vary in the appropriate age range they target. This further complicates the ability to track developmental progress across time.

In reviews of the childhood career development literature (e.g., Hartung, Porfeli, & Vondracek, 2005; Watson & McMahon, 2005), a number of prime targets for future inquiry have been proposed, yet the assessment tools necessary to conduct such research remain sparse (Schultheiss, 2008). Further development of childhood career assessment procedures would help to broaden the focus of career inquiry to include a more complete lifespan perspective (Schultheiss & Stead, 2004) and to facilitate research that would add to our knowledge of childhood career development and interventions that promote progress (Watson *et al.*, 2015b). This is important given that children are just beginning to learn about work and to be socialised into the workforce (Stead & Schultheiss, 2010). It is also important that measures are not used exclusively to identify deficits or to encourage premature decision making (cf., Watson *et al.*, 2015b). Instead, they should be used to encourage exploration and the development of knowledge, skills, and adaptability to enhance the development of children and early adolescents who are flexible and effective problem solvers and lifelong learners. Ultimately, this could help to expand future career options and the ability to take advantage of future opportunities for career growth and progress (Schultheiss & Stead, 2004).

A number of challenges remain that interfere with the development and use of childhood career assessment procedures. There are often very few career professionals employed in elementary and middle schools to address the career needs of students. When those professionals are available, it is not unusual for them to be embedded in the context of school environments which have competing agendas, such as those related to academic achievement and other domains of childhood and early adolescent growth and development (e.g., social, emotional). Many schools also face challenges associated with competitive educational environments, coupled with less than sufficient resources to reach the desired academic outcomes. Finally, it is difficult for many to conclude that there is an urgent need to allocate scare resources to address the career issues, concerns, and progress of children when the choice of a career is many years in the future.

References

Betz, N. E. (2006). Developing and using parallel measures of career self-efficacy and interests with adolescents. In F. Pajares & T. Urdan (Eds.), *Self-efficacy beliefs of adolescents* (pp. 45–74). Greenwich, CT: Information Age Publishing.

Ferrari, L., Ginerva, M. C., Santilli, S., Nota, L., Sgaramella, T. M., & Soresi, S. (2015). Career exploration and occupational knowledge in Italian children. *International Journal for Educational and Vocational Guidance, 15,* 113–130.

Ferrari, L., Nota, L., Schultheiss, D. E., & Stead, G. B. (2015, August). *Validation and cultural relevancy of the childhood career development scale.* Paper presented at the American Psychological Association Convention, Toronto, Canada.

Ferrari, L., Nota, L, Schultheiss, D. E., Stead, G. B., & Davis, B. L. (under review). Validation of the childhood career development scale among Italian middle school students.

Ferrari, L., Nota, L., & Soresi, S. (2002). Idee ed atteggiamenti sul futuro scolastico-professionale: uno strumento per l'analisi dei livelli di indecisione di persone di eta compresa fra i 15 e i 19 anni [The questionnaire "Ideas and attitudes on school-career future:" An instrument for the analysis of career indecision in 15 to 19 year old students]. *Giornale Italiano di Psicologia dell'Orientamento, 3,* 20–31.

Flum, H., & Blustein, D. L. (2000). Reinvigorating the study of vocational exploration: A framework for research. *Journal of Vocational Behavior, 56,* 380–404.

Fouad, N. A., & Smith, P. L. (1997). Reliability and validity evidence for the middle school self-efficacy scale. *Measurement and Evaluation in Counseling and Development, 30,* 17–31.

Gibson, D. M. (2005). The use of genograms in career counseling with elementary, middle, and high school students. *The Career Development Quarterly, 53,* 353–362.

Gillies, R. M., McMahon, M., & Carroll, J. (1998). Evaluating a career education intervention in the upper elementary school. *Journal of Career Development, 24,* 267–287.

Gysbers, N. C., Heppner, M. J., & Johnson, J. A. (2003). *Career counseling: Process, issues and techniques* (2nd ed.). Boston: Allyn & Bacon.

Gysbers, N. C., & Moore, E. J. (1987). *Career counseling: Skills and techniques for practitioners.* Englewood Cliffs, NJ: Prentice Hall.

Hartung, P. J. (2015). Life design in childhood: Antecedents and advancement. In L. Nota & J. Rossier (Eds.), *Handbook of the life design paradigm: From practice to theory, from theory to practice* (pp. 89–102). Göttingen, Germany: Hogrefe Publishing.

Hartung, P. J., Porfeli, E. J., & Vondracek, F. W. (2005). Child vocational development: A review and reconsideration. *Journal of Vocational Behavior, 66,* 385–419.

Hartung, P. J., Porfeli, E. J., & Vondracek, F. W. (2008). Career adaptability in childhood. *The Career Development Quarterly, 57*(1), 63–74.

Helwig, A. A. (2004). A ten-year longitudinal study of the career development of students: Summary findings. *Journal of Counseling and Development, 82,* 49–57.

Heppner, M. J., O'Brien, K. M., Hinkelman, J. M., & Humphrey, C. F. (1994). Shifting the paradigm: The use of creativity in career counseling. *Journal of Career Development, 21,* 77–86.

Howard, K. A. S., & Walsh, M. E. (1999). *Children's conceptions of the school-work relationship.* Paper presented at the Meeting of the American Psychological Association, Boston, MA.

Howard, K. A. S., & Walsh, M. E. (2010). Conceptions of career choice and attainment: Developmental levels in how children think about careers. *Journal of Vocational Behavior, 76,* 143–152.

Jantzer, A. M., Stalides, D. J., & Rottinghaus, P. J. (2009). An exploration of social cognitive mechanisms, gender, and vocational identity among eighth graders. *Journal of Career Development, 36,* 114–138.

Ji, P. Y., Lapan, R. T., & Tate, K. (2004). Vocational interests and career efficacy expectations in relation to occupational sex-typing beliefs for eighth grade students. *Journal of Career Development, 31,* 143–154.

Lapan, R. T., Adams, A., Turner, S., & Hinkelman, J. M. (2000). Seventh graders' vocational interest and efficacy expectation patterns. *Journal of Career Development, 26*, 215–229.

Lapan, R. T., & Turner, S. L. (1999). *Mapping vocational challenges career development program.* Unpublished manuscript.

McMahon, M., & Rixon, K. (2007). The career development of rural Queensland children. *Australian Journal of Career Development, 16*, 39–49.

McMahon, M., & Watson, M. (2001). *Revised career awareness survey.* Unpublished manuscript.

McMahon, M., & Watson, M. (2005). Occupational information: What children want to know. *Journal of Career Development, 31*, 239–249.

Nota, L., & Soresi, S. (2004). Improving the problem-solving and decision-making skills of a high indecision group of young adolescents: A test of the "Difficult: No Problem!" training. *International Journal for Educational and Vocational Guidance, 4*, 3–21.

Porfeli, E. J., Hartung, P. J., & Vondracek, F. W. (2008). Children's vocational development: A research rationale. *The Career Development Quarterly, 57*, 25–37.

Rohlfing, J. E., Nota, L., Ferrari, L., Soresi, S., & Tracey, T. J. G. (2012). Relation of occupational knowledge to career interests and competence perceptions in Italian children. *Journal of Vocational Behavior, 81*, 330–337.

Savickas, M. L., & Hartung, P. J. (2012). *My career story: An autobiographical workbook for life-career success.* Kent, OH: Vocopher. Retrieved from http://www.vocopher.com.

Savickas, M. L., & Jarjoura, D. (1991). The career decision scale as a type indicator. *Journal of Counseling Psychology, 38*, 85–90.

Schultheiss, D. E. P. (2008). Current status and future agenda for theory, research and practice of childhood career development. *The Career Development Quarterly, 57*, 7–24.

Schultheiss, D. E. P., Palma, T. V, & Manzi, A. J. (2005). Career development in middle childhood: A qualitative inquiry. *The Career Development Quarterly, 53*, 246–262.

Schultheiss, D. E. P., & Stead, G. B. (2004). Childhood career development scale: Construction and psychometric properties. *Journal of Career Assessment, 12*, 113–134.

Soresi, S., & Nota, L. (2001). *Optimist: Introduzione, interessi e valori* [Optimist: Introduction, interests and values]. Firenze, Italy: Iter-Organizzazioni Speciali.

Soresi, S., & Nota, L. (2013). *A qualitative instrument to assess occupational knowledge in children: Occupational knowledge interview.* Paper presented at the Counselling and Career Counselling Conference. University of Padua, Padua, Italy.

Stead, G. B., & Davis, B. L. (2015). Qualitative career assessments: Research evidence. In M. McMahon & M. Watson (Eds.), *Career assessment: Qualitative approaches* (pp. 21–30). Rotterdam, The Netherlands: Sense Publishers.

Stead, G. B., & Schultheiss, D. E. P. (2003). Construction and psychometric properties of the childhood career development scale. *South African Journal of Psychology, 33*, 227–235.

Stead, G. B., & Schultheiss, D. (2010). Validity of childhood career development scale scores in South Africa. *International Journal for Educational and Vocational Guidance, 10*, 73–88.

Super, D. E. (1990). A life-span, life-space approach to career development. In D. Brown, L. Brooks & Associates (Eds.), *Career choice and development* (2nd ed., pp. 197–261). San Francisco, CA: Jossey-Bass.

Todt, E., & Mesa, M. (1988). *Die Verankerung der Schulfachinteressen in den allgemeinen und in den Freizeitinteressen von Schuelern und Schuelerinnen der 7. bis 10. Klassenstufe* (The relation of interests in school subjects to the general and leisure interests of students of the 7th through 10th grades). Unpublished paper. Giessen, Germany: University of Giessen.

Tracey, T. J. G. (2002). Personal globe inventory: Measurement of the spherical model of interests and competence beliefs. *Journal of Vocational Behavior, 60*, 113–172.

Tracey, T. J. G., Lent, R. W., Brown, S. D., Soresi, S., & Nota, L. (2006). Adherence to RIASEC structure in relation to career exploration and parenting style: Longitudinal and ideothetic considerations. *Journal of Vocational Behavior, 67*, 248–261.

Tracey, T. J. G., & Ward, C. C. (1998). The structure of children's interests and competence perceptions. *Journal of Counseling Psychology, 45*, 290–303.

Trice, A., Hughes, M., Odom, K., Woods, K., & McGlellan, N. (1995). The origins of children's career aspirations: IV. Testing hypotheses from four theories. *The Career Development Quarterly, 43*, 307–322.

Turner, S. L., & Lapan, R. T. (2002). Career self-efficacy and perceptions of parent support in adolescent career development. *The Career Development Quarterly, 51*, 44–55.

Turner, S. L., & Lapan, R. T. (2003). The measurement of career interests among at-risk inner-city and middle-class suburban adolescents. *Journal of Career Assessment, 11*, 405–420.

Turner, S. L., & Lapan, R. T. (2005). Evaluation of an intervention to increase non-traditional career interests and career-related self-efficacy among middle-school adolescents. *Journal of Vocational Behavior, 66*, 516–531.

Vondracek, F. W., & Skorikov, V. B. (1997). Leisure, school, and work activity preferences and their role in vocational identity development. *The Career Development Quarterly, 45*, 322–340.

Watson, M., & McMahon, M. (2004). Matching occupation and self: Does matching theory adequately model children's thinking? *Psychological Reports, 95*, 421–431.

Watson, M., & McMahon, M. (2005). Children's career development: A research review from a learning perspective. *Journal of Vocational Behavior, 67*, 119–132.

Watson, M., Nota, L., & McMahon, M. (2015a). Child career development: Present and future trends. *International Journal for Educational and Vocational Guidance, 15*, 95–97.

Watson, M., Nota, L., & McMahon, M. (2015b). Evolving stories of child career development. *International Journal for Educational and Vocational Guidance, 15*, 175–184.

Wood, C., & Kaszubowski, Y. (2008). The career development needs of rural elementary school students. *The Elementary School Journal, 108*, 431–444.

Part 5

Facilitating career exploration and development

Chapter 13

School-based approaches promoting children's career exploration and development

Richard T. Lapan, Becky L. Bobek, and John Kosciulek

This chapter focuses on school-based approaches that promote career exploration and development in children up to the age of 14. Evidence is also presented supporting the premise that career development interventions that deeply engage children in meaningful, personally relevant explorations of self and possible educational and world-of-work futures positively impact academic achievement. Children face formidable career development challenges and opportunities that will unfold for them as they move into adolescence. Among other challenges and opportunities, they will need to organise their high school studies around future educational and career pathway goals, select the right high school to attend, begin to create a career identity, participate in work-based learning experiences, and ultimately make truly informed decisions about which postsecondary educational and career training program to attend. There are two key career development transitions occurring approximately between ages 6 through 11 and then ages 12 through 14 that, when successfully negotiated, provide the adolescent significant adaptive advantages. Children who have mastered age-appropriate career exploration and development tasks during these transitions are more likely to proactively and successfully take advantage of opportunities and navigate potential career development obstacles that adolescence both presents to them and demands of them.

Support for these two transitions and related career development constructs comes from a recently developed holistic framework designed to promote education and work readiness from childhood through to successful adult participation in the workforce (Camara, O'Connor, Mattern, & Hanson, 2015). Based on a comprehensive multidisciplinary review of empirical research, theory, and input from experts in diverse fields, four broad domains were identified (*Core Academic Skills, Cross-Cutting Capabilities, Behavioural Skills*, and *Education and Career Navigation*). Each of these domains were found to significantly influence developmental pathways leading to education and work success. This chapter draws from the *Education and Career Navigation* domain (the knowledge and skills needed to make informed decisions, plan, and navigate one's journey through valued educational and career pathways) to present a model for understanding and promoting children's exploration within two key career development transitional stages.

The chapter is organised into four major sections. First, the two developmental transitions characteristic of this age range are described and supporting research cited. Second, critical career development constructs operative at each transition are discussed and prioritised. Third, examples of knowledge and skills specifying what learners should know and be able to do will illustrate the developmental progression across these two transitions and the more complex cognitive processing experienced by young students as they reach the end of childhood and enter adolescence. Strategies will be identified that teachers can use to promote more complex processing by their students. Fourth, promising school-based practices and interventions will be identified for all children, including those with disabilities.

Career development transitions

This section focuses on two major career development transitions during childhood. The first occurs between the ages of 6 to 11 and is characterised by increasing career awareness, the beginning formation of critical beliefs and expectations that will shape later career development, and the engagement of children in meaningful career exploratory actions. The second transition occurs between the ages of 12 to 14 and is characterised by more intentional efforts at educational planning connected to exploratory actions and access to relevant educational and career information.

Ages 6 through 11: Awareness, beliefs, and general exploration

Generally, by approximately nine years of age, children are becoming aware of and knowledgeable about different career futures that may one day be available to them. Formative expectations and beliefs begin to crystallise and start to shape how children understand themselves in relation to school and future possibilities. These young learners are beginning to become aware of their own interests and abilities. While it must be noted that individuals vary greatly in their rate of development, a growing body of research supports the position that these career exploration and development issues are (on average) clearly operative and influential by at least nine years of age (e.g., Alliman-Brissett, Turner, & Skovholt, 2004; Bigler, Averhart, & Liben, 2003; Care, Deans, & Brown, 2007; Hartung, Porfeli, & Vondracek, 2005; Schultheiss, Palma, & Manzi, 2005; Watson & McMahon, 2005). For example, Cook and colleagues (1996) found that by eight to nine years of age lower-income African American boys living in an urban setting had a significant discrepancy between what they aspired to one day attain and what they actually expected to achieve. These children had the same high level of career aspirations as eight- to nine-year-olds from a more affluent suburban community. However, when compared to more financially advantaged children, these lower-income children had lower expectations that they would actually be able to attain these high career aspirations (and did not understand school to be a means of helping them to reach these dreams).

Ages 12 to 14: Career information, exploration, and educational planning

The cultural and contextual landscape of many schools, families, and communities now demand 12- to 14-year-olds to build upon this first career transition in specific ways. Children develop at different rates and have varying levels of preparation but reach a point where many are required to make certain decisions (e.g., what type of and which high school to attend, which educational and career pathway to pursue in high school). This is a very significant decision point in which options and constraints vary greatly across different communities and cultures. More informed decisions made during this transition lead to greater likelihood of high school and postsecondary success. Successful navigation of the transition from middle school to secondary school is a key marker of future educational and career success (ACT, 2007). Children perform better in school if they are able to discuss and explore career and educational planning issues with their families. Children at this age who engage in more meaningful career exploration and development experiences have better outcomes when they get to their chosen high school and then later in college, as well as during their current academic studies (e.g., Akos, 2005; Eccles, Vida, & Barber, 2004; Lapan *et al.*, 2016).

This developmental transition requires children to build upon the aspirations, beliefs, and expectations from the earlier transition to now become more self-directed and intentional about their educational planning. Career information expands. In optimal situations, children use a growing awareness of personal characteristics, contextual supports, and early work experiences (e.g., lawn mowing and child care – 'babysitting') to explore and then make tentative commitments to follow a particular educational direction in high school. Growth in understanding of self and the world of work now includes new developments such as an emerging awareness of interest patterns, a better understanding of the influence of factors such as gender and socioeconomic status, access to an expanding range of information about the world of work, and the consideration of negative possibilities in work such as job dissatisfaction, role strain, and schedule demands on one's life. Research supports the important and dynamic nature of this transition period and how successful navigation enhances children's chances for success as they move into adolescence (e.g., Akos, Konold, & Niles, 2004; Hartung *et al.*, 2005; Hill, Ramirez, & Dumka, 2003; Howard, *et al.*, 2011; Keller & Whiston, 2008; Patton, Bartrum, & Creed, 2004; Porfeli & Lee, 2012; Rowan-Kenyon, Swan, & Creager, 2012; Weisgram & Bigler, 2006). Specific career-related constructs discussed next shape children's ability to successfully navigate the 6- to 11-year-old and 12- to 14-year-old career development transitions.

Critical career constructs at each developmental transition

A comprehensive review of the research and literature identified 20 evidence-supported constructs related to career development that influence individuals as they progress from childhood through to adult success and satisfaction in the workforce (Bobek & Zhao, 2015). Subject matter experts (SME) were surveyed to better understand which of these 20 constructs were more important at each of 10 critical career transitions (e.g., transition from middle school to high school, from high school to college, or from postsecondary training to work). SMEs (n = 256) were recruited from K–12 schools, postsecondary institutions, and workforce groups. SMEs rated each of the 20 constructs in relation to how important the construct was for successfully navigating the particular transitions for which they were an SME.

Figure 13.1 rank-order results of navigation constructs for Grades K–5 and Grades 6–8 transitions presents the ranking results (based on mean ratings) for the top-five constructs that SMEs identified as being most important for helping children navigate the age 6 to 11 and 12 to 14 transitions. SMEs at both transitions identified the same five constructs as being most important. Differences between the five highest-ranked constructs were not statistically significant.

Each of the five top-rated constructs plays both unique and interacting roles with the other constructs to assist children. Personal Attributes refer to those self-knowledge characteristics that contribute to self-referent thoughts, decisions, and behaviours (e.g., interests, values, personality, and skills and abilities). Expectations highlight those anticipatory beliefs that children use to attribute cause and effect relationships between educational decisions, actions, and consequent

Rank Order	Grades K–5	Grades 6–8
1	Personal Attributes	Expectations
2	Expectations	Awareness
3	Self-Efficacy	Self-Efficacy
4	Exploration	Personal Attributes
5	Awareness	Exploration

Figure 13.1 Rank-order results of top-five education and career navigation domain constructs for grades K–5 and grades 6–8 transitions

outcomes (e.g., expectations of being able to positively influence educational and occupational choices). Self-Efficacy Beliefs point to children's self-perceptions of the ability to successfully execute specific academic and career-related tasks. Exploration engages children in seeking and processing educational and career information in ways that are guided by a developing understanding of self. Awareness focuses on those moments or states of feeling and perceiving that help children to become conscious of themselves, possible education and career futures, and the connections or disconnections between them. While SMEs judged the top-five constructs to be the same for both transitions, the next section will illustrate how these constructs manifest themselves differently in a developmental progression across the two transitions and become increasingly complex through the type of cognitive processing that is possible as the child matures and the surrounding contexts shape career development.

What learners should know and be able to do at each developmental transition

Two constructs (Self-Efficacy Beliefs and Exploration) will be used to illustrate the developmental progression of critical career constructs across the two transitions. In addition, examples of teaching strategies are suggested that can be used to encourage the cognitive processing related to these constructs at the K–5 and Grades 6–8 transitions. These strategies are informed by models used to understand the cognitive demands associated with different curriculum activities and learning tasks (Marzano & Kendall, 2008; Webb, 2002, 2007). While there are multiple ways in which cognitive processing complexity or cognitive complexity has been defined, the definition used here juxtaposes cognitive complexity and simplicity:

> an aspect of a person's cognitive functioning which at one end is defined by the use of many constructs [ways of perceiving the world] with many relationships to one another (complexity) and at the other end by the use of few constructs with limited relationships to one another (simplicity).
>
> (Pervin, 1984, p. 507)

This broad conceptualisation of cognitive processing can be used to understand differences in the way in which career constructs manifest themselves at transitions between the ages of 6 and 11 and 12 to 14. For younger children, career development tasks require less complexity and fewer relationship connections than tasks for older children. This is evidenced by examples of knowledge and skill statements that follow, which are part of a much larger set of statements for constructs across the kindergarten to career continuum that have been developed for the *Education and Career Navigation* domain of the holistic framework (Bobek & Zhao, 2015).

Self-Efficacy Beliefs have consistently been found to be pivotal in promoting personal agency and successful educational and career transitions across the lifespan (Lent & Brown, 2013). These task-specific perceptions of ability are fundamental to progressing through the elementary school transition where such beliefs begin to shape children's understanding of themselves and possible future pathways and the middle school transition where these beliefs take on nuances and more complexity to play a key formative role in the decision-making process, wherein high school plans evolve and decisions are made.

Before 12 years of age, children should be able to accomplish the following: 'Explain how confident you are that you will do well in each of your school subjects.' To be successful, children need information about their performance accomplishments related to different school subjects and the experiences they have with subject-specific tasks. Drawing on this knowledge, children then use their ability to describe how well they think they will do in their academic subjects. This would not require extended processing or conceptual transformation of the knowledge. Children could briefly explain or describe their level of confidence in each of their academic subjects. Counsellors and teachers could question and listen to children and require children to produce academic products where learners are able to explain their answers in a relatively straightforward manner.

Before 15 years of age, children should be able to complete the following task: 'Determine how your level of confidence in a subject can influence which classes you will take in high school.' Here more complex cognitive processing is required, as it relies on the knowledge that is needed to establish one's belief about one's ability to do well in various subjects as well as the ability to connect this information to a future state involving selection of high school classes. Analysing subject-specific information in relation to a future purpose demands greater cognitive complexity. Children would need to articulate their reasoning from this analysis and use supporting evidence to make new connections. Children could debate, assess, and think more deeply about these connections. Counsellors and teachers could act as information resources, question students, and then guide student discussions. Children's work products could include activities such as written reports and panel discussions.

Exploration has been identified as a critical strategy for engaging children in school and facilitating identity development (Flum & Kaplan, 2006). Using an exploratory approach, children are able to seek out and process educational and occupational information guided by an emerging understanding of oneself. By 12 years of age, children should be able to complete the following: 'Explore one or more occupations based on what you like to do.' Children use knowledge of their emerging interests to search for or discover information about occupations related to those preferences. Cognitively, a relatively limited number of connections need to be made wherein children contrast or compare occupations based on interests and classify and sort careers into meaningful categories. Here children are actively learning about the world of work within the personal context of their interests. These children are beginning to construct tentative narratives about who they are in relation to their environment and to make early exploratory choices that arise from competing and conflicting options. Counsellors and teachers can ask questions and reinforce the learning through assignments such as journaling to reflect on the occupations they have explored, creating a blog to share what they are finding and how it relates to them, and meeting people working in occupations of interest to them.

Before 15 years of age, children should be able to complete the following task: 'Research the educational requirements of occupations that you would like to pursue.' This involves children investigating the education needed for desired future occupation alternatives. Cognitively, there is more complexity in these relationships as children sort through, coordinate, and analyse information about the self, education, and occupations. Through this increasingly complex set of connections, children create personal relevance between their aspirations and the world of work and education. Children use reflection and synthesise information as they explore possible occupations and consider decisions that have unpredictable and unexpected outcomes (e.g., making a decision to commit oneself to a specific career pathway). Children would engage in research, take risks, formulate a proposal, and create a plan to guide their high school studies. Counsellors and teachers can help children analyse information about themselves and the environment and evaluate children's work. Learners could create academic products such as multi-paragraph essays, creative media products, and coherent narrative stories related to future possible selves (Markus & Nurius, 1986). Examples of high-level writing assignments completed by middle school children are presented in the next section as part of promising interventions.

Promising school-based career development practices and interventions

Four promising intervention practices are highlighted that can be utilised in schools to assist children to successfully transition through career development challenges and opportunities. These are guidance classroom curriculum, integrating career development into the academic curriculum, individualised learning plans, and engaging parents and families. First, guidance classroom curriculum has become a recommended approach in the United States and is now quite common in both elementary and middle schools. Coming from the seminal work of Gysbers and Henderson (2012) and now embraced and incorporated into the national model of the American School Counselor Association (2012), professional school counsellors deliver classroom lessons on a wide range of critical career development issues facing students and families (e.g., from understanding career interests to thinking about how to pay for postsecondary education). These lessons are delivered in classrooms and small group settings and can be brought to scale across an entire school. Small to moderate effects have been consistently found for classroom curriculum and small group instruction that engage children in activities embedded in sound career development research (e.g., Brown & Ryan Krane, 2000; Turner & Lapan, 2005; Whiston, Tai, Rahardja, & Eder, 2011). For example, in a study of seventh grade Swiss students, Hirschi and Läge (2008) used the

Cognitive Information Processing Approach (Sampson, Reardon, Peterson, & Lenz, 2004) to deliver nine teaching modules in a structured group workshop format. Positive gains for children were found in the development of their vocational identity and career exploration. Also, delivering guidance classroom curriculum with appropriate and effective accommodations will greatly enhance the career self-efficacy and exploration for students with disabilities. For example, children on the autism spectrum can be successfully included in classroom guidance lessons by pacing activities and discussions, intentionally facilitating interaction between a student with autism and other students, and using visual as well as verbal information and cues. Children with sensory impairments can be engaged in classroom lessons by identifying and securing appropriate assistive technology (e.g., screen readers for students with visual impairments, interpreters for students with hearing impairments).

Second, integrating career development into the academic curriculum has the potential to also impact student academic achievement and become a sustainable approach across the whole school or school district. For example, Woolley, Rose, Orthner, Akos, and Jones-Sanpei (2013) developed a career-relevant instructional strategy to more deeply engage middle school children by increasing the perceived relevance of the academic curriculum to possible jobs and occupations. *CareerStart* classroom lessons help teachers and students connect the curriculum to real-world adult jobs (Woolley *et al.*, 2013). This exploration process blends academic learning with a career development approach that leads youth to better understand the relevance between what they are learning and realistic, attainable careers where the academic skills covered in the curriculum are actually used. While findings have not been significant in relation to gains in reading, this approach has found significant gains in end-of-grading term mathematics tests scores.

Lapan *et al.* (2016) developed a promising middle school approach for infusing theory and research-supported career development constructs and practices into standards-based English Language Arts (ELA) classroom instruction. An interdisciplinary team (teachers, school counsellors, multimedia specialist, and special education teacher) collaborated to carry out this eight-week curriculum. Career agency emerged as a critical nuanced construct for children and was strongly related to standardised test scores, ELA end-of-year grades, and positive gains in sixth- to seventh-grade test scores. The culminating project in this curriculum required students to synthesise, reflect, and write a multi-paragraph essay about their college and career dreams and how they were preparing themselves to deal with the challenges awaiting them in high school. The two examples that follow illustrate how students used a standards-based writing curriculum to produce essays that personalised and organised relationships around themes of career concern and emotional well-being (Savickas, 2013). The first paragraph was titled 'Life Is Good' and the second as 'Life Is Upset.':

> My life is a bright purple book, with a white question mark that pops on the cover. Each page is silky smooth with a gold border around the edges. As I open my book and jump in, I begin to walk. As I am walking I hear

many stories of the struggles I will face and already have. In the sky I see myself fighting those struggles and in the end I come out on top. This makes me optimistic for what the future will hold. I stop to feel the soft warm air as it touches my cheek. Then I take a deep breath in and smell nothing but my aspirations. As I walk deeper into my book I taste success, something I longed for, this is the best feeling in the world.

I'm standing in the middle of the road waiting for something. I gaze up at the white clouds and I notice it's colour change from a happy blue to a mean grey. The icy raindrops hit my skin like a t.v. smashing into a wall. The wind was moving the trees as if it wants to pull it by the roots. That's when it hit me a whirlwind is coming. My life is just like that whirlwind it goes round and round. The whirlwind was too fast because I had to manage a lot of things especially when I lost my grandmother. Way before she left my life was so great and fun I never had whirlwind. After she left my life went downhill. That is when the whirlwind had just begun. I was very optimistic that it would slow down. I was wrong.

These essays personalised and made the learning of standards-based ELA curriculum more relevant to the lives of these children. They were able to use the integrated curriculum to both achieve academically and grow personally. Analysis of their writings revealed that these 12- and 13-year-old children were motivated to explore and grapple with key career development challenges (e.g., developing a positive time perspective and dealing with the challenges of self-direction). Career development interventions that can be united with standards-based curricula have great potential for capitalising on the synergy possible between an interdisciplinary team of educators and bring the benefits of sound career development practices to scale and to a central sustainable position in schools. Career development programming that is integrated into the academic curriculum could also include social and independent-living skills training, career awareness information and exercises, career counselling, community experiences (e.g., job-site visits, accessing public transportation), career mentoring, and work study. These factors have all been shown to be predictors of both in-school academic success and positive post-school career outcomes for children with disabilities.

Third, individualised learning plans (ILPs) have been identified as a possible promising practice. There is a growing hope and some supporting research in the United States that to aid children in their transition to high school, every student should complete an ILP by the end of middle school (Hammond *et al.*, 2013). The Rennie Center (2011) outlined ILPs as student-driven planning and self-monitoring tools providing youth the opportunity to develop postsecondary goals, explore college and career options, and become an autonomous self-regulated learner. ILPs are seen as a strategy to enhance youth's college and career readiness. Solberg, Phelps, Haakenson, Durham, and Timmons (2012) highlighted how ILPs have two basic parts: a portfolio document that is created and annually updated as well as a process that assists students to more deeply engage in self-exploration of interests, skills, and values. ILPs can also assist children with disabilities to master key self-advocacy and self-determination skills that research has found to be strongly connected to both in-school and post-school success (National Secondary Transition Technical Assistance Center, 2011).

Fourth, engaging parents and families in the career exploration and development of children is a practice that also warrants greater attention and research. Parents have significant influence on the thoughts, beliefs, and behaviours of their children (Lapan, 2008). Early in their development, children learn about work directly and indirectly from their parents and family. Adults convey work attitudes (e.g., work is fun or work is drudgery, certain types of work are stereotypically appropriate for males or females) and work behaviours (e.g., bringing projects home at night, wearing a uniform to work) throughout their daily lives with their offspring. Research also shows that children are more likely to report aspirations similar to their parents (Trice, Hughes, Odom, Woods, & McClellan, 1995), and a large majority have ideas about the preparation needed for occupations that are also similar to their parents (Otto, 2000). Given the important role parents play in influencing children's career development, it is critical to involve parents in intentional, planned, and goal-oriented approaches that will enable them to be more effective. Based on a study with German students (Schmitt-Rodermund & Vondracek, 1999), engaging in joint activities with parents between the ages of 6 and 12 years positively relates to greater breadth of exploration during childhood, which is linked to greater exploration and career planning during later adolescence. Further, building coordinated and collaborative efforts between schools and parents of children with disabilities has the potential to optimise the career exploration, understanding, and confidence so clearly needed by these young people (Morningstar *et al.*, 2010).

A number of parental strategies that facilitate child career exploration and development have been suggested. One strategy involves having conversations with children that would allow parents to share accurate information about educational pathways and occupations (Lapan, 2008; Niles & Harris-Bowlsbey, 2013). This would require increasing the capacities of parents to understand different aspects of the world of work and education (Levine & Sutherland, 2013). Herr, Cramer, and Niles (2004) identify other strategies such as parents encouraging children to examine their interests, values, and skills and providing work opportunities at home and in the community. While it is clear that parents and family are crucial to the career development of children and there are relevant strategies for involving parents in this process, it is not as clear which methods are most effective. These are important areas for future research.

Conclusion

Career exploration and development play important roles in facilitating children's academic, motivational, and self-regulatory growth. Research is beginning to articulate a much clearer picture of the transitions and career constructs that

School-based approaches and child career development 169

shape this development. Children have adaptive advantages when they know and are able to perform (at a level of complexity and depth appropriate to their age) foundational career development tasks characteristic of the age 6 to 11 and 12 to 14 transitions. Career exploration and developmental activities are more than add-on enrichment practices. They have the potential to add unique value for children and their families. Schools would take a step forward by more fully implementing evidence-supported strategies that capitalise on the synergy possible between interdisciplinary teams of educators. Such career exploration and development practices can be brought to scale and sustained across schools and school districts to benefit all children as they progress towards being college and career ready.

References

ACT. (2007). *Impact of cognitive, psychosocial, and career factors on educational and workplace success.* Iowa City, IA. Retrieved from http://act.org/research/policymakers/pdf/Cognitive Noncognitive.pdf

Akos, P. (2005). The unique nature of middle school counseling. *Professional School Counseling, 9*, 95–103.

Akos, P., Konold, T., & Niles, S. G. (2004). A career readiness typology and typal membership in middle school. *The Career Development Quarterly, 53*, 53–66.

Alliman-Brissett, A. E., Turner, S. L., & Skovholt, T. M. (2004). Parent support and African American adolescents' career self-efficacy. *Professional School Counseling, 7*, 124–132.

American School Counselor Association. (2012). *ASCA national model: A framework for school counseling programs.* Alexandria, VA: American School Counselor Association.

Bigler, R. S., Averhart, C. J., & Liben, L. S. (2003). Race and the workforce: Occupational status, aspirations, and stereotyping among African American children. *Developmental Psychology, 39*, 572–580.

Bobek, B., & Zhao, R. (2015). Education and career navigation. In W. Camara, R. O'Connor, K. Mattern, & M. A. Hanson (Eds.), *Beyond academics: A holistic framework for enhancing education and workplace success.* ACT Research Report Series. Retrieved from http://www.act.org/research/researchers/reports/pdf/ACT_RR2015–4.pdf

Brown, S. D., & Ryan Krane, N. E. (2000). Four (or five) sessions and a cloud of dust: Old assumptions and new observations about career counseling. In S. D. Brown & R. W. Lent (Eds.), *Handbook of counseling psychology* (3rd ed., pp. 740–766). New York, NY: Wiley.

Camara, W., O'Connor, R., Mattern, K., & Hanson, M. A. (Eds.). (2015). *Beyond academics: A holistic framework for enhancing education and workplace success.* ACT Research Report Series. Retrieved from http://www.act.org/research/researchers/reports/pdf/ACT_RR2015–4.pdf

Care, E., Deans, J., & Brown, R. (2007). The realism and sex type of four-to five-year-old children's occupational aspirations. *Journal of Early Childhood Research, 5*, 155–168.

Cook, T. D., Church, M. B., Ajanaku, S., Shadish, W. R., Kim, J. R., & Cohen, R. (1996). The development of occupational aspirations and expectations among inner city boys. *Child Development, 67*, 3368–3385.

Eccles, J. S., Vida, M. N., & Barber, B. (2004). The relation of early adolescents' college plans and both academic ability and task-value beliefs to subsequent college enrollment. *The Journal of Early Adolescence, 24*, 63–77.

Flum, H., & Kaplan, A. (2006). Exploratory orientation as an educational goal. *Educational Psychologist, 41*, 99–110.

Gysbers, N. C., & Henderson, P. (2012). *Developing and managing your school guidance and counseling program* (5th ed.). Alexandria, VA: American Counseling Association.

Hammond, C., Drew, S., Withington, C., Griffith, C., Swiger, C., Mobley, C., & Sharp, J. (2013). *Programs of study as a state policy mandate: A longitudinal study of the South Carolina personal pathway to success initiative.* National Research Center for Career and Technical Education. Louisville, KY: University of Louisville.

Hartung, P. J., Porfeli, E. J., & Vondracek, F. W. (2005). Child vocational development: A review and reconsideration. *Journal of Vocational Behavior, 66*, 385–419.

Herr, E. L., Cramer, S. H., & Niles, S. G. (2004). *Career guidance and counseling through the lifespan – Systematic approaches* (6th ed.). Boston, MA: Allyn & Bacon.

Hill, N. E., Ramirez, C., & Dumka, L. E. (2003). Early adolescents' career aspirations: A qualitative study of perceived barriers and family support among low-income, ethnically diverse adolescents. *Journal of Family Issues, 24*, 934–959.

Hirschi, A., & Läge, D. (2008). Using accuracy of self-estimated interest type as a sign of career choice readiness in career assessment of secondary students. *Journal of Career Assessment, 16*, 310–325.

Howard, K. A., Carlstrom, A. H., Katz, A. D., Chew, A. Y., Ray, G. C., Laine, L., & Caulum, D. (2011). Career aspirations of youth: Untangling race/ethnicity, SES, and gender. *Journal of Vocational Behavior, 79*, 98–109.

Keller, B. K., & Whiston, S. C. (2008). The role of parental influences on young adolescents' career development. *Journal of Career Assessment, 20*, 1–20.

Lapan, R. T. (2008). *More than a job: Helping your teenagers find success and satisfaction in their future careers.* Alexandria, VA: American Counseling Association.

Lapan, R. T., Marcotte, A. M., Storey, R., Carbone, P. E., Loher-Lapan, S., Guerin, D., . . . Mahoney, S. (2016). Infusing career development to strengthen middle school English language arts curricula. *The Career Development Quarterly, 64*, 126–139.

Lent, R. W., & Brown, S. D. (2013). Social cognitive model of career self-management: Toward a unifying view of adaptive career behavior across the lifespan. *Journal of Counseling Psychology, 60*, 557–568.

Levine, K. A., & Sutherland, D. (2013). History repeats itself: Parental involvement in children's career exploration. *Canadian Journal of Counselling and Psychotherapy, 47*, 239–255.

Markus, H., & Nurius, P. (1986). Possible selves. *American Psychologist, 41*, 954–969.

Marzano, R. J., & Kendall, J. S. (Eds.). (2008). *Designing and assessing educational objectives: Applying the new taxonomy.* Thousand Oaks, CA: Corwin Press.

Morningstar, M. E., Frey, B. B., Noonan, P. M., Ng, J., Clavenna-Deane, B., Graves, P., . . . Williams-Diehm, K. (2010). A preliminary investigation of the relationship of transition preparation and self-determination for students with disabilities in postsecondary educational settings. *Career Development for Exceptional Individuals, 33*, 80–94.

National Secondary Transition Technical Assistance Center (NSTTAC). (2011). *Predictors of in-school and post-school success.* Charlotte, NC: Author. Retrieved from http://nsttac.org/sites/default/files/assets/pdf/pdf/ebps/PredictorsInOutOfSchool_Jan2013.pdf

Niles, S. G., & Harris-Bowlsbey, J. (2013). *Career development interventions in the 21st century* (4th ed.). Upper Saddle River, NJ: Pearson.

Otto, L. B. (2000). Youth perspectives on parental career influence. *Journal of Career Development, 27*, 111–118.

Patton, W., Bartrum, D. A., & Creed, P. A. (2004). Gender differences for optimism, self-esteem, expectations and goals in predicting career planning and exploration in adolescents. *International Journal for Educational and Vocational Guidance, 4*, 193–209.

Pervin, L. A. (1984). *Personality: Theory and research* (4th ed.). New York, NY: John Wiley & Sons.

Porfeli, E. J., & Lee, B. (2012). Career development during childhood and adolescence. *New Directions for Youth Development, 134*, 11–22.

Rennie Center for Education Research & Policy. (2011). *Student learning plans: Supporting every student's transition to college and career.* Cambridge, MA: Rennie Center for Education Research & Policy.

Rowan-Kenyon, H. T., Swan, A. K., & Creager, M. F. (2012). Social cognitive factors, support, and engagement: Early adolescents' math interests as precursors to choice of career. *The Career Development Quarterly, 60*, 2–15.

Sampson, J. P., Reardon, R. C., Peterson, G. W., & Lenz, J. G. (2004). *Career counseling and services: A cognitive information processing approach.* Belmont, CA: Thomson/Brooks/Cole.

Savickas, M. L. (2013). Career construction theory and practice. In S. D. Brown & R. W. Lent (Eds.), *Career development and counseling: Putting theory and research to work* (2nd ed., pp. 147–183). Hoboken, NJ: John Wiley & Sons.

Schmitt-Rodermund, E., & Vondracek, F. W. (1999). Breadth of interests, exploration, and identity development in adolescence. *Journal of Vocational Behavior, 55*, 298–317.

Schultheiss, D. E. P., Palma, T. V., & Manzi, A. J. (2005). Career development in middle childhood: A qualitative inquiry. *The Career Development Quarterly, 53*, 246–262.

Solberg, V. S., Phelps, L. A., Haakenson, K. A., Durham, J. F., & Timmons, J. (2012). The nature and use of individualized learning plans as a promising career intervention strategy. *Journal of Career Development, 39*, 500–514.

Trice, A. D., Hughes, M. A., Odom, C., Woods, K., & McClellan, N. C. (1995). The origins of children's career aspirations: IV. Testing hypotheses from four theories. *The Career Development Quarterly, 43*, 307–322.

Turner, S. L., & Lapan, R. T. (2005). Evaluation of an intervention to increase non-traditional career interests and career-related self-efficacy among middle-school adolescents. *Journal of Vocational Behavior, 66*, 516–531.

Watson, M., & McMahon, M. (2005). Children's career development: A research review from a learning perspective. *Journal of Vocational Behavior, 67*, 119–132.

Webb, N. L. (2002). *Depth-of-knowledge levels for four content areas.* Retrieved from http://schools.nyc.gov/NR/rdonlyres/2711181C-2108–40C4-A7F8–76F243C9B910/0/DOK-FourContentAreas.pdf

Webb, N. L. (2007). Issues related to judging the alignment of curriculum standards and assessments. *Applied Measurement in Education, 20*, 7–25.

Weisgram, E. S., & Bigler, R. S. (2006). Girls and science careers: The role of altruistic values and attitudes about scientific tasks. *Journal of Applied Developmental Psychology, 27*, 326–348.

Whiston, S. C., Tai, W. L., Rahardja, D., & Eder, K. (2011). School counseling outcome: A meta-analytic examination of interventions. *Journal of Counseling and Development, 89*, 37–55.

Woolley, M. E., Rose, R. A., Orthner, D. K., Akos, P. T., & Jones-Sanpei, H. (2013). Advancing academic achievement through career relevance in the middle grades: A longitudinal evaluation of CareerStart. *American Educational Research Journal, 50*, 1309–1335.

Chapter 14

Targeted career exploration and development programmes

Anthony Barnes and Barbara McGowan

In this chapter, we make the case for early career exploration and development programmes that can benefit children with additional needs such as those who have learning difficulties and disabilities or who come from socio-economically deprived backgrounds. We discuss the reasons for the disappointingly piecemeal nature of many initiatives that make examples of good practice activities and programmes hard to come by. From recent projects and research, we distil the key features of effective practice in meeting the specific needs of disadvantaged children up to the age of 14. Finally, we reflect on what more could be done to provide sustained and consistent support for children with additional needs to promote their well-being and enable them to participate fully in society and economic life.

Acting on a concern for equality, diversity, and inclusion

The career development profession has a long-standing commitment to fairness and social justice (Arthur & Collins, 2014; Irving & Malik, 2005). This goes some way towards explaining the field's commitment to raising aspirations, strengthening aspirational capability, boosting self-esteem, improving social mobility, strengthening engagement in learning, and closing the attainment gap for disadvantaged children. Current practice in school-based career exploration and development activities is still focused mainly on the latter stages of compulsory schooling. What is becoming increasingly apparent from recent research is that career interventions can have a greater impact and make more of a difference to children's education and employment prospects if they are started earlier (Barnes, 2015).

The lens of equality, diversity, and inclusion helps us to clarify the intended benefits of improving access to career exploration and development programmes for all children. Multicultural societies such as the United States and Canada have articulated the moral and social case for promoting harmony and integration, but much attention has been focused also on the business argument. Companies that approach equality and diversity in a strategic way are able to widen their talent pool, stimulate innovation and creativity, improve customer care, and strengthen their global economic competitiveness (Department for Business, Innovation and Skills, 2013). Career programmes which develop the 'soft' skills that employers are looking for such as working in a team and presenting oneself well to others can lay the foundations of children's future employability.

A concern for equality, diversity, and inclusion begins to address the issues faced by individuals living in poverty, living in care ('looked after children'), being a young carer themselves (e.g., looking after a parent), and having special educational needs or health problems. Ofsted, the education inspectorate in England, has argued that these issues require a full response from the school system (Ofsted, undated). Early career programmes for children can tackle these social exclusion issues by improving self-esteem and self-efficacy, raising aspirations and attainment, widening horizons, engaging families, and developing and promoting 'active inclusion' strategies to break down the barriers to participation and hence minimising the effect of contextual factors on a child's progress (Levine, Sutherland, & Cole, 2015).

In the United Kingdom, the Equality Act (2010) places a statutory duty on publicly funded schools to advance equality of opportunity, foster good relations across all people, and eliminate harassment and discriminatory practices. It is designed particularly to support and uphold the interests of children with protected characteristics defined as race, disability, sex, religion or belief, sexual orientation, pregnancy and maternity, and gender reassignment. The Equality and Human Rights Commission (EHRC, 2012a) asserts that implementing this duty will help schools to tackle attainment gaps, reduce inequalities in school exclusions, promote participation, engage children in learning, tackle bullying, and improve career learning and progression.

Whilst much of the aforementioned will be recognisable in career programmes for the over-14 age range, much work still needs to be done to establish a coherent rationale for undertaking preventive work with children up to the age of 14. Where no compulsion or incentive exists to firmly ground career education in the primary or elementary curriculum, it depends on the vision, commitment, and goodwill of staff in the school (often battling against competing priorities and lack of funding) and/or external partner agencies (such as charitable organisations, enlightened employers, and careers guidance services) to sustain it. It also requires the establishment of a fully fledged career development culture in schools. Education systems that require primary schools to teach career education – such as British Columbia and Ontario (Canada), the Czech Republic, Denmark, and, more recently, Croatia, Estonia, and Hungary – will probably recognise that legislation by itself is not enough. Countries such as New Zealand, some American states (e.g., Missouri and Georgia), England, and Scotland that have voluntary guidelines and resources recognise that take-up is often patchy.

Providing programmes to tackle socio-economic disadvantage

The Equality and Human Rights Commission in the United Kingdom has gone some way to supporting and developing practice through *Equal Choices,*

Equal Chances, a career education resource available online (EHRC, 2012b). It illustrates a number of features of effective practice in early career interventions:

1 It seeks to enable schools to tackle 'occupational segregation' by encouraging children aged 9 to 11 in England to think more broadly about the sorts of gender roles they can occupy in employment. An example would be by arranging for children to talk to men and women who work in non-stereotypical jobs. Resources include teachers' notes, posters, and lesson activities clustered into five learning areas with accompanying PowerPoint presentations and lesson materials. An additional resource is 'Pass It On', an engaging short video telling children to pass on the message to other children that they do not have to follow gender-determined career choices nor those indicated by social status, ethnicity, culture or disability.

2 It helps to tackle one of the critical barriers to the career development of children with a range of specific needs by raising awareness of the necessity to change the perceptions of the rest of the population about who can do what in society. Changing negative attitudes to 'difference' in the workforce is one of the biggest challenges that those with disabilities, mental health problems, and others face.

3 Whilst *Equal Choices, Equal Chances* is a 'one-size-fits-all' resource, it offers teachers and career development professionals the opportunity to customise the material to meet the identified needs of individuals and groups with whom they are working. The aims of career exploration and development are essentially the same for all children; what differs are the ways of getting there (i.e., the pedagogical and guidance approaches employed), the rate of progress that children are able to make, and how far they can get.

The expectation for children using *Equal Choices, Equal Chances* is that they should be able to:

- recognise and accept individual differences and uniqueness;
- tell their own story and imagine their dreams and hopes for the future;
- identify when stereotyping and discrimination are taking place and develop emotional recognition to respond appropriately, including strategies to challenge these;
- challenge preconceptions about who does different jobs and why they work;
- identify and describe some of the jobs done in their community; and
- recognise and embrace diversity in the local workforce.

The programme seeks to achieve the aforementioned expectations via a range of approaches that teachers and career development professionals will recognise as embracing features of good practice, including activities to:

Targeted career exploration and development programmes 175

- promote self-awareness and personal reflection;
- engage children and young people in respecting equality, diversity, and inclusion;
- promote career awareness and career exploration; and
- engage parents and employers.

The key features of effective practice in career exploration and development programmes that promote equal opportunities for children include teacher awareness of:

- cultural sensitivity in terms of religious, cultural, and moral values of the children they teach and support;
- materials that avoid stereotypes, use gender-free terms and portray different lifestyles;
- cultural tradition not being sufficient justification to continue stereotyping and discrimination and that children have a right to challenge this;
- the need to widen children's access to inspirational role models; and
- the need to boost children's social and cultural capital. The Aspires 10–13 project, for example, specifically looks at how to build children's science capital.

(Archer, 2013)

In 2009–10, the then Department for Children, Schools and Families (DCSF) funded a pathfinder research project to discover if planned career interventions for 10- and 11-year-olds in socio-economically deprived areas could help tackle problems such as stereotyped thinking about subject and career choice, poverty of aspiration and low attainment, disengagement from school, and unsuccessful transitions. In recognition of their different starting points, each of the 38 participating schools from seven local authority areas was given considerable freedom and flexibility to decide how to deliver the project. They all drew on a rich vein of previously published guidance in England (DES, ED, & Welsh Office, 1987; DfES, 2001; HMI, 1988; Law & McGowan, 1999; National Curriculum Council, 1990; SCAA, 1995). The evaluation of the pathfinder research project by the National Foundation for Educational Research (NFER) involved case study visits to seven schools and a survey administered in three termly sweeps to over 4,500 children in all participating (i.e., treatment) schools and comparison schools (Wade et al., 2011).

The range of activities undertaken by the schools included:

- University visits – This experience had a subtle impact on children and parents who knew little or nothing about university education. On one visit, children experienced a 'lesson' in a laboratory about the evolution of birds' beaks using tweezers and chopsticks! The university gave children disposable cameras to take pictures of themselves on campus as a permanent reminder that university was a place where people like them could go. Another school arranged for photographs of children in mini-academic gowns as a similar message to families.

- Drama and role-play workshops – Children put on performances for their parents about their career dreams and aspirations.
- Cultural trips – These activities were inspired by ideas of boosting children's cultural capital. One school in a deprived area on the outskirts of a large city took children into the city centre to visit museums and other cultural centres. Another school took children on a trip on a train. For many children, this was the first time they had experienced such things.
- Employer-led activities – A human resources director ran a confidence-building workshop with children.
- Career fairs – One school organised an afternoon for parents to come into school to answer questions about their jobs. Parents showed children the equipment they used, the products they made, and their work clothes. One mother brought examples of training shoes she designed. A father who worked in a dental lab brought examples of the dentures he made. The children drew pictures and wrote about what had interested them most.
- Assemblies – Most schools held assemblies presented by the children themselves to celebrate and showcase what they had been doing. Such activities can influence the culture and ethos of the school.
- Career games – Several schools ran the *Make It Real* game (www.realgame. co.uk).
- Circle time – Talking in a group provided emotional support and reflective time to process learning experiences such as transitions, e.g., 'What I will miss about leaving this school is . . .', 'What I hope to find at my new school is . . .'

The external evaluation conducted by NFER for the Department concluded that "the programme has the potential to help 'close the gap' for disadvantaged pupils, (and) encourage schools to develop a curriculum and practices that best suit their circumstances" (Wade *et al.*, 2011, p. 8). The survey methodology succeeded in measuring the impact of quite small changes, which was remarkable given the short period of the classroom trial (effectively about eight months) and the fact that the career-related learning interventions were only a small part of the total curriculum experience for children. The use of multi-level modelling enabled the researchers to examine the impact of the project on six general outcomes:

1. Stereotypical thinking

This was identified as an issue because of its ability to get in the way of children seeing their own and their friends' possibilities. All children showed a general improvement (i.e., their thinking became less stereotypical) across time, but the change was much bigger in the participating schools as the project progressed. Boys benefited most, but girls in the pathfinder schools also became less stereotypical in their thinking than those in the comparison schools. Girls and the more academically 'successful' children were generally less stereotypical in their thinking.

2. Career-related learning effectiveness

Pathfinder schools generally rated career-related learning effectiveness more highly than the comparison schools. There was a greater impact on children with special education needs and gifted and talented children in the pathfinder schools. This analysis is particularly relevant to issues of targeting and value for money for future career exploration and development programmes.

3. Children's confidence in their ability to work effectively

Generally, children showed significantly improved confidence over time (and especially those with English as an additional language, for example, recent immigrants) but this was not confined to the pathfinder schools. However, socio-economically deprived children in pathfinder schools showed a greater improvement in confidence as the project progressed.

4. Parental aspirations for their children

Generally, children felt that their parents developed higher aspirations for them, but this improvement was not maintained, and by the end of the pathfinder, the levels had returned to the baseline. This finding that the pathfinder had made no difference is perhaps not surprising given the case study evidence of relatively weak involvement of parents in the programme. In future work, it would be highly desirable to find out if a more focused and deliberate policy of engaging parents produced more discernible effects.

5. Attitude to learning

Children in both participating and comparison schools registered less positive attitudes to learning as the project progressed, so there is no evidence that the programme mitigated that effect. Children in receipt of free school meals (FSM) showed a significantly greater decline in their attitude to learning, but the reasons for this are not clear. It may be a reaction to school work becoming harder, but it would be interesting to explore what other kinds of career-related interventions could make a difference.

6. Confidence in ability to do different jobs

This was a measure of 'self-efficacy', i.e., what children felt they 'could do' rather than what they would 'like to do' or were 'likely to do'. Children were presented with picture questions about five levels/types of jobs: professional, associate professional, skilled, customer service/operative, and elementary (low skill). All children generally became more confident, but there were significant differences regarding gender, special educational needs, and age group in terms of children's confidence to do different types/levels of jobs. There was particular evidence of value-added impact within pathfinder schools relating to children receiving FSM and ten-year-olds, who showed a significant increase in confidence in their ability to do a professional job in the future. Boys in pathfinder schools showed a greater increase in confidence than girls concerning their ability do a skilled job in the future. In the focus groups, some children said that they were now working harder and making connections that they had not made before, e.g., between getting on at school and getting a good job. Howard and Walsh's (2011) work on children's cognitive reasoning applied to career development was published too late to inform the project but provides a useful framework for future projects to assess the impact of career interventions on children's career thinking.

The pathfinder research project also showed evidence of children's improved career management skills such as teamwork and the ability to work autonomously. It also registered improved attendance and attainment with a perception in some schools that this had helped to improve School Attainment Test results for 11-year-old children. This last benefit was widely expected to win the support of senior leaders in schools to the programme! Eleven-year-old children also showed increased self-confidence and reduced concerns, especially around the transition to secondary school, with children receiving FSM showing a greater improvement in confidence than their non-FSM peers.

Generally, schools and local authorities felt the project had exceeded expectations: children benefited, teachers enjoyed it, and useful links with local businesses and universities had been forged. What we can learn from the pathfinder research project is that:

- it is more important with this age group to focus on learning outcomes which promote children's self-awareness and career exploration than on inappropriate questioning such as 'Do you know what you want to be yet?' The pathfinder used a framework of learning outcomes which has influenced the development of other frameworks such as the Framework for Careers, Enterprise and Employability (Career Development Institute, 2015);
- career-related learning is more effective when it is carefully planned and sustainably embedded in the mainstream curriculum using the same rigour that would be applied to other subjects;
- ready-made activities can help practitioners with the initial capacity building in their schools but many teachers quickly found that both they and the children were inspired by their experience of the pathfinder to design new activities around existing curriculum hotspots. For example, one school already held an Enterprise week for 10- to11-year-olds and grafted careers activities onto it, rather than the other way round;

- some unexpectedly successful activities happen serendipitously. For example, the survey questionnaire that the children completed gave rise to much interesting discussion between teachers and children. As teachers grew in confidence, they were able to capitalise on everyday and informal classroom opportunities to talk about careers. One parent told researchers that the activities the school arranged had been an enabling trigger for conversations with her daughter about careers. It would be advantageous if future projects could explore how schools can engage and empower parents as co-partners in promoting their children's career exploration and development;
- the expected hesitancy from class teachers about participating in the pathfinder research project because of their own lack of knowledge about careers and labour-market information or the lack of training received beforehand did not emerge. Most teachers did not feel the need for extended formal training. They learnt what to say and do from shared and discussed experiences with the children – a classic example of teachers and children learning together rather than the teachers telling children everything that they know about a subject; and
- a single school year is not long enough to bring about sustained change in how the majority of schools promote career exploration and development. Most pathfinder schools indicated that they wanted to carry on providing some career activities, but the loss of external funding, the break-up of the supporting infrastructure, and competing school priorities meant that some schools made limited further progress.

Raising the career aspirations of children whose families are living in poverty requires structured, extensive engagement with parents, especially mothers. An analysis by Flouri and Panourgia (2012) of more than 11,000 children taking part in the Millennium Cohort Study shows that children's resilience is related to their career aspirations at age seven. They found that more ambitious children from poor backgrounds have fewer behaviour problems than their equally disadvantaged peers. They also discovered that career aspirations are related to the level of the mother's qualifications and not to family poverty *per se*.

Providing programmes for children with special educational needs and disabilities

Article 23 of the United Nations Convention on the Rights of the Child states, "A young person with special needs has the right to special care, education and training to help him or her enjoy a full and decent life in dignity and achieve a greater degree of self-reliance and social integration"(UNICEF, 1990, p. 8). Effective schools will have strategies in place to access the resources provided by charities and education and health bodies and to draw up individual education and health-care plans. Accurate, early diagnosis and assessment of a specific learning difficulty or disability is vital for identifying relevant support that will protect the child from later failure to make progress in education, training, and employment. For example, dyslexia affects children of all abilities, girls as well as boys (although it is more common in boys), in different ways, and with varying levels of severity. As important as experts are in the diagnosis and assessment of dyslexia, it is the everyday support by teachers and their assistants that makes the real difference to the child's career and life chances. They can:

- improve the child's literacy skills (vital for employability);
- maintain their motivation and self-esteem and help them overcome frustration and barriers;
- nurture the strengths that dyslexic children may display, for example, verbal communication skills (good for acting), lateral thinking skills (good for problem solving); physical skills (good for sport), or spatial skills (good for design, building, and construction).

The career development needs of children with learning difficulties and disabilities vary greatly, but the features of good practice in the design and implementation of programmes for these children include elements applicable to all children, such as:

- structuring transition programmes. From a career development perspective, the transfer from one phase or stage of education to the next is a rite of passage for all children akin to transitions such as the move from school or university to work. Feeder and take-up schools will usually make reciprocal practical arrangements to facilitate a smooth transition for children (and families). It may involve competition for places in the preferred choice of secondary or high school with long-term consequences for their life chances. Above all, it involves psychological challenges like coping with anxiety and building a new identity as the child adjusts to their new situation (Evangelou *et al.*, 2008). Not all teachers and school leaders view transition explicitly from this career development perspective, although practices encountered in special schools often come close. To facilitate the transition for children with learning difficulties and disabilities, teachers will deploy strategies such as physically accompanying them on visits to the new schools, rehearsing with them the journey they will take, identifying each small step, and building in relevant support;
- modifying teaching approaches where necessary to meet children's needs, as in choosing relevant and motivating tasks, providing frequent rewards to boost engagement, recapping and recording to reduce reliance on memory and consolidating learning. Some groups of learners have additional and specific needs. For example, it is helpful where there are children with autistic spectrum disorders to create low-arousal areas in the classroom to minimise distraction, prepare these children for unfamiliar situations, and provide literal explanations to prevent misunderstandings. Similarly, for children with severe learning difficulties, it is important to use multi-sensory approaches to

facilitate learning such as letting children touch the food mixer that the cook uses, hearing the sound it makes, showing the cook using it (or a picture of it), and smelling the blended ingredients in the mixer;

- incorporating opportunities across the curriculum for the development of basic/life skills, for example, literacy, numeracy, and social relationships;
- providing opportunities for children to have purposeful interactions with a range of adults, for example, with support staff and visitors as well as with teachers;
- adopting focused teaching situations where teachers and teaching support staff work closely with specific individuals and groups while the rest of the class are self-directed;
- providing opportunities for engaging parents/carers as co-partners in children's career learning and development;
- developing children's self-advocacy skills to enable them to recognise that they have a voice and allowing their voices to be heard. For example, by helping children to maintain their own portfolio where they can record goals, plans, and reflections and use these in making real choices and decisions such as ensuring their wishes are taken into account when choosing where and what to study;
- embedding career exploration and development activities in the whole curriculum. The formal curriculum, whether it is subject and/or topic based, provides ample scope for careers inputs; without this approach, it is doubtful whether schools could allocate sufficient stand-alone time to career learning to have the level of impact required. Examples of integrated or embedded activities are included in Box 14.1. The whole curriculum offers opportunities related to wider school life such as the school's ethos and its extracurricular and enrichment activities.

Box 14.1 Embedding career-related learning in subject-based topics

English – the media
- writing for different audiences, spoken presentation of a news story about work; working in a small group to prepare an information page about part-time jobs while still at school for a young person's website; researching job roles on a newspaper; investigating opportunities for disabled people to work in television

Maths – the retail sector
- visiting a large local store to research which jobs involve financial recording and analysis, surveying customer shopping patterns; investigating pricing and display strategies; costing a basket of goods; finding

out about all jobs in the store including opportunities for people with learning difficulties or disabilities; understanding customer care skills

Geography – the airport
- investigating industries located on and around the airport; investigating the transport infrastructure; investigating airport jobs linked to the protection of the environment; finding out about people who work at the airport, including opportunities for people with learning difficulties or disabilities

History – the town
- using historical methods such as looking at buildings, old photos, maps, directories, and censuses to compare jobs and businesses in a part of the town today with a previous era; gaining basic insights into occupational and labour-market change and possible implications for their future working lives

Information and communications technology – games
- making simple games, animations, presentations, and stories; exploring job roles and pathways into the gaming industry

Science – space
- investigating space and space exploration; creating a moon buggy; finding out how astronauts train; exploring jobs in the space industry, including ways into them

Continuing challenges

The studies mentioned in this chapter have shown the potential benefits of developing career exploration and development provision for children with additional needs. The examples of good practice highlight the positive impact these approaches can have on all children. Yet challenges still remain for career development professionals in seeking to make an impact. Scattered activities lack the penetration of coherent programmes. Career learning is often a low-priority area with a lack of incentives in terms of both funding and policymaking for schools to do more. Career exploration and development programmes are more commonplace for children in the 12 to 14 age group than for 5- to 11-year-olds, but even so, many schools focus on the career development needs of the 14 plus age group without recognising the value of undertaking earlier work. Funding models often ignore the higher costs incurred in dealing with problems that could have been averted. In some cases, a stigma or negativity towards children with additional needs is the barrier; such negativity can be compounded when initiatives are not implemented well enough and are perhaps linked to a deficit in initial professional training.

Not doing sufficient preventive work with vulnerable, disadvantaged, and at-risk children early enough is to risk higher costs to the well-being of individuals and society in the longer term. This latter point is clearly demonstrated in children who have offended. A disproportionate number of children in the United Kingdom who enter the youth justice system after the age of ten have mental health problems, learning difficulties and disabilities, and other impairments such as attention deficit hyperactive disorder, lack of communication skills, and drug problems (Talbot, 2010). Many of these vulnerable children benefit from the supervision and safeguarding treatments of the statutory agencies that are there to protect, support, and rehabilitate them, but a significant number of 10- to 14-year-olds are put at further risk by inappropriate incarceration and contact with adult offenders. Bodies such as the Prison Reform Trust and the Howard League for Penal Reform campaign for more innovative practice towards children who have offended when they enter the youth justice system to avoid the confusion caused to them by the number of expert professionals handling their cases. Byrne and Brooks (2015) in a working paper for the Howard League advocate the development of an informal restorative and integrated strategy for supporting those children based on 'authentic relationships' as the catalyst for change. They make a compelling case, which has implications for the development of career-related strategies for child offenders. The Centre for Justice Innovation (2015) is interested in whether, instead of formally processing children in the youth justice system with the present additional costs and frequently unintended consequences of children adopting and internalising a 'deviant' identity, a 'diversionary approach' might be more effective. This suggests that helping children to gain qualifications by keeping them in mainstream schooling could stop them from acquiring a criminal record which would damage their labour-market prospects. More research is needed, but this is an approach which career development professionals through their training in narrative methods would be equipped to make a significant contribution. (McMahon, Watson, & Bimrose, 2010). This is not about a career adviser drawing up a career plan for the child as a 'quick fix' with limited effectiveness. It is about ensuring that children who offended are able to have a sustained relationship with a career adviser, who in turn facilitates the training of their professional colleagues such as social care workers and youth offending teams who are the main first-in-line helpers for the child.

Conclusion

In the past, career exploration and development programmes for children with additional needs have all too easily been treated as low priority. The growing weight of evidence that well-planned programmes can make a difference to the life chances of the individuals concerned is compelling. Programmes that are underpinned by the principles of equality, diversity, and inclusion are also likely to be more effective than those that are not. More than that, such programmes have the capacity to make a real difference to the happiness and well-being of children in their personal, social, and working lives.

References

Archer, L. (2013). What shapes children's science and career aspirations age 10–13? *ASPIRES project interim report*. Retrieved from http://www.kcl.ac.uk/sspp/departments/education/research/aspires/aspires-summary-spring-2013.pdf

Arthur, N., & Collins, S. (2014). Diversity and social justice: Guiding concepts for career development practice. In B. C. Shepard & P. S. Mani (Eds.), *Career development practice in Canada: Perspectives, principles and professionalism* (pp. 77–103). Toronto: CERIC.

Barnes, A. (2015). *There's a job to be done: Career matters*, 3.3, 18–19. Stourbridge: Career Development Institute.

Byrne, B., & Brooks, K. (2015). *Post YOT youth justice*. Howard League What is justice? Working Papers 19/2015. Retrieved from https://d19ylpo4aovc7m.cloudfront.net/fileadmin/howard_league/user/pdf/What_is_justice_/HLWP_19_2015.pdf

Career Development Institute. (2015). *Framework for careers, enterprise and employability*. Retrieved from http://www.thecdi.net/write/Framework/BP385-CDI_Framework-v7.pdf

Centre for Justice Innovation. (2015). *Valuing youth diversion: Making the case*. Retrieved from http://www.justiceinnovation.org/sites/default/files/attached/Valuing%20Youth%20Diversion%20A%20Toolkit_0.pdf

Department for Business, Innovation and Skills. (2013). *The business case for equality and diversity: A survey of the academic literature*. Retrieved from https://www.gov.uk/government/uploads/system/uploads/attachment_data/file/49638/the_business_case_for_equality_and_diversity.pdf

Department for Education and Skills. (2001). *First impressions: Career-related learning in primary schools*. London: DfES.

DES, ED & Welsh Office. (1987). *Working together for a better future*. London: HMSO.

Equality Act. (2010). London: The Stationery Office. Available at http://www.legislation.gov.uk/ukpga/2010/15/contents

Equality and Human Rights Commission. (2012a). *Public sector equality duty guidance for schools in England*. Retrieved from http://www.equalityhumanrights.com/sites/default/files/documents/EqualityAct/PSED/public_sector_equality_duty_guidance_for_schools_in_england_final.pdf

Equality and Human Rights Commission. (2012b). *Equal choices, equal chances*. Retrieved from http://www.equalityhumanrights.com/private-and-public-sector-guidance/education-providers/primary-education-resources

Evangelou, M., Taggart, B., Sylva, K., Melhuish, E., Sammons, P., & Siraj-Blatchford, I. (2008). *What makes a successful transition from primary to secondary school?* (DCSF). Retrieved from http://www.ioe.ac.uk/successful_transition_from_primary_to_secondary_report.pdf

Flouri, E., & Panourgia, C. (2012). *Do primary school children's career aspirations matter? The relationship between family poverty, career aspirations, and emotional and behavioural problems*. CLS Working Paper 2012/5. Institute of Education, University of London. Retrieved from

http://www.cls.ioe.ac.uk/library-media%5Cdocuments%5CCLS%20WP%202012
(5)%20-%20Do%20primary%20school%20children's%20career%20aspirations%20
matter%20-%20E%20Flouri%20and%20C%20Panourgia%20-%20Sept%202012.pdf

Her Majesty's Inspectorate. (1988). *Careers education and guidance from 5 to 16: Curriculum matters 10.* London: HMSO.

Howard, K. A. S., & Walsh, M. E. (2011). Children's conceptions of career choice and attainment: Model development. *Journal of Career Development, 38*(3), 256–271.

Irving, B. A., & Malik, B. (Eds.). (2005). *Critical reflections on career education and guidance: Promoting social justice within a global economy.* Abingdon: Routledge Falmer.

Law, B., & McGowan, B. (1999). *Opening doors: A framework for developing career-related learning in primary and middle schools.* Cambridge: CRAC/NICEC.

Levine, K., Sutherland, D., & Cole, D. (2015). *Career exploration in elementary years: It's not too early.* Retrieved from http://contactpoint.ca/2015/10/career-exploration-in-elementary-years-its-not-too-early/

McMahon, M., Watson, M., & Bimrose, J. (2010). *Stories of careers, learning and identity across the lifespan: Considering the future narrative of career theory.* The Institute of Career Guidance. Retrieved from http://www.agcas.org.uk/assets/download?file=2609&parent=1031

National Curriculum Council. (1990). *Careers education and guidance: Curriculum guidance 6.* York: NCC.

Ofsted. (Undated). *Evaluating educational inclusion: Guidance for inspectors and schools.* London: Ofsted. Retrieved from http://www.naldic.org.uk/Resources/NALDIC/Teaching%20and%20Learning/EvaluatingEducationalInclusion.pdf

School Curriculum and Assessment Authority. (1995). *Looking forward: Careers education and guidance in the curriculum.* London: SCAA.

Talbot, J. (2010). *Seen and heard.* London: Prison Reform Trust. Retrieved from http://www.prisonreformtrust.org.uk/Portals/0/Documents/SeenandHeardFinal%20.pdf

UNICEF. (1990). *The United Nations convention on the rights of the child.* Retrieved from http://www.unicef.org.uk/Documents/Publication-pdfs/UNCRC_PRESS200910web.pdf

Wade, P., Bergeron, C., White, K., Teeman, D., Sims, D., & Mehta, P. (2011). *Key stage 2 career related learning pathfinder evaluation.* London: Department for Education. Retrieved from https://www.gov.uk/government/uploads/system/uploads/attachment_data/file/182663/DFE-RR116.pdf

Chapter 15

Career development learning in childhood

Theory, research, policy, and practice

Ewald Crause, Mark Watson, and Mary McMahon

Childhood is a time of career exploration where career development learning begins as children begin to observe the world around them and realise that work is a part of adult life. While children are not expected to make premature decisions regarding an anticipated career path, there is a need to provide career learning activities that will assist children to explore possible career interests and the interrelatedness of the future world of work (Beale, 2000). Career development learning, as the term suggests, is a developmental learning process that evolves throughout individuals' lives (Turner & Lapan, 2005). Such learning includes interventions used by career practitioners, for example, career education, to facilitate age- and situation-appropriate career behaviours across the lifespan (Herr, 2001). Career development learning, however, is not confined to formal career activities, such as career education, but is inclusive of informal opportunities (Watson & McMahon, 2007a) such as watching a television show or observing parents. This suggests two distinct career development learning categories – namely, intentional (i.e., formal career intervention) and unintentional (i.e., what children see and hear vicariously) (Patton & McMahon, 2014).

The renewed emphasis on child career development (e.g., Hartung, Porfeli, & Vondracek, 2005, 2008; Howard & Walsh, 2011; McMahon & Watson, 2008; Porfeli & Lee, 2012; Watson & McMahon, 2005; Watson, McMahon, & Stroud, 2012; Watson, Nota, & McMahon, 2015a, b) mostly provides a theoretical perspective with limited information provided on career development learning for this developmental stage. The persistent disconnect between what theory proposes and what practice dictates has been lamented in more recent literature on child career development. For instance, Watson *et al.* (2015b), in their conclusion to the latest journal special issue on child career development, state that there is a need for "larger scale interventions as well as the evaluation of career programs" (p. 179) in order to build an evidence base for career interventions that enhance children's career development learning. The call for more evaluation echoes that of earlier calls in the literature (Schultheiss, 2005; Watson *et al.*, 2015b).

While other chapters in this book clearly motivate for the relevance of childhood in lifespan career development, the present chapter explores career development learning in childhood. The chapter starts with a broad overview of career development learning in childhood. Subsequently, the chapter considers career theory, research, practice, and policy from which a set of potential guidelines for facilitating career development learning in childhood are offered.

Childhood career development learning

Turner and Lapan (2013) state that career development is a process of learning across the lifespan and that learning is foundational to child career development. The skills and competencies that children learn provide them with foundations that have "been built over time" (Harkins, 2001, p. 173) for later career decision making in adolescence and young adulthood. Childhood can be seen as an "ideal time" for career development learning as it is unencumbered by the pressures of actual career decision making (Porfeli & Lee, 2012, p. 20). Indeed, the focus of career development learning in childhood should be on self- and world-of-work awareness rather than decision making.

Career development learning has not received sufficient attention to date as noted in Hartung *et al.'s* (2005) review of childhood career research. Similarly, Watson and McMahon (2005), recognising the need for a greater emphasis on childhood career development learning, specifically used learning as an organising framework for their research review of child career development and identified a need for a greater understanding of what children learn and how children learn. Subsequently, Watson and McMahon (2007a) considered how career development learning is systemically embedded in the experiences of children. They suggested that a learning perspective could provide a more holistic understanding of how learning, development, and experience recursively interrelate in childhood career development. Further, Patton and McMahon (2014) suggest that emphasis needs to be placed on learning rather than on career programs or career education. The two forms of career development learning, intentional and unintentional, need to be considered in relation to career theory, research, policy, and practice in order to develop a holistic understanding of how career development learning occurs in childhood. Career theory and career development learning is considered next.

Career theory and career development learning

A challenge in the development and design of age-appropriate career development learning programs for children is to effectively integrate insights from the complimentary theoretical fields of child development and childhood career development, as well as learning theory. It is salient to briefly examine the seminal work of major child development theorists (Erikson, 1985; Piaget, 1970, 1977), childhood career development theorists (Gottfredson, 2002, 2005; Savickas, 2005, 2013; Super, 1980, 1990), and learning theorists (e.g., Kolb, 1984; Vygotsky, 1978). A detailed examination is not possible within the word limit constraints of this chapter and readers are referred to the original works referenced here.

In the field of child development, the theories of Erikson (1985) and Piaget (1970, 1977) are undoubtedly influential contributions, although their developmental focus differs. Erikson's theory focussed on psychosocial development through eight identifiable stages, while Piaget focussed on cognitive development through four successive stages. Both theorists proposed that children need to successfully complete developmental tasks associated with these age-related stages. Central concepts related to the developmental tasks of both theories include exploration and curiosity, which are pivotal in the development of career development learning programs for children.

Learning has featured in career theory. The emphasis, however, has been predominantly on unintentional learning. Specifically, career theory suggests that children mainly learn experientially through observation and play. Further, holistic theories (e.g., Patton & McMahon, 2014; Super, 1990) remind us that the contextual learning environments of children vary and that, for some children, career learning experiences are limited and limiting. Similar to Erikson and Piaget, Super identified a series of developmental stages across the lifespan, one of which, the growth stage, applies to children. Within the growth stage, Super identified four developmental tasks for children related to their future orientation (i.e., becoming future focused, increasing self-control, developing self-motivation to achieve, and developing competent work habits and attitudes). Gottfredson's (2002, 2005) theory also identified stages in which children's occupational aspirations develop over time through a learning process of circumscription and compromise. Gottfredson suggests that such learning may result in children developing assumptions based on gender and social status that may limit their career development.

More recent lifespan theories that consider childhood career development are Savickas's (2005, 2013) career construction theory (see Chapter 5) and Howard and Walsh's (2010, 2011) vocational reasoning model. Savickas's theory affirms and adapts Super's stages and tasks, while Howard and Walsh describe six levels of vocational reasoning, three of which apply to career development in childhood. The latter theory is described in greater detail in Chapter 5 of this book. Central to these career theories is that children begin to develop an understanding of themselves in adult roles through concepts such as curiosity and exploration. Moreover, these theories emphasise the contextual and experiential nature of career development learning in childhood and its developmental progression from fantasy to more realistic thinking.

In the field of learning, the work of Vygotsky (1978) and Kolb (1984) offer differing but useful insights for understanding career development learning. For example, Vygotsky's theory of learning and cognitive development emphasises the social contextual nature of learning, while Kolb's experiential learning theory emphasises the importance of grounding learning in experience. Experiential learning is increasingly supported by technology, and developing career learning

Career development learning in childhood   189

programs in the twenty-first century requires attention to learning through technology (Crause, 2013). Mayer's (2001) theory of multimedia learning acknowledges how technological elements can combine in a cohesive learning experience. Common to these learning theories is their emphasis on learning through interactive experiences with others and with technology.

Over a decade and a half ago, Magnuson and Starr (2000) considered theory in relation to children's career development learning and suggested strategies that had implications for career practice with elementary school children. These included encouraging curiosity within children, scaffolding learning onto the existing experience and knowledge of children, and developing social understanding in terms of self-awareness and awareness of others. Despite more recent theoretical developments, these strategies remain relevant.

In summary, based on central theoretical constructs from child, career, and learning theories, components that can inform potential guidelines for the development of career learning programs include the following: career development learning is appropriate for children from a young age because they are curious and seek to understand the world and imagine themselves in adult roles that they observe in their families and in the community; theory provides a rationale and theoretical grounding for career development learning programs for children; career development learning needs to be age appropriate and purposeful in the development of skills and knowledge; experiential learning actively involves children and harnesses their natural curiosity; a broad range of contextual learning experiences may be incorporated into career learning programs; and self-awareness, rather than decision making, needs to be emphasised. Theory, however, provides only one element that could guide the development of career development learning programs for children; career research also has a role to play.

Career research and career development learning

The past two decades have been characterised by considerable research on career development in childhood, resulting in further integration of early career behaviour into lifespan and systemic models of career (Ferreira, Santos, Fonseca, & Haase, 2007; Hartung et al., 2008; Howard & Walsh, 2010, 2011; McMahon & Watson, 2008; Porfeli & Lee, 2012; Skorikov & Patton, 2007). Similar to theory, research has focused more on unintentional learning. Children's career development research highlights the critical significance of career development learning during childhood (Hartung et al., 2005; Porfeli, Hartung, & Vondracek 2008; Watson & McMahon, 2005). For instance, career development begins much earlier in the lifespan than generally assumed, and what children learn about work has an influence on the career choices they make later as adolescents and young adults (Schultheiss, 2008). Drawing from the extant body of childhood career development research, several findings can inform our understanding of career development learning in childhood as well as suggest implications for the development of career development learning programs in elementary schools.

First, research suggests that children possess the necessary readiness to begin learning about careers (Beale, 2003) and that age-appropriate career learning activities need to move beyond the provision of child-friendly information. Children should be provided with opportunities and freedom to explore and wonder about the future and their future selves (Howard & Walsh, 2011; Magnuson & Starr, 2000). Further, career learning activities should assist children to build bridges (or scaffolds) to more complex learning, moving from what children know to what is not yet known. Second, research suggests a multidisciplinary approach in which researchers, program developers, policymakers, and educators work towards a common goal to provide elementary school children with meaningful career learning experiences (Beale, 2003; Ferreira *et al.*, 2007; Gillies, McMahon, & Carroll, 1998; McMahon & Carroll, 2001; McMahon & Watson, 2008). In addition, children need to experience both intentional and unintentional career development learning activities in which exploration, curiosity, awareness, and achievement of age-appropriate career developmental tasks are encouraged (Hartung *et al.*, 2005, 2008; McMahon & Watson, 2008).

Third, research indicates that children's career aspirations are shaped by their career awareness, which may be limited (Watson & McMahon, 2005, 2007a, b) and circumscribed by inappropriate or even inaccurate representations of careers (Gottfredson, 2002, 2005). Thus career development learning programs need to address and redress children's misconceptions of the world of work related to gender equity, cultural diversity, and equal opportunity irrespective of socioeconomic background. Fourth, research suggests that children need to develop an awareness of how personal agency can influence future career decision making. This can be accomplished through intentional career learning experiences that encourage age-appropriate career exploration, awareness, aspirations, interests, and adaptability.

Fifth, research indicates that children's career development learning is a recursive process between children and a variety of contextual influences (McMahon & Watson, 2009). Children may be supported in the development of age-appropriate career skills to cope with and benefit from these contextual influences (Gillies *et al.*, 1998). Finally, sixth, research indicates that career learning programs for children may be supported by technology-based learning activities, supportive learning environments, and developmentally appropriate activities which can provide a variety of positive learning experiences (Cooper, 2005; Keengwe & Onchwari, 2009). Technology-based learning activities support the child as a unique individual and encourage exploration, experimentation, risk taking, critical thinking, decision making, and problem solving. Moreover, technology-based learning activities may offer quick feedback and new challenges, build on previous learning, encourage reflection and metacognition, and support social interaction (Appel & O'Gara, 2001; Clements & Samara, 2002; Downes, Arthur, & Beecher, 2001).

In summary, career research may strengthen the rationale for offering career development learning programs for children as well as provide potential guidelines for developing intentional career learning programs for children. One recommendation from research involves the consideration of policy to which we now turn.

Career policy and career development learning

At the level of policy, childhood career learning has been subsumed in a broader focus on lifelong career guidance which, along with the learning derived from it, is seen by numerous governments as a key policy element in promoting a learning society that equips individuals for employability and lifelong learning (Hooley & Watts, 2011; Watts & Sultana, 2004). National policy initiatives that include reference to career learning in childhood indicate policymakers' commitment to equipping children and adolescents with age-appropriate skills and knowledge necessary for successful future transitions. For example, the European Union advocates lifelong guidance (Council of the European Union, 2004), the Australian government funded the development of the Australian Blueprint for Career Development (MCEECDYA, 2010) which offers suggestions as to the content and potential outcomes of career development learning programs through their identification of age-appropriate competencies, and the South African government, through its Life Orientation Curriculum, advocates that career development learning begins in primary school (Department of Education, 2002). Despite such policy initiatives, the career development needs of elementary school children remain largely unmet (Sharf, 2013).

In summary, policy statements indicate several components that may inform potential guidelines for career development learning programs and may provide a rationale for the provision of career development learning programs for children. Specifically, career learning needs to be accessible to individuals of all ages (including children) and sensitive to the different developmental needs of individuals from childhood through to adulthood. While theory, research, and policy offer components that may inform potential guidelines for stimulating career development learning, it is in practice that intentional career development learning occurs.

Career practice and career development learning programs

In career practice, intentional career development learning is explicit. However, in reality, more is written about career development learning programs than the learning process that takes place within such programs. Clearly there is an increasing need for relevant, timely, and comprehensive career development learning programs throughout the lifespan, including childhood (Feller, Russell, & Whichard, 2005; Sharf, 2013), as a means to learn realistic career information, challenge career gender stereotypes, and educate parents about their role in children's career development (Porfeli & Lee, 2012). Career development learning in schools creates pathways to future career success (Knight, 2015). The career development learning of children can be influenced by schools through the formal provision of intentional career development learning (Patton & Porfeli, 2007) that more clearly links academic learning areas with a variety of careers (Schultheiss, Palma, & Manzi, 2005).

Less attention has been devoted to providing career learning programs for children. Possible reasons for the slower evolvement of career development learning programs for children may be found in misconceptions about intentional career learning programs and their implementation during childhood. There are three points worth noting in this regard. First, while there is a misconception that children are disconnected from the future world of work, there are those who see this as a benefit for career development learning in that this developmental stage could be ideal for career exploration precisely because it is absent from the burden of having to make an immediate commitment (Porfeli & Lee, 2012). Second, although children are not expected to make premature career decisions, there is still a need to provide them with career exploration activities that will assist them in thinking about and broadening their possible career interests as well as the interrelatedness of the world of work to the primary school learning environment (Beale, 2000). Third, the need for career development learning becomes critical when one considers Porfeli *et al.'s* (2008) comment on the neglected status of children's career development, particularly given its theoretical recognition as foundational for future lifespan career development.

As reflected in the Blueprint frameworks developed in countries such as Canada (National Steering Committee for Career Development Guidelines and Standards, 2004) and Australia (MCEECDYA, 2010), career development learning programs need to focus on building the competencies needed for future planning, goal setting, and decision making, with an important output being to prevent children from foreclosing on career choices before they thoroughly explore the world of work and gain an understanding of their own self-interest (Knight, 2015). The Blueprint frameworks identify age-appropriate career management competencies across the lifespan and provide a resource that can underpin the development of career learning programs inclusive of those for primary school children. For instance, Hooley, Watts, Sultana, and Neary (2013) considered the Blueprint frameworks developed in Canada, the United States, and Australia and found that common to all three were the three core elements of career learning areas, a learning model, and developmental levels, and four contextual elements of resources, community of practice, service delivery approach, and policy connection.

A persistent issue remains in relation to the provision of career development learning programs for children. Specifically, the facilitators of such programs (e.g., teachers) may not have the necessary skills and knowledge. Moreover, parents and other stakeholders may not see the necessity of career development learning in childhood given its seeming remoteness from future transitions such as leaving school and workforce entry (Porfeli & Lee, 2012).

A criticism of the career field generally is the nature of its evidence base (Watts & Sultana, 2004). Thus a prerequisite in implementing career development learning programs with children is research evidence supporting the effectiveness of such interventions. Considering the limited evidence base for career development learning programs for elementary school children (Gillies *et al.*, 1998; Hynes & Hirsch, 2012; Watson & McMahon, 2007a), this remains a clear and pressing need.

The implementation of career learning programs does not have to come at the expense of academic learning (Mekinda, 2012). Career development learning programs should not be seen as additional or *ad hoc* to mainstream academic learning (which would most likely result in it being largely marginalised) but should rather be viewed as the common theme that links existing curriculum foci (i.e., literacy, numeracy, and life skills). Indeed, career development learning programs must be moved "from a peripheral role as an enrichment activity to a central role as a required element of the curriculum" (Peterson, Sampson, & Reardon, 1991, p. 64).

In summary, components that may inform potential guidelines for developing career development learning programs for children may be drawn from practice. Foremost among these is the appropriateness of career development learning for children. In addition, career development learning may be supported by a sound rationale and an evidence base and is most likely to succeed when facilitators (e.g., teachers) are well supported and receive appropriate training.

Potential guidelines: Synthesising theory, research, policy, and practice

As evident in this brief overview of theory, research, policy, and practice, components may be abstracted that could guide the development of career development learning programs for children. Indeed a synthesis of core components from these four interrelated areas offers eight holistic guidelines.

First, career learning is not only relevant to childhood but provides foundational skills and knowledge that will contribute to the successful transition into the later career developmental stages of adolescent and adult decision making and career development (Porfeli & Lee, 2012; Watson & McMahon, 2007b). Thus the career learning process should start in the early primary school grades (Harkins, 2000) or even earlier. Second, a rationale for career development learning in childhood must be informed by evidence from theory, research, policy, and best practice. This rationale needs to be written for stakeholders (e.g., parents, teachers, and education authorities) who may have no background in career development and who may question the relevance of career learning in childhood given its distance from adulthood (Porfeli & Lee, 2012; Watson &

McMahon, 2007b) and its need for time allocation in already crowded curricula (McMahon & Carroll, 1999). Career development learning programs, however, may assist children in relating their school curricula to future work requirements (Hynes, 2012).

Third, key stakeholders, including education authorities, teachers, parents, and community members, need to be consulted about the career development learning needs of children, involved where possible in the development and delivery of the career development learning program, and kept informed about learning outcomes. Fourth, career development learning programs must be age appropriate and contain clearly defined learning outcomes that subsequently provide a foundation for evaluation and reporting.

Fifth, experiential career development learning processes that harness children's curiosity and facilitate their career exploration are essential. Sixth, career learning programs should be contextualised. Parents and members of the broader community may be involved and site visits may support children's career development learning (e.g., Beale, 2003). Where site visits are not feasible, worksite simulation may be effective in helping children to expand their list of future career choices and to understand the ramifications of those decisions (Harkins, 2000). Such worksite simulations may be provided through technology-based learning activities. Seventh, facilitators of career learning programs should be supported with appropriate resources and training, as they may not have background skills and knowledge in career development. Eighth, evaluation of outcomes needs to be systematically undertaken in order to develop an evidence base that can be reported to key stakeholders and should go beyond criteria such as enjoyment and ease of use to considering learning outcomes in relation to career awareness, future focus, self-awareness, world-of-work knowledge, and decision-making skills. Evidence-based career learning programs require an iterative process beginning with a needs assessment of key stakeholders, the development of theory- and research-based learning materials, trialling, review and evaluation, refinement and revision, and the subsequent administration of the program and further evaluation.

While these proposed guidelines could be viewed as discrete elements in a process of developing and implementing career development learning programs for children, they actually exist in a recursive relationship that involves feedback loops. For example, parental involvement may enhance their understanding of childhood career learning. This in turn may assist parents in being more aware of and enhancing the unintentional career learning of their children and motivate them to advocate for the place of career development learning in the curriculum. Just as child career development learning is contextually located, so too is the development of career development learning programs for children. In this chapter, these proposed potential guidelines are contextually located in theory (child development, career, and learning), research, policy, and practice. Synthesising the components from each of these has provided an opportunity to propose a set of integrated and holistic guidelines.

Conclusion

There is evidence from theory, research, policy, and practice that career learning is appropriate and essential for children. Indeed, an orientation and openness to the future lived in the present and respectful of the past is a critical dimension of career development that first emerges during childhood (Hartung *et al.*, 2005). Early experiences related to the world of work can provide a foundation for later learning and ensure that children's knowledge frameworks will be more fully developed when they reach young adulthood (Harkins, 2001). Career learning programs may increase an awareness of the benefits of achieving at school as well as the relationship between future work and learning, facilitate the development of age-appropriate career skills in understanding and using career information, facilitate the recognition of personal responsibility in acquiring good work habits, and create an awareness of why people work.

Challenges remain in the development and implementation of career development learning programs for children who are just beginning to learn about the world of work. Regardless, there is a need to provide children with career learning activities that will assist them in thinking about possible career interests and the interrelatedness of the future world of work with the present realities of their primary school education (Beale, 2000). The specific benefits to children themselves and society more broadly of being able to effectively manage career decisions and transitions cannot be understated. Intentional career development learning helps children build concepts that will serve them throughout their lives (Harkins, 2001). Indeed, failing to attend to intentional career development learning in childhood may be a "missed opportunity" (Porfeli & Lee, 2012, p. 20) to adequately prepare them with important skills and knowledge for managing their future career development in adolescence and adulthood. Theory, research, policy, and practice attest to the need to provide intentional career development learning in childhood, and each offers suggestions for sound development and implementation of career development learning programs for children. Drawing on these suggestions from theory, research, policy, and practice, the guidelines proposed in this chapter may contribute to the successful development and implementation of intentional career development learning programs for children and guide school personnel such as school counsellors, school psychologists, teachers and administrators.

References

Appel, A., & O'Gara, C. (2001). *Technology and young children: A review of literature.* Retrieved from http://ict.aed.org/infocenter/pdfs/technologyandyoung.pdf

Beale, A. V. (2000). Elementary school career awareness: A visit to a hospital. *Journal of Career Development, 27*, 65–72.

Beale, A. V. (2003). It takes a team to run a restaurant: Introducing elementary students to the interrelatedness of occupations. *Journal of Career Development, 29*, 211–220.

Clements, D. H., & Samara, J. (2002). The role of technology in early childhood learning. *Teaching Children Mathematics, 8*, 340–343.

Cooper, L. Z. (2005). Developmentally appropriate digital environments for young children. *Library Trends, 54*, 286–302.

Council of the European Union. (2004). Draft resolution of the Council and of the representatives of the Member States meeting within the council on strengthening policies, systems and practices in the field of guidance throughout Europe.

Crause, E. (2013). *The effect of using a computer-based exploration tool on children's career development learning*. Port Elizabeth: Unpublished doctoral dissertation, Nelson Mandela Metropolitan University.

Department of Education. (2002). *Revised national curriculum statement grades R-9 (Schools)*. Pretoria, South Africa: Department of Education.

Downes, T., Arthur, L., & Beecher, B. (2001). Effective learning environments for young children using digital resources: An Australian perspective. *Information Technology in Childhood Education Annual, 1*, 139–153.

Erikson, E. H. (1985). *Childhood and society* (35th Anniversary ed.). New York: Norton.

Feller, R. W., Russell, M., & Whichard, J. A. (2005). Career techniques and interventions: Themes from an international conversation. *The Career Development Quarterly, 54*, 36–47.

Ferreira, J. A., Santos, E. J., Fonseca, A. C., & Haase, R. F. (2007). Early predictors of career development: A 10-year follow-up study. *Journal of Vocational Behavior, 70*, 61–77.

Gillies, R. M., McMahon, M. L., & Carroll, J. (1998). Evaluating a career education intervention in the upper elementary school. *Journal of Career Development, 24*, 267–287.

Gottfredson, L. S. (2002). Gottfredson's theory of circumscription, compromise, and self-creation. In D. Brown & Associates (Eds.), *Career choice and development* (4th ed., pp. 85–149). San Francisco, CA: Jossey-Bass.

Gottfredson, L. S. (2005). Applying Gottfredson's theory of circumscription and compromise in career guidance and counseling. In S. D. Brown & R. W. Lent (Eds.), *Career development and counseling: Putting theory and research to work* (pp. 71–100). New Jersey, NJ: John Wiley & Sons.

Harkins, M. A. (2000). Career education in primary grades: Building work-readiness through an experiential curriculum. *Childhood Education, 76*, 219–224.

Harkins, M. A. (2001). Developmentally appropriate career guidance: Building concepts to last a lifetime. *Early Childhood Education Journal, 28*, 169–174.

Hartung, P. J., Porfeli, E. J., & Vondracek, F. W. (2005). Child vocational development: A review and consideration. *Journal of Vocational Behavior, 66*, 385–419.

Hartung, P. J., Porfeli, E. J., & Vondracek, F. W. (2008). Career adaptability in childhood. *The Career Development Quarterly, 57*, 63–74.

Herr, E. L. (2001). The impact of national policies, economics, and school reform on comprehensive guidance programs. *Professional School Counseling, 4*, 236–245.

Hooley, T., & Watts, A. G. (2011). *Careers work with young people: Collapse or transition? An analysis of current developments in careers education and guidance for young people in England*. International Centre for Guidance Studies (iCeGS). Retrieved from http://www.derby.ac.uk/files/careers_transition_paper.pdf

Hooley, T., Watts, A. G., Sultana, R. G., & Neary, S. (2013). The "Blueprint" framework for career management skills: A critical exploration. *British Journal of Guidance and Counselling, 41*, 117–131.

Howard, K., & Walsh, M. E. (2010). Conceptions of career choice and attainment: Developmental levels in how children think about careers. *Journal of Vocational Behavior, 76*, 143–152.

Howard, K., & Walsh, M. E. (2011). Children's conceptions of career choice and attainment: Model development. *Journal of Career Development, 38*, 256–271.

Hynes, K. (2012). Next steps for research and practice in career programming. *New Directions for Youth Development, 134*, 107–114.

Hynes, K., & Hirsch, B. J. (2012). *Career programming: Linking youth to the world of work.* San Francisco, CA: Jossey-Bass.

Keengwe, J., & Onchwari, G. (2009). Technology and early childhood education: A technology integration professional development model for practicing teachers. *Early Childhood Education Journal, 37*, 209–218.

Knight, J. L. (2015). Preparing elementary school counselors to promote career development: Recommendations for school counselor education programs. *Journal of Career Development, 42*, 75–85.

Kolb, D. A. (1984). *Experiential learning: Experience as the source of learning and development.* Englewood Cliffs, NJ: Prentice Hall.

Magnuson, C. S., & Starr, M. F. (2000). How early is too early to begin life career planning? The importance of the elementary school years. *Journal of Career Development, 27*, 89–101.

Mayer, R. E. (2001). *Multimedia learning.* New York, NY: Cambridge University Press.

MCEECDYA. (2010). *The Australian Blueprint for Career Development.* Prepared by Miles Morgan Australia. Canberra, Australia: Commonwealth of Australia. Retrieved from https://www.education.gov.au/australian-blueprint-career-development

McMahon, M., & Carroll, J. (1999). Implementing a developmental career education program using a K-12 framework. *Australian Journal for Career Development, 8*, 38–44.

McMahon, M., & Carroll, J. (2001). K-12 career education programs: From rhetoric to practice. In W. Patton & M. McMahon (Eds.), *Career development programs: Preparation for lifelong career decision making* (pp. 73–84). Melbourne: Acer Press.

McMahon, M., & Watson, M. (2008). Children's career development: Metaphorical images of theory, research, and practice. *The Career Development Quarterly, 57,* 75–83.

McMahon, M., & Watson, M. (2009). Career psychology research challenges: A systems theory response. *South African Journal of Psychology, 39*, 184–194.

Mekinda, M. A. (2012). Support for career development in youth: Program models and evaluations. *New Directions for Youth Development, 134*, 45–54.

National Steering Committee for Career Development Guidelines and Standards. (2004). *Canadian standards and guidelines for career development practitioners code of ethics.* Retrieved from http://www.career-dev-guidelines.org

Patton, W., & McMahon, M. (2014). *Career development and systems theory: Connecting theory and practice* (3rd ed.). Rotterdam, The Netherlands: Sense Publishers.

Patton, W., & Porfeli., E. J. (2007). Career exploration during childhood and adolescence. In V. B. Skorikov & W. Patton (Eds.), *Career development in childhood and adolescence* (pp. 47–70). Rotterdam, The Netherlands: Sense Publishers.

Peterson, G. W., Sampson, J. P., & Reardon, R. C. (1991). *Career development and services: A cognitive approach.* Pacific Grove, CA: Brooks/Cole.

Piaget, J. (1970). *Science and education and the psychology of the child.* New York: Orion.

Piaget, J. (1977). *The development of thought: Equilibrium of cognitive structures.* New York, NY: Viking Press.

Porfeli, E. J., Hartung, P. J., & Vondracek, F. W. (2008). Children's vocational development: A research rationale. *The Career Development Quarterly, 57*, 25–37.

Porfeli, E. J., & Lee, B. (2012). Career development during childhood and adolescence. *New Directions for Youth Development, 134*, 11–22.

Savickas, M. L. (2005). The theory and practice of career construction. In S. Brown & R. Lent (Eds.), *Career development and counseling: Putting theory and research to work* (pp. 42–70). Hoboken, NJ: Wiley.

Savickas, M. L. (2013). Career construction theory and practice. In R. W. Lent & S. D. Brown (Eds.), *Career development and counseling: Putting theory and research to work* (2nd ed., pp. 147–183). Hoboken, NJ: John Wiley & Sons.

Schultheiss, D. E. (2005). Elementary career intervention programs: Social action initiatives. *Journal of Career Development, 31*, 185–194.

Schultheiss, D. E. (2008). Current status and future agenda for the theory, research, and practice of childhood career development. *The Career Development Quarterly, 57*, 7–24.

Schultheiss, D., Palma, T. V., & Manzi, A. J. (2005). Career development in middle childhood: A qualitative inquiry. *The Career Development Quarterly, 53*, 246–262.

Sharf, R. S. (2013). *Applying career development theory to counseling* (6th ed.). Pacific Grove, CA: Brooks/Cole.

Skorikov, V. B., & Patton, W. (2007). Future directions in research on career development during childhood and adolescence. In V. B. Skorikov & W. Patton (Eds.), *Career development in childhood and adolescence* (pp. 325–336). Rotterdam, The Netherlands: Sense.

Super, D. E. (1980). A life-space, life-space approach to career development. *Journal of Vocational Behavior, 16*, 282–298.

Super, D. E. (1990). A life-span, life-space approach to career development. In D. Brown & L. Brooks (Eds.), *Career choice and development: Applying contemporary theory to practice* (2nd ed., pp. 197–262). San Francisco, CA: Jossey-Bass.

Turner, S, L., & Lapan, R. T. (2005). Promoting career develoment and aspirations in school-age youth. In S. D. Brown & R. W. Brooks (Eds.), *Career development and counseling: Putting theory and research to work* (pp. 417–440). Hoboken, NJ: John Wiley & Sons.

Turner, S. L., & Lapan, R. T. (2013). Promotion of career awareness, development and school success in children and adolescents. In S. D. Brown & R. W. Lent (Eds.), *Career development and counseling* (pp. 539–564). Hoboken, NJ: John Wiley & Sons.

Vygotsky, L. S. (1978). Mental development of children and the process of learning. In M. Cole, V. John-Steiner, S. Scribner, & E. Sauberman (Eds.), *L.S. Vygotsky: Mind in society* (pp. 7–8). Cambridge: Harvard University Press.

Watson, M., & McMahon, M. (2005). Children's career development: A research review from a learning perspective. *Journal of Vocational Behavior, 67*, 119–132.

Watson, M., & McMahon, M. (2007a). Children's career development learning: A foundation for lifelong career development. In V. B. Skorikov & W. Patton (Eds.), *Career development in childhood and adolescence* (pp. 29–46). Rotterdam, The Netherlands: Sense Publishers.

Watson, M., & McMahon, M. (2007b). School and work: Connections made by South African and Australian primary school children. *South African Journal of Education, 27*, 565–577.

Watson, M., McMahon, M., & Stroud, L. (2012). Career development in children. In J. Hardman (Ed.), *Child and adolescent development: A South African socio-cultural perspective* (pp. 269–286). CapeTown, South Africa: Oxford University Press.

Watson, M., Nota, L., & McMahon, M. (2015a). Child career development: Present and future trends. *International Journal for Educational and Vocational Guidance, 15*, 95–97.

Watson, M., Nota, L., & McMahon, M. (2015b). Evolving stories of child career development. *International Journal for Educational and Vocational Guidance, 15*, 175–184.

Watts, A. G., & Sultana, R. G. (2004). Career guidance policies in thirty-seven countries – contrasts and common themes. *International Journal for Educational and Vocational Guidance, 4*, 105–122.

Chapter 16

Epilogue

Mary McMahon and Mark Watson

Writing the concluding chapter for this book is indeed a privilege, as it provides us with an opportunity to celebrate the strength of the field of child career development. Moreover, it provides an opportunity to celebrate the first book solely devoted to child career development; this book represents a landmark publication.

The purpose of this chapter is to conclude the book. Following on from the book's previous chapters and the directions for the field set out in the special issue of the *International Journal for Vocational Education and Guidance* in 2015 (Watson, Nota, & McMahon, 2015), we could wonder what more can be said. This chapter, therefore, is intentionally short and draws together our impressions of the field based on the content of the book.

At the outset, several observations can be made about the book. First, as reflected in the book's authorship that represents seven countries, developed and developing, and all continents, child career development is a topic of relevance internationally. This is not an insignificant point, because throughout the history of the field, the literature has been primarily western and dominated by publications from the US context. The authorship of this book reflects significant internationalisation of the field of child career development through the collaborations evident in the chapter authorship. Such collaborations suggest that national barriers are being crossed in an effort to achieve a more international and nuanced understanding of child career development in different contexts.

We would like to make three further observations about the authorship of this book. First is the dedication of a number of authors, names that are well known to those familiar with the field, who, over many years, have continued to research in a field that was described in Chapter 1 of this book as the "Cinderella" of career development. A debt of gratitude is owed to these authors for not only keeping this underemphasised field alive but also for advancing it and continuing to innovate. Second, succession planning is evident through the mentoring of emerging authors in the field as reflected in several chapters' authorship. The calibre of the mentors and the strength of the contributions in this book provide confidence in the future of the field of child career development. Third, this book reflects multidisciplinary interest in child career development with contributions from authors in disciplines such as psychology and education, which can only serve to strengthen the field as it moves forward.

Although the broader field of career development has been criticised for the cursory attention it has paid to child career development, the present first comprehensive collation of career theory, research, and practice reminds us that a substantial body of literature does in fact exist and provides a firm foundation on which the field can build. Successive reviews of child career development have tended, somewhat apologetically, to acknowledge shortcomings in the field. This observation can be made of any field and perhaps is more reflective of the relatively limited nature of special issues. The breadth and depth of contributions that has been possible in this book clearly attests, however, to the productivity and rigour of a relatively small group of authors from this subfield of career development who have shepherded child career development forward and provided a firm foundation for its future growth.

It is timely, given the comprehensive nature of this book, to review and reconsider the most recent critique of the field – namely, that in the concluding article of the special issue of the *International Journal for Vocational Education and Guidance* in 2015 (Watson *et al.*, 2015). This concluding article considered four themes, each of which warrant comment in this chapter: advances in child career development theory, innovations in practice and assessment related to child career development, child career development in diverse settings, and policy implications of child career development theory, research, and practice.

In terms of *child career development theory*, Trice and Greer (Chapter 2) remind us that, while some theories may seem outdated, constructs such as imitation, identification, fantasising, compromising, crystallising, and conscripting remain relevant today. Further, such constructs may have application in theoretical advances proposed from the perspective of the constructivist worldview, which is influential in current thinking in career psychology. A conclusion drawn about the contributions to the special issue was their recognition of context which is strikingly evident in the emerging theoretical perspectives presented in this book – namely, Hartung's chapter on career construction theory (Chapter 3), Patton's chapter on systems and relational approaches (Chapter 4), and McMahon and Watson's chapter on children as storytellers (Chapter 6).

Across these chapters, the contextual and relational nature of the process of child career development is evident, as is children's potential to story their experiences and to begin the construction of occupational identities that influence subsequent career development in adolescence and adulthood. While Patton (Chapter 4) and previous reviews (e.g., Hartung, Porfeli, & Vondracek, 2005; Watson & McMahon, 2005) suggest a need for greater understanding of the process of child career development, the emerging theory of Howard and her colleagues, the Concepts of Career Choice and Attainments Model (CCCA; Chapter 5) has begun to provide answers to this vexed question by focusing on how children conceptualise the process of career development and how they reason differently over time. Moreover, this emerging model is founded on a research base and addresses a need for closer links between theory and research. It seems, therefore, that in this emerging body of theory, a solid core of constructs is consistent across most theoretical approaches; a more cohesive story of child career development is beginning to emerge, and its process is becoming better understood. Each of these emerging theoretical perspectives suggest fertile ground for future research and a foundation for theory-based practice.

In terms of *innovations in practice and assessment* related to child career development, we are reminded of the importance of career development learning in childhood. Crause and his colleagues (Chapter 15) remind us that much career development learning in childhood is unintentional and emphasises the need for intentional career development learning which can be provided through career learning programs. In this regard, Chapters 13 and 14 provide promising examples of programs. Lapan and his colleagues (Chapter 13) identify a broad range of benefits that may be derived from career exploration and development in childhood, including academic, motivational, and self-regulatory growth and benefits to children and to their families. Barnes and McGowan (Chapter 14) draw attention to children with additional needs and emphasise how career learning programs can support such children, promote their wellbeing, and assist them in engaging fully in society. Further, this chapter focuses on a group whose needs have been neglected in theory, research, and practice; in career development in general; and in child career development in particular.

The relationship between career intervention and career assessment instruments is emphasised in Chapters 11 and 12, where a growth in the number of career assessment instruments for children is evident. In their comprehensive review of a number of quantitative and qualitative career assessment instruments, Stead and Schultheiss (Chapter 12) explain how career assessment may be used to better target scarce resources. Similarly, Tracey and Sodano (Chapter 11) note that career assessment may be used to design appropriate interventions. These authors also explicate the unique characteristics related to the valid assessment of children. Both chapters on assessment stress the importance of developing instruments specifically for children. In this regard, the predominant emphasis on quantitative assessment is evident with Stead and Schultheiss reminding us that career assessment should not be used to guide children into premature career decision making or to identify deficits.

In terms of *child career development in diverse settings*, messages are delivered consistently throughout this book about the necessity of considering the context in which career development occurs. Striking among these messages is that delivered by Bakshi in Chapter 10. This chapter, with its focus on child career development in developing countries, provides a salutary reminder about the western, privileged nature of much of our theory, research, and practice and challenges us to think more broadly about who we serve and our potential role in advocacy for the field. Liu and McMahon (Chapter 9) consider the familial context in terms of both theory and research. Family, as a primary influence on child career development, has received comparatively little attention in both theory and research and remains a promising topic for future research. That career aspirations begin in childhood is well known. What is less well known is where aspirations begin. Flouri and her colleagues (Chapter 8) begin to answer this question when they discuss gender, ethnicity, and parental socioeconomic status as antecedents and predictors of aspirations. These authors remind us that it is unclear whether aspirations predict career trajectories or reflect historical and societal contexts. This remains an area in need of future research.

A pervasive theme running across all chapters of the book is child career development research, which is the focus of Oliveira and her colleagues (see Chapter 7). Reflecting a link between research and theory, these authors used the Living Systems Theory of Vocational Behavior and Development (LSVD; Vondracek, Ford, & Porfeli, 2014) as a framework to structure their review of research published since the 2008 review. These authors demonstrate the research emphasis at the personal and microsystem levels and the more limited nature of research related to the broader context of child career development, which attests to the value of the research conducted by Flouri and her colleagues and the need for further research in this more neglected area.

In terms of *policy implications of child career development theory, research, and practice*, the field has yet to tell a convincing story about the need for intentional career development learning in childhood so that policymakers understand the importance of this lifespan phase. Throughout the book, there is little mention of policymakers who have the potential to influence curriculum and research funding. Telling a convincing story of child career development to policymakers is dependent on the language in which it is told in order that they receive our message. For too long, the story of the field has been largely told to those in the field. Language is critical in the telling of stories, and so we may need to learn a new language in order to convince policymakers of the inherent worth of child career development and its value in terms of individual good and public good (Watts, 1999). Further, convincing stories of the value of providing career development learning in childhood must be evidence based if policymakers are to invest public money in our field. Strengthening the evidence base that attests to the value of investment in child career development learning programs remains a critical need. Policy-driven curriculum and better research funding have the potential to considerably advance the field, and successful advocacy with policymakers remains a goal worth aiming for.

As reflected by this brief synopsis of the chapters, it seems that the comprehensive nature of this book has painted both a paradoxical picture of child career development theory, research, and practice as one of rigour, consolidation, and hope and also as one of a "fragmented constellation of scientific camps dispersed across disciplines" that "lacks a strong consensus on a dominant theoretical paradigm" (Oliveira *et al.*; Chapter 7). Further, just as the book is presented in sections – that is, theory, assessment, research, and practice – so too are these elements largely 'siloed' in the literature. For example, throughout the book, few examples of theory-research, theory-practice, research-practice relationships are presented, and this remains a challenge for the field of child career development.

Conclusion

While Cinderella found hope for a better future through a glass slipper, it is unlikely that such a slipper will ensure a better future for child career development. What is going to ensure the future of the field is the depth of scholarship reflected in this book and the dedication of the researchers who have steadily progressed it. This first book on child career development is indeed a milestone. In closing this chapter and this book, we hope that any subsequent text will reflect consolidation, innovation, and extension in this vital field of child career development.

References

Hartung, P. J., Porfeli, E. J., & Vondracek, F. W. (2005). Child vocational development: A review and consideration. *Journal of Vocational Behavior, 66*, 385–419.

Vondracek, F. W., Ford, D. H., & Porfeli, E. J. (2014). *A living systems theory of vocational behavior and development.* Rotterdam, The Netherlands: Sense Publishers.

Watson, M., & McMahon, M. (2005). Children's career development: A research review from a learning perspective. *Journal of Vocational Behavior, 67*, 119–132.

Watson, M., Nota, L., & McMahon, M. (2015). Evolving stories of child career development. *International Journal for Educational and Vocational Guidance, 15*, 175–184.

Watts, A. G. (1999). The economic and social benefits of career guidance. *Educational and Vocational Guidance Bulletin, 63*, 12–19.

Index

academic performance 107, 136
academic pressure 122
academic self-concept 93, 94
Acquiring the Basic Habits of Industry 18
action theory 20, 42
actor, agent, author 29–31
actor, self as 29–30
adolescence, pivotal concept of 114
Affiliation 135–6
agent, self as 30
Agreeableness 136
Akos, P. T. 166
Alonso, A. 94
"ambient" messages 106
American School Counselor Association (ASCA) 53
association, reasoning and 50, 52, 54
attitudes, beliefs, and competencies (ABCs) 27–8
author, self as 30–1
Axelrad, S. 12

Bandura, A. 40
Barbaranelli, C. 40
Baron, A. S. 93
Beale, A. V. 54
Beaman, L. 95
Betz, D. E. 96
'big-fish/little-pond' effect 93
Big Five 135–6
Block, K. 93
Blueprint competencies 53
Blustein, D. L. 39, 40, 41, 116
Bordin, E. S. 16, 17
boundaries, tolerable 20
Brook, J. S. 105

capacity stage 12
career adaptability 27–8, 30

career assessment: aspects of career development 134–5; CAIS development 137–8; children's interests 131–3; overview 129; personality dispositions 135–7; psychological constructs 129–30; self-esteem and self-efficacy 133–4
career choice, cognitive developmental approach to 50
career construction theory: career adaptability 27–8; constructivism and social constructionism 25–6, 35; cornerstones 25; differences, development, and design 26–9; future orientation 28; identity construction and 65; intentionality 28–9; orientation 27–8; overview 24–5; reputation development 27; self-making 27, 29–31; three psychological principles 24–5
career development: discrimination 121–2; ethnic identity 121–2; in family contexts 101–9; family of origin influences 39–40; overview 34–5; as a rational process 11; relational perspectives 39–43; religious identity 121–2; systems theory perspectives 35–9; violence 121–2; Western developed country perspective 115
career development assessment: overview 143–4; qualitative measures 148–52; quantitative measures 144–8
career development learning: career policy and 191; career practice 191–3; defined 186; foundational nature of 187–9; overview 186–7; potential guidelines 193–4; research focus 189–91
Career Development Quarterly, The (2008) 3
career development theory: overview 34–5; poverty, phenomenon of 115–16; relational perspectives 39–43; research implications 109; systems perspectives 35–9

career development transitions 160–1
career exploration: career development transitions 160–1; characteristics of 74–5; critical constructs 162–3; developmental progression 163–5; eight developmental conflicts 18; narrative approaches to 56; overview 159–60; research overview 73–83; school-based practices and interventions 165–8
career exploration and development programmes: continuing challenges 182–3; equality, diversity, and inclusion 172–3; overview 172; socio-economic disadvantage and 173–9; special needs and disabilities 179–81; subject-based topics and 181–2
Career Exploration Scale (CES) 146
Career Family Tree 148
career guidance theory, culture specificity 115–17
Career Guidance: Who Needs It, Who Provides It, Who Can Improve It (Ginzberg) 13
career maturity 14
career orientation 27–8
Career Pattern Study (Super) 14
career role models 67
career self-efficacy 106
career socialisation opportunities 107
CareerStart (classroom lessons) 166
Castine, E. 43
Catholic private schools 94
changing workplace 21
Child and Adolescent Interpersonal Survey (CAIS) 137
child career development: macro-contexts of developing countries 117–23; research 1–7; role of school 122–3; role of the family 118–22; in world contexts 114–17
child career development theories: Anne Roe 14–16; conclusions 21; contemporary approaches to 20–1; Donald Super 13–14; Havighurst and Erikson 17–19; John Holland 16–17; Linda Gottfredson 19–20; occupational choice (1951) 12–13; overview 11
childhood: assessment of psychological constructs 129–31; definition of 1–3; deprivation of 114–15; typical career aspirations 11
Childhood and Society (Erikson) 18
Childhood Career Development Scale (CCDS) 134, 144–5

child labour phenomenon 120–1
child–parent interaction categories 15
children as storytellers 63–4
children's aspirations: development of 89–90; individual differences in 90–2; overview 89; role of parents 92–3; role of the broader context 93–6
circumscription 19–20
cognitive developmental approach 50
Collin, A. 34
community influences 107–8
compromise, career development and 14
Conceptions of Career Choice and Attainment (CCCA) model 149; description 50–2; empirical support for 52–3; future of 57; implications for intervention 53–7; overview 48; theoretical foundation 48–50
conception-to-death vision of development 17
constructivism 35
constructivism-social constructionism 24
contextualist action theory 42
Cotter, E. W. 20
Croft, A. 93
culture–relationship paradigm 41

decent work concept 118
De Leeuw, E. D. 130
Deutsch, M. 105
developing world, career development: culture specificity 115–17; macro-contexts 117–23; overview 114–15; population numbers 117
developmental conflicts 18
developmental-contextual framework 36–7, 104
developmental psychology 14, 17
developmental systems theory (DST) 37
developmental tasks concept 17
diffusion, Erikson's definition of 19
direct/indirect career messages 106, 118–19
discrimination, career development and 121–2
division of labour 104–5
Dominance 135–6
Dominick, M. 91
Duflo, E. 95
Durham, J. F. 167

Edler, E. 94
Ellsworth, R. A. 91

emotional support 106
Engaging Parents in Career Conversations Framework (EPiCC) that 67
English Language Arts (ELA) classroom instruction 166
environmental-societal system influences 108
Equal Choices, Equal Chances (online resource) 173–5
equality, diversity, and inclusion 172–3
Erikson, Erik 17–19, 188
ethnic identity 121–2
external resources and barriers 116
Extroversion 136

family-class background 105–6
family of origin influences: career research and child career development 104–9; career theory and child career development 102–3; child career development 118–22; overview 101; parental 'cultural capital' 92–3; predictability of 39, 63; theory, research, and practice 109
family socioeconomic status (SES) 92, 108
family systems interfaces 107–9
fantasy choice stage 12
father-mother relationship 106
fidelity, Erikson's definition of 19
Five-Factor Model (FFM) 135–6
Flanagan, S. 43
Foley, P. F. 20
Ford, D. H. 35–6, 37, 74
Fowler, Therese 2
functional pleasure basis 12
future orientation 28

Gender and Social Class Model (GSCM) 116
gender development of children 104–5
gender differences: career related outcomes 116–17; career self-efficacy 106; child labour 120–1; children's aspirations and 90–1; household labour 93; identity crisis 19; literacy rates 122; parental role models 11; pathfinder research 177–8; premature foreclosure of ideas 132–3; STEM occupations 94, 95–6; stereotypical thinking 176–7; stories as construction tools 64
gender-related attitudes 104–5
gender-role attitudes 105
geographical location influences 109

Gibson, D. 94
Gibson, D. M. 148
Ginsberg, S. W. 12
Ginzberg, E. 12, 49
Ginzberg, Eli 11
Ginzberg, W. 49
Goldstein, B. 60
Gottfredson, Linda 19–20, 49
Gottfredson, L. S. 1, 64
Gottfredson's theory of circumscription and compromise 89–90
'grand' theory 20
Greene, Graham 29
Gysbers, N. C. 165

Haakenson, K. A. 167
Happenstance Learning Theory 20
Hartung, P. J. 2–3
Havighurst, Robert 17–19
Hayes, A. R. 94
Heflin, E. N. 52
Henderson, P. 165
Heppner, M. J. 116
Herma, J. L. 12
Hirschi, A. 165–6
Holland, John 16–17, 131–2
Howard, K. A. S. 43, 48, 50, 52, 66, 188
Howard, K. A. W. 150
Hughes, M. A. 52
human rights violations 114, 121

Ideas and Attitudes on School/Career Future measure (IASCF) 146–7
identity crisis 18, 19
individual differences 24
individual identity 34
individualised learning plans (ILPs) 167
informal economy 118, 119
intentionality 28–9
interaction, reasoning and 51, 56–7
interests, development of 131
interest stages 12
internal resources and barriers 116
International Journal for Educational and Vocational Guidance 4
International Programme on the Elimination of Child Labour (IPEC) 121
Interpersonal Circumplex (IPC) 135–6
interpersonal dimensions 135–6
Interpersonal Theory 135–6
Inventory of Children's Activities (ICA) 131–2, 133–4, 147

208 Index

Jones-Sanpei, H. 166
Joshi, H. 95
Jung, A.-K. 116

Keller, B. K. 104
Kolb, D. A. 188
Krumboltz, J. D. 20, 103
Kuhnm T. S. 20
Kuwabara, M. 57

Läge, D. 165–6
Lapan, R. T. 166, 187
Lee, B. 61
Leonard, D. 95
Lerner, R. M. 36
Li, Y. 94
Life Career Assessment 149
life-space theory 102
lifespan approach to developmental psychology 17
lifespan development 24
lifespan orientation 14
life themes 30–1
literacy rates 122
Living Systems Theory of Vocational Behaviour and Development (LSVD) 37, 74–5
Luke, C. 20

McAdams, D. P. 61, 62
McClellan, N. C. 52
McMahon, M. 2–4, 7, 38–9, 40, 66, 187
Mael, F. 94
magical thinking 50, 54
Magnuson, C. S. 189
Making of a Scientist, The (Roe) 14
Manzi, A. J. 52, 152
Mapping Vocational Challenges Career Development Program (MVC) 145–6
Marsh, H. W. 93
Mau, W. C. 91
media, as source of career information 107
Middle School Self-Efficacy Scale (MSSES) 145
Mitchell, L. K. 103
mother-child relationship 106, 107
multi-level modeling 176–7
My Career Story (Savickas and Hartung) 67, 150

Nagengast, B. 93
narratability, self and 31

narrative identity: children as storytellers 63–4; development of 61–3; introduction 60–1; theory, research, and practice 64–8
National Vocational Guidance Association 13
non-traditional occupational aspirations 105
Nota, L. 4, 66, 147

Occupational Awareness Inventory (OAI) 134
Occupational Choice: An Approach to a General Theory (Ginzberg *et al.*) 12, 13
Occupational Choice theory 12–13
occupational identity formation 62, 63
Occupational Knowledge Interview (OKI) 151–2
Occupational Knowledge Scale (OKS) 147
Odom, C. 52
O'Hara, R. P. 49
orientation to internal, unique self 20
orientation-to-sex role 19
orientation to size and power 19
orientation to social valuation 20
Orthner, D. K. 166
Owings, N. 52

paid and unpaid labour 104–5
Palma, T. V. 52, 152
Pande, R. 95
parent-child relationship 106
parenting-personality-profession proposition 15
parents: aspirations and stereotypes 105–6, 177; involvement of 107; as role models 67, 92–3, 118–19; sexual orientation 104–5; work participation 119
Pastorelli, C. 40
Patton, W. 38, 40, 43
Peisach, E. 105
People-Things interest dimension 132
Personal Globe Inventory 147
personality, career development and 21
personality dispositions 135–6
person-context interactions 37–8
Person-Environment fit tradition 136
person-environment matching system 16–17
Phelps, L. A. 167
Phipps, B. J. 52
Piaget, Jean 188
play, role of 123
Popadiuk, N. E. 35

Porfeli, E. J. 2–3, 36, 37, 40, 61, 74
poverty, phenomenon of 115–16
Power and the Glory, The (Greene) 29
premature work experiences 120–1
Prezioso, M. S. 40
private schools 94
psychological constructivism 25–6
Psychology of Occupations, The (Roe) 14
psychosocial moratorium 19
Pulkkinen, L. 91
pure association 50, 54
purpose, Erikson's definition of 18

Quatman, T. 94

realistic choice stage 12
reasoning, common approaches to 50
Redekop, F. 20
religious identity 121–2
Revised Career Awareness Survey (RCAS)
    151
RIASEC (Realistic, Investigative, Artistic,
    Social, Enterprising, and Conventional)
    interest types 131–2, 133–4
Richardson, M. L. 41
Roe, Anne 14–16, 21, 102–3
Rogers, K. 94
Rose, R. A. 166
rote learning 17

Savickas, M. L. 188
Schaeffer, C. 41
Schmader, T. 93
school-based career development practices
    and interventions 165–6
school-level achievement, aspiration and 93
school quality 107
Schultheiss, D. 40, 41, 43, 134
Schultheiss, D. E. P. 52, 135, 152
Sekaquaptewa, D. 96
self-determination and agency 36
Self-Efficacy Beliefs and Exploration 163–4
self-esteem/self-efficacy 133–4
self-in-relation construct 41
self-making 29–31
Seligman, L. 52
sequence, reasoning and 50–1, 52, 55–6
Signorella, M. L. 94
single-sex education 94
Skorikov, V. B. 38, 43, 62
Smith, L. B. 57
Smith, M. 94

social class 105–6, 116–17
Social Cognitive Career Theory (Lent, 2013)
    20, 103
social learning theory 103
socio-economic disadvantage 173–9
socioeconomic status (SES) 92, 108
Sodano, S. M. 131, 137
Solberg, V. S. 167
Soresi, S. 147
special needs and disabilities 179–81
Starr, M. F. 189
Statistical Information and Monitoring
    Programme on Child Labour (SIMPOC)
    121
Stead, G. B. 134, 135
STEM occupations 94, 95–6
stereotypical thinking 176–7
storytelling 2
subject-based topics 181–2
Sullivan, A. 95
Super, D. E. 1, 13–14, 49, 102, 134, 144
supportive parenting 106
Survey of Interest and Plans (SIP) 148–9
systemic interaction 51
systems theory 35–6, 38–9
Systems Theory Framework 104

technology in the workplace 21, 117–23
temperament and aspiration 91
tentative choice stage 12
theoretical 'revolution' 20
'Theory of Vocational Development'
    (Super) 13
Tiedeman, D. V. 49
Timmons, J. 167
Todt Vocational Questionnaire (TVQ) 147
tolerable-effort boundary 20
tolerable-level boundary 20
tolerable-sex-type boundary 20
Topalova, P. 95
Tracey, T. J. G. 131, 137
Trice, A. D. 52
Turner, S. L. 187

Valach, L. 20, 41, 42
vicarious learning 26
violence: career development 121–2
Vittorio-Caprara, G. 40
vocational maturity 20
Vocational Preference Inventory
    (Holland) 16
vocational psychology, history of 11

210 Index

Vondracek, F. W. 2–3, 36, 37, 61, 62, 74
Vygotsky, L. S. 188

Walsh, M. E. 43, 48, 50, 52, 66, 150, 188
Watson, C. M. 94
Watson, M. 2–4, 38–9, 40, 66, 187
Weinstock, L. 52
Whiston, S. C. 104
Whiteman, M. 105

Williams, J. C. 54
Woods, K. 52
Woolley, M. E. 166
work, changing world of 21
work environment clusters 16
work-life balance 119

Young, R. A. 20, 34, 35, 41, 42
young adults, economic theory and 116